SUPREME GLOBAL SCHOOL
Near Ameen Hospital, Nagsen Colony, Roshan Gate,
Aurangabad, (M.S.), India-431001

HYPERTENSION

Written by

Mohammed Taufeeque Shaikh
(Corresponding Author)

Co-authors:

Noman Arif Shaikh
Ibaadur Rahmaan Shaikh
Nasreen Bano
Fouzia Shaikh
Mohammed Akbar Quadri

DEDICATED TO HUMANITY

Every day sees humanity more victorious in the struggle with space and time.

Acknowledgement

This review would not have been possible without the support, guidance and encouragement of several individuals and organizations. I would like to take this opportunity to extend my heartfelt thanks and appreciation to all who contributed to its creation. First and foremost, I am deeply grateful to mentors, collaborators and co-authors for their unwavering support and invaluable insights throughout this journey. Their expertise and constructive feedback helped shape the direction and content of this book. I would like to thank Supreme Global School for providing the necessary resources and facilities to conduct research. Although I would like to extend my thanks and gratitude to Unique Coaching Institute for provision of constant moral and ethical support. The dedication and professionalism of the staff, who assisted me in accessing relevant materials and data, played an essential role in this project.

A special note of gratitude goes to family, friends and colleagues for their patience, understanding and encouragement during the long hours spent on this book. Their emotional support kept me grounded and motivated. I am also grateful to the reviewers and editors who offered their acritical perspectives and ensured the high quality of the manuscript. Their knee insights and attention to detail have greatly enhanced the final version of this book. Finally, I would like to acknowledge the contributions of the publishing team for their belief in this project and their efforts to bring this work to fruition. To all those who have contributed directly or indirectly, thank you for your generosity, wisdom, and support.

INDEX

1. Introduction to Hypertension

Hypertension commonly known as high blood pressure, is a chronic medical condition where the force of the blood against the walls of the arteries is consistently too high. This increased pressure can lead to various health problems, particularly heart disease, stroke, and kidney failure, making it a leading cause of mortality worldwide. Hypertension continues to be a critical global health issue, disproportionately affecting low- and middle-income countries. The condition's widespread prevalence, coupled with its potential for severe complications, underscores the need for continued public health efforts in prevention, early detection, and effective management to reduce the global burden of hypertension.

1.1 Prevalence of Hypertension:

Hypertension is a prevalent global health issue, affecting approximately 1.4 billion adults worldwide. Its prevalence increases with age, lifestyle factors, and rising obesity rates, making it a leading risk factor for cardiovascular diseases.

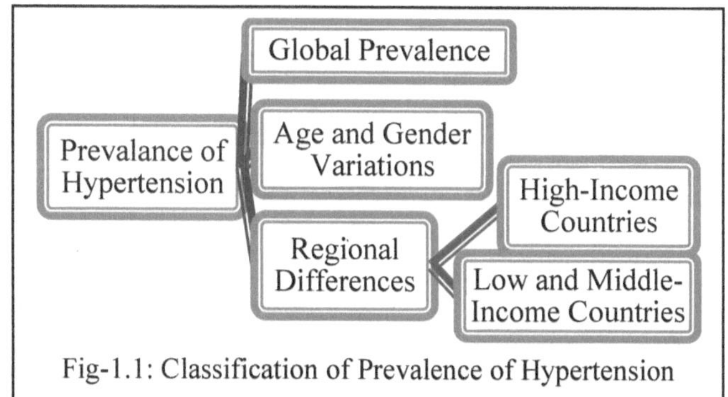

Fig-1.1: Classification of Prevalence of Hypertension

Effective public health strategies are essential to address hypertension and reduce its impact on populations.

a) Global Prevalence:

Hypertension is a major global health issue. As of recent estimates, around 1.13 billion people worldwide are affected. The prevalence varies by region, with higher rates observed in low- and middle-income countries due to factors like lifestyle, diet, and limited access to healthcare. Overall, approximately 30-45% of adults globally have hypertension, making it a leading risk factor for cardiovascular diseases, stroke, and kidney failure. Efforts to improve awareness, prevention, and treatment are critical in addressing this public health challenge. As a recent estimates, about 1 in 4 men and 1 in 5 women have hypertension globally. The condition is more prevalent in adults over 30 years old, though it is increasingly being diagnosed in younger populations.

b) Age and Gender Variations:

Generally, hypertension is less common in young adults but can be influenced by lifestyle factors. In middle-aged adults, risk increases with many developing hypertensions due to weight gain, sedentary lifestyle, and stress. In older adults, the prevalence is highest, often linked to arterial stiffness and comorbidities. The prevalence of hypertension rises sharply with age, particularly among individuals over 50 years old. Blood pressure typically rises with age. Men tend to have higher rates in women often equal or surpass those in men. In young adults, hypertension rates are similar in both genders, though men may have slightly higher rates. In middle age, women tend to have lower rates until menopause, after which their risk increases significantly, often surpassing that for men. In older adults, women generally have higher rates of hypertension compared to men, likely due to hormonal changes and longer life expectancy.

c) Regional Differences:

Regional differences are based on economy of geographical area or specific countries.

i. **High-income countries:** The prevalence of hypertension has stabilized or decreases slightly due to better healthcare systems, lifestyle modifications and widespread use of antihypertensive medications.

ii. **Low-and middle-income countries:** The prevalence of hypertension has increased dramatically due to urbanization, sedentary lifestyles, poor dietary habits, and limited access to healthcare. In some LMICs, over 40% of adults may suffer from hypertension.

1.1.1 Global Impact of Hypertension:

a) Morbidity and Mortality:

Hypertension is a leading contributor to morbidity and mortality globally, significantly increasing the risk of cardiovascular diseases. It is a major risk factor for cardiovascular diseases (CVD), which are responsible for over 17.9 million deaths annually. It significantly increases the risk of heart attack, stroke, heart failure, and atherosclerosis.

i. **Stroke:** Hypertension is the leading cause of ischemic and haemorrhagic stroke. It accounts for around 50% of all stroke cases worldwide.

ii. **Kidney Diseases:** Hypertension is a primary contributor to chronic kidney disease (CKD) and end-stage renal disease, further increasing global healthcare burdens.

b) Global Disease Burden:

Hypertension contributes to around 9.4 million deaths annually. The condition is ranked as the single largest contributor to global disease burden, as defined by the World Health Organization (WHO) and is the most significant risk factor for premature death. According to the Global Burden of Disease Study, high systolic blood pressure accounts for a considerable percentage of total disability-adjusted life years (DALYs), representing the loss of both quality and quantity of life.

1.1.2 Economic and Healthcare Burden:

a) Cost of Hypertension:

The direct and indirect costs associated with hypertension are immense, including the costs of medical treatment, hospitalizations for related complications (e.g. heart disease, stroke) and lost productivity due to disability and premature death. For example, in the United States alone, the annual cost of hypertension exceeds $131 billion.

b) Health System Strain:

In countries with high rates of hypertension, healthcare systems are often strained by the demand for ongoing management, medications such as heart failure and kidney disease.

1.1.3 Uncontrolled Hypertension:

Uncontrolled hypertension is defined as consistently high blood pressure levels that remain above the target despite treatment, presents significant health challenges and risks. This condition often stems from a variety of factors, including poor adherence to prescribed medications, lifestyle choices such as high salt intake, obesity, sedentary behaviour, excessive alcohol consumption and smoking. Additionally, underlying medical issues such as chronic kidney disease, hormonal imbalances, or sleep apnoea can contribute to resistance against conventional treatments. The consequences of uncontrolled hypertension are severe, leading to an increases risk of cardiovascular diseases, including heart attacks and strokes, as well as potential damage to vital organs like the kidneys and eyes.

This state not only diminishes the quality of life for affected individuals but also places a considerable burden on healthcare systems due to the need for more intensive management and treatment of associated complications. Effective management strategies are crucial and should include regular monitoring of blood pressure, medications, such as adopting a heart-healthy diet, engaging in regular physical activity, and reducing stress. Public health initiatives aimed at increasing awareness and access to health are also essential to address the growing prevalence of uncontrolled hypertension worldwide. Globally, around 46% of adults with hypertension are unaware they have the condition. Even among those who are aware, less than 1 in 5 people have their blood pressure adequately controlled, leading to a persistently high risk of complications. In low-and middle-income countries, access to diagnostic tools and treatments is often limited, and this contributes to greater burden of untreated and uncontrolled hypertension compared to high-income nations.

1.1.4 Social and Behavioural Risk Factors:

The increasing prevalence of hypertension in many regions can be attributed to modern lifestyles, including:

a) High Sodium intake:

Processed foods and high-salt diets contribute significantly to elevated blood pressure level.

b) Sedentary lifestyles:

Urbanization has led to more sedentary behaviours, decreasing physical activity and increasing obesity rates, both of which are risk factors for hypertension.

c) Tobacco and alcohol consumption:

Smoking and excessive alcohols consumption remain significant contributors to hypertension and related cardiovascular conditions.

1.2 Global Initiatives and Public Health Responses:

Several global organizations, including the World Health Organization (WHO) and the International Society of Hypertension (ISH), are actively working to reduce the burden of hypertension through awareness campaigns, improved treatment guidelines, and advocating for healthier public policies. WHO's Global Health Initiative and the HEARTS technical package aim to improve the prevention and management of cardiovascular diseases, particularly in low- and middle-income countries. These initiatives emphasize:

- Hypertension screening in primary healthcare settings.
- Lifestyle interventions such as salt reduction and promoting physical activity.
- Improved access to affordable medications to ensure better control of hypertension.
- Education campaigns to raise awareness about hypertension, its risks, and its management.

1.3 Future Trends:

Hypertension is a major public health challenge globally. The World Health Organization (WHO) estimates that 1.28 billion adults aged 30-79 worldwide suffer from hypertension. With its prevalence rising due to factors such as aging populations, sedentary lifestyles, and dietary changes, addressing hypertension has never been more critical. As medical science progress, the landscape of hypertension treatment, diagnosis, and management is set to change. Several emerging trends are shaping the future of hypertension, influenced by technological advancements, research innovations, and a greater understanding of lifestyle factors. With increasing rates of obesity, unhealthy diets, and sedentary behaviours globally, the number of people living with hypertension is projected to rise significantly by 2030, especially in developing regions. Efforts to curb this trend are focused on population-wide prevention through healthier environments and better management practices in healthcare.

1.3.1 Personalized Medicine and Genomics:

Personalized medicine and genomics are revolutionizing the approach to hypertension by tailoring treatment strategies to an individual's genetic profile. Research has identified specific genetic variations that influence blood pressure regulations, responsiveness to antihypertensive medications and susceptibility to hypertension-related complications. By integrating pharmacogenomic insights, healthcare providers can select medications that are more likely to be effective for a particular patient, minimizing trial and error approaches and reducing adverse effects. Additionally, personalized lifestyle recommendations based on genetic predispositions can enhance the effectiveness of interventions, such as dietary changes and exercise regimens.

This tailored approach not only improves blood pressure control but also promotes better long term health outcomes by addressing the unique needs of each patient. One of the most promising future trends in hypertension management is the move toward personalized medicine. The future of hypertension treatment is leaning towards personalized medicine, where therapies are tailored to individual patient profiles. Genetic research is uncovering how variations in genes affect blood pressure regulations and medication response. As pharmacogenomics becomes more integrated into clinical practice, healthcare providers will be able to prescribe medications that are more effective and have fewer side effects for everyone. This approach could significantly improve outcomes and reduce the burden of hypertension-related complications.

1.3.2 Digital Health and Wearable Technology:

Digital health and wearable technologies play a transformative role in managing hypertension by offering innovative solutions for continues monitoring and proactive care. Devices such as smartwatches, fitness bands, and specialized blood pressure monitors allow users to track their blood pressures, heart rate and physical activity throughout the day. Many of these wearables feature advanced sensors that provide accurate, real-time data, which can be crucial for identifying fluctuations in blood pressure that may require medical attention. Moreover, these technologies often integrate with mobile health applications, enabling users to log their daily habits, medications, and lifestyle choices. This comprehensive data collection facilities a better understanding of individual patterns and triggers related to hypertension. Users can set reminders for medication, receive personalized insights based on their health data with healthcare providers for more informed consultations. Telehealth services further enhance this landscape by allowing remote consultations, which can be particularly beneficial for patients in rural or undeserved areas. By combining wearables with telemedicine, healthcare professionals can monitor patient progress more closely and make timely adjustments to treatment plans, improving adherence and outcomes.

1.3.3 Advances in Pharmacological Treatments:

Recent advances in pharmacological treatments for hypertension reflect a multifaceted approach to managing this prevalent condition, emphasizing efficacy, safety, and patient adherence. Among the most notable developments is the emergence of dual-acting angiotensin receptor-neprilysin inhibitors (ARNIs), which have demonstrated superior outcomes in reducing both blood pressure and cardiovascular morbidity compared to traditional therapies. These agents not only block the angiotensin II receptor but also inhibit neprilysin, leading to increased levels of beneficial peptides that promote vasodilation and diuresis.

Additionally, the integration of long-acting formulations for commonly prescribed medications, such as thiazide diuretics, calcium channel blockers and ACE inhibitors addresses patient adherence by minimizing the frequency of dosing. This is particularly crucial given that hypertension often requires lifelong management, and complex regimens can lead to poor compliance. Combination therapies are gaining traction as well, allowing for lower doses of multiple agents to achieve optimal blood pressure control while reducing the risk of side effects. For instance, fixed-dose combinations that pair an ACE inhibitor with a calcium channel blocker or a diuretic are becoming standard practice, offering synergistic effects that enhance overall efficacy.

1.3.4 Gut Microbiome and Hypertension:

The gut microbiome has emerged as a critical player in the pathophysiology of hypertension, influencing blood pressure regulation through various mechanisms. Research indicates that the composition and diversity of gut bacteria can significantly affect systemic inflammation, metabolic processes, and vascular function. Certain microbial populations are linked to the production of short-chain fatty acids (SCFAs), such as butyrate, which possess anti-inflammatory properties and can enhance endothelial function, thereby promoting vasodilation. Conversely, dysbiosis, or an imbalance in gut microbial communities, has been associated with increased production of harmful metabolites like trimethylamine-N-oxide (TMAO), which may contribute to vascular inflammation and hypertension.

Additionally, the gut microbiome interacts with dietary components, modulating how nutrients are metabolized and affecting blood pressure outcome. For example, high-fibre diets can promote beneficial microbial growth and SCFA production, leading to improved blood pressure control. Ongoing studies are exploring the potential of probiotics and prebiotics as therapeutic interventions to restore a healthy microbiome and mitigate hypertension. By understanding the intricate relationship between gut health and blood pressure, researchers hope to develop novel, microbiome-targeted strategics that offer a complementary approach to conventional antihypertensive treatments. This area of research highlights the importance of a holistic view of health, emphasizing the gut's role in systemic conditions like hypertension.

1.3.5 Nutritional Interventions and Lifestyle Modifications:

Nutritional interventions and lifestyle modifications play a vital role in the management and prevention of hypertension, significantly complementing pharmacological treatments. A primary dietary approach is the DASH (Dietary Approaches to Stop Hypertension) diet, which emphasizes the consumption of fruits, vegetables, whole grains, lean proteins, and low-fat diary while reducing saturated fats, cholesterol, and sodium intake. This diet has been shown to lower blood pressure effectively due to its rich content of potassium, magnesium and fibre which promote vascular health.

Additionally, reducing sodium intake to less than 2,300 milligrams per day, and ideally around 1,500 milligrams for those with hypertension, can lead to substantial improvements in blood pressure levels. Lifestyle modifications also include regular physical activity, such as aerobic exercise, which have been associated with lower systolic and diastolic blood pressure through mechanisms like improved endothelial function and reduced vascular resistance. Weight management is crucial, as even modest weight loss can lead to significant reductions in blood pressure for overweight individuals. Furthermore, limiting alcohol intake and quitting smoking are essential strategies, as both can exacerbate hypertension and contribute to cardiovascular risk. Stress management techniques, such as mindfulness, yoga and deep beathing exercise, can also positively impact blood pressure by promoting relaxation and reducing sympathetic nervous system activation. Collectively, these nutritional and lifestyle interventions create a comprehensive approach to hypertension management, fostering long-term health benefits and enhancing quality of life.

1.3.6 Focus on Preventive Strategies:

Preventive strategies for hypertension emphasizing early intervention and lifestyle modifications to reduce the risk of developing high blood pressure and its associated complications. Central to these strategies is the promotion of a heart-healthy diet, such as the DASH diet, which prioritizes the intake of fruits, vegetables, whole grains, lean proteins, and low-fat dairy while minimizing sodium, sugar and saturated fat. Regular physical activity is equally important, with recommendations suggesting at least 150 minutes of moderate aerobic exercise weekly, which not only helps maintain a healthy weight but also enhances cardiovascular health. Monitoring body weight and maintaining a BMI within the normal range are critical, as even modest weight loss can significantly lower blood pressure.

Additionally, reducing alcohol consumption and quitting smoking are vital, as both habits contribute to increased blood pressure and cardiovascular risk. Stress management techniques, including mindfulness, meditation and yoga can further mitigate hypertension risk by promoting relaxation and reducing sympathetic nervous system activity. Regular health screening for blood pressure and related risk factors allows for early detection and timely intervention, fostering a proactive approach to health. Community awareness programs and educational initiatives also play a crucial role in disseminating information about the importance of these preventive measures, encouraging individuals to adopt healthier lifestyle before hypertension develops. Collectively, these strategies aim to create a supportive environment for individuals to make informed choices, thereby reducing the prevalence of hypertension and improving overall public health outcomes.

1.3.7 Integration of Behavioural Science:

The integration of behavioural science into hypertension management has become increasingly important in addressing the complex interplay between lifestyle factors, patient adherence and health outcomes. Behavioural science provides insights into how psychological, social and environmental factors influence individuals' choices and behaviours related to hypertension prevention and treatment. For instance, understanding the role of motivation and self-efficiency can help healthcare providers design tailored interventions that empower patients to adopt healthier lifestyles, such as improved dietary habits and increased physical activity. Techniques such as motivational interviewing can facilitate open dialogue, helping patients to explore their ambivalence about making changes and enhancing their commitment to treatment plans.

Additionally, behavioural strategies like goal setting, self-monitoring and feedback mechanisms can reinforce positive health behaviours, making it easier for patients to track their progress in managing their blood pressure. Social support systems, including family involvement and peer support groups, can also enhance adherence to treatment regimens by providing encouragement and accountability. Furthermore, addressing behavioural barriers, such as stress, depression and anxiety is crucial as these factors can adversely affect blood pressure control. By incorporating behavioural science into hypertension care, healthcare providers can develop comprehensive, patient-centred approaches that not only focus on pharmacological treatment but also address the underlying behaviours and lifestyle choices that significantly impact blood pressure management. This holistic perspective ultimately aims to improve patient engagement, enhance treatment adherence, and promote better health outcomes in the long term.

1.3.8 Integration of technology:

The integration of technology in hypertension management has transformed how patients monitor their health and engage with healthcare providers. Wearable devices, such as smartwatches and fitness trackers, enable continuous monitoring of heart rate and physical activity, while blood pressure monitors with Bluetooth connectivity allow users to track their readings in real-time and share data with healthcare professionals. Mobiles health applications provide platforms for patients to log their dietary habits, medication adherence and lifestyle factors offering insights that can guide personalized treatment plans. Telemedicine has also emerged as a crucial tool, allowing patients to consult with healthcare providers remotely, facilitating timely adjustments to treatment without the need for in-person visits.

Additionally, artificial intelligence and machine learning algorithms are being employed to analyse large datasets from wearable devices and electronic health records, identifying trends and predicting individual risk factors for hypertension. These technological advancements not only enhance patient engagement and education but also enable more proactive and tailored interventions, ultimately leading to improved adherence and better management of blood pressure. Furthermore, technology can support community health initiatives by facilitating outreach and education, helping to raise awareness about hypertension prevention and control in broader populations. Overall, the integration of technology in hypertension management represents a significant leap forward, enhancing both patient outcomes and healthcare efficacy.

1.3.9 Lifestyle interventions:

Lifestyle interventions are essential in managing hypertension and include dietary changes, increased physical activity, weight management and stress reduction. Following the DASH (Dietary Approaches to Stop Hypertension) diet, which emphasizes fruits, vegetables, whole grains and low sodium options, can significantly lower blood pressure. Regular aerobic exercise, such as walking or recycling for at least 150 minutes a week, helps improve cardiovascular health. Maintaining a healthy weight is crucial, as even modest weight loss can lead to significant reductions in blood pressure.

Additionally, stress management techniques like mindfulness, yoga and deep breathing can help mitigate the impact of stress on blood pressure levels. Collectively, these lifestyle changes empower individuals to take control of their health and reduce the risk of hypertension-related complications. Preventing and managing hypertension through lifestyle modifications will continue to gain emphasis. Future trends will likely focus on holistic health approaches, integrating diet, exercise. And mental health into hypertension management. Innovations in digital health platforms can provide personalized diet plans and exercise regimens. Furthermore, community-based programs aimed at promoting healthy lifestyles will be essential, particularly in addressing health disparities among different populations.

1.3.10 Policy and Public Health Initiatives:

Policy and public health initiatives play a crucial role in addressing hypertension at the population level, aiming to reduce its prevalence and associated health complications. Comprehensive public health campaigns focus on raising awareness about hypertension, its risk factors and the importance of regular screening. These initiatives often promote lifestyle modifications, such as healthy eating, regular physical activity, and smoking cessation, through community programs and partnerships with local organizations. On a broader scale, public health policies will play a crucial role in combating hypertension. Governments and health organizations are expected to increase efforts in awareness campaigns, emphasizing the importance of regular blood pressure monitoring and the impact of hypertension on overall health. Initiatives such as sugar taxes, regulations on processed foods, and improvements in healthcare access will contribute to reducing risk factors associated with hypertension.

Moreover, educational programs targeting healthcare professionals enhance their effectively, ensuring they are equipped to provide evidence-based recommendations and support. Funding for research into hypertension prevention and management strategies is vital, as it helps develop innovative solutions and evaluate the effectiveness Of existing programs. Collaboratives efforts involving from various sectors, including education, agriculture, and urban planning are also essential to create environments that support healthy lifestyles, such as developing safe recreational spaces and improving access to nutritious foods. By fostering a comprehensive approach that combines education, policy changes, and community engagement, these initiatives aim to mitigate the burden of hypertension and improve overall public health outcomes.

1.3.11 Research and innovation:

Innovations in hypertension management are rapidly transforming how the condition is diagnosed, monitored and treated, ultimately aiming to improve patient outcomes. One of the key advancements is the development of digital health technologies, including smart blood pressure monitors that can sync with smartphones to provide real-time data tracking. These devices allow patients to monitor their blood pressure easily and share their readings with healthcare providers, facilitating timely interventions. Telemedicine has also gained traction, enabling patients to consult with healthcare professionals remotely, which is particularly beneficial for those in underserved areas. This accessibility helps ensure continuous care and fosters patient engagement in their health management.

Additionally, artificial intelligence and machine learning are increasingly being utilized to analyse large datasets, providing insights into patient risk factors and predicting hypertension-related complications, allowing for more personalized treatment approaches. Ongoing research into the pathophysiology of hypertension will likely yield new insights into prevention and treatment. Studies focusing on the microbiome, inflammation and other emerging areas could reveal novel therapeutic targets. Moreover, advancements in drug development may lead to new classes of antihypertensive medications with improved efficacy and safety profiles. Pharmacological innovations such as new classes of antihypertensive drugs, offer improved efficacy and fewer side effects. For example, dual-acting agents like angiotensin receptor-neprilysin inhibitors (ARNIs) have shown

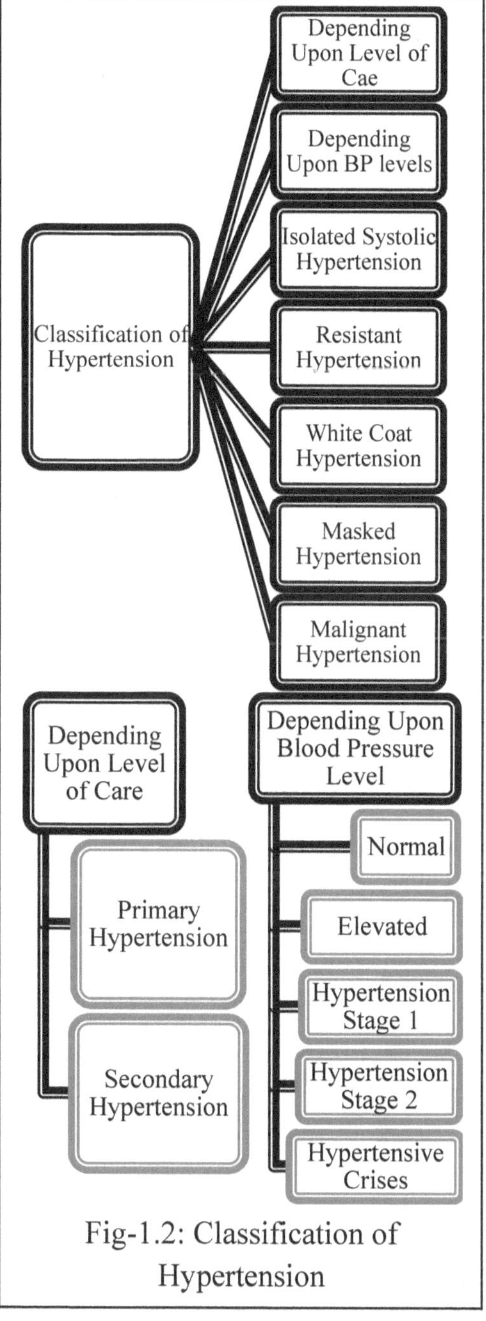

Fig-1.2: Classification of Hypertension

promising results in controlling blood pressure while providing cardiovascular protection. Moreover, research into gut microbiome's role in hypertension has opened new avenues for therapeutic strategies, including probiotics and dietary interventions aimed at restoring microbial balance to support blood pressure regulation. Overall, these innovations represent a comprehensive approach to hypertensive approach to hypertension management, focusing on technology, personalized medicine and lifestyle interventions, which together enhance the effectiveness of treatment and improve patient quality of life.

1.4 Classification of Hypertension:

Hypertension is classified into several categories based on blood pressure measurements, primarily using systolic and diastolic values.

1.4.1 Primary and secondary hypertension:

The two major categories are Primary (Essential) Hypertension and Secondary Hypertension, which additional sub-classifications based on blood pressure severity and specific conditions. Primary hypertension accounts for about 90-95% of cases and typically develops gradually over many years, with no identifiable cause, often influenced by genetic, lifestyle and environmental factors. Secondary hypertension, which constitutes about 5-10% of cases, results from identifiable conditions.

a) Primary (Essential) Hypertension: `

- **Definition:** This is the most common form of hypertension, accounting for about 90-95% of cases. If develops gradually over many years and has no identifiable direct cause
- **Contributing Factors:** Genetics, age, lifestyle factors (diet, stress, lack of physical activity)
- **Characteristics:** Primary hypertension tends to be long-term, often requires lifelong management, and is influenced by multiple environmental and genetic factors.

b) Secondary Hypertension:

- **Definition:** This type of hypertension is caused by an underlying medical condition or specific external factors. It accounts for about 5-10% of hypertension cases.
- **Characteristics:** Secondary hypertension can develop suddenly and may be more severe than primary hypertension. Treating the underlying cause can often normalize blood pressure levels.
- **Common Causes:**

Sr. No.	Causes	Specifications
1.	Kidney disease	Conditions like chronic kidney disease or renal artery stenosis.
2.	Endocrine disorders	Hyperthyroidism, Cushing's syndrome, pheochromocytoma, primary aldosteronism.
3.	Medications	Nonsteroidal anti-inflammatory drugs (NSAIDs), steroids, oral contraceptives, decongestants.
4.	Sleep apnoea	Obstructive sleep apnoea can lead to hypertension.
5.	Vascular conditions	Aortic coarctation or other vascular disorders.

Table-1.1: Common Causes of Secondary Hypertension

1.4.2 Classification Based on Blood Pressure Levels:

Blood pressure is typically measured in millimetres of mercury (mmHg) and is recorded as two values:

- **Systolic pressure:** The pressure in the arteries when the heart beats
- **Diastolic pressure:** The pressure in the arteries when the arteries between heartbeats

The hypertension can be categorized into following several stages based on these readings:

Category	Systolic BP (mmHg)	Diastolic BP (mmHg)
Normal	<120	<80

Elevated	120-129	<80
Hypertension Stage 1	130-139	80-89
Hypertension Stage 2	>140	>90
Hypertensive Crisis	>180	>120

Table-1.2: Classification of Blood Pressure Levels

1.4.2 Isolated Systolic Hypertension (ISH):

- **Definition:** A condition where only the systolic blood pressure is elevated (>130 mmHg) while the diastolic pressure remains normal (<80 mmHg).
- **Prevalence:** This form of hypertension is more common in older adults due to the stiffening of arteries with age.
- **Risks:** ISH is strongly associated with an increased risk of cardiovascular events such as heart attack or stroke.

1.4.3 Resistant Hypertension:

- **Definition:** Hypertension that remains elevated despite the use of three or more antihypertensive medications from different classes, including a diuretic, at optimal doses.
- **Causes:** Common reasons include medication non-adherence, secondary causes of hypertension, and lifestyle factors such as excessive salt intake or obesity.
- **Management:** Requires through evaluation to rule out secondary causes and may involve the use of additional medications or interventions like renal denervation.

1.4.4 White Coat Hypertension:

- **Definition:** Blood pressure readings are elevated in a clinical setting but normal when measured outside the doctor's office.

- **Prevalence:** Occurs in about 10-30% of patients with high office BP readings.
- **Significance:** Although often considered less dangerous, individuals with white coat hypertension may still be at risk of developing sustained hypertension and cardiovascular disease over time.

1.4.5 Masked Hypertension:

- **Definition:** The opposite of white coat hypertension, where blood pressure readings are normal in the clinical setting but elevated outside the office.
- **Prevalence:** Found in about 10-20%of patients.
- **Risks:** Masked hypertension is associated with a higher risk of cardiovascular events than white coat hypertension and often goes undetected without home or ambulatory blood pressure monitoring.

1.4.6 Malignant (Accelerated) Hypertension:

- **Definition:** A rare and severe form of hypertension characterized by very high blood pressure (usually>180/120 mmHg) that results in the damage to organs, particularly the heart, kidneys, and brain. It is considered a medical emergency.
- **Symptoms:** May include severe headaches, blurred vision, chest pain, and difficulty in breathing.
- **Complications:** If left untreated, it can lead to life-threatening complications such as stroke, heart failure, or kidney failure.
- **Management:** Immediate medical intervention is required to lower blood pressure and prevent further organ damage.

In conclusion, hypertension remains a significant over a billion people worldwide and serving as a major risk factor for cardiovascular diseases, stroke and renal failure. The complexity of hypertension is underscored by its multifactorial etiology, encompassing genetic predisposition, environmental influences, and lifestyle choices such as diet, physical activity, alcohol consumption and stress makes hypertension a particularly challenging condition to address. Recent advancements in research and clinical practice are reshaping the approach to hypertension management. The development of novel antihypertensive medications, including newer classes like angiotensin receptor-neprilysin inhibitors (ARNIs) and combination therapies, has improved treatment efficacy and reduced side effects.

Additionally, technological innovations, such as remote blood pressure monitoring and mobile health applications, facilitate real-time tracking and empower patients to take an active role in managing their health. Personalized medicine, driven by insight from genomics, is revolutionizing hypertension treatment by allowing healthcare providers to tailor interventions based on individual genetic profiles. This approach not only enhances medications, further improving patient outcomes. For instance, understanding specific genetic markers can guide dietary choices and physical activity plans that align with a patient's unique needs. Public health initiatives are vital in promoting awareness and education about hypertension, advocating for routine screenings and implementing community-based programs that encourage lifestyle modifications.

Efforts such as the DASH (Dietary Approaches to Stop Hypertension) diet and community exercise programs have demonstrated effectiveness in lowering blood pressure in populations at risk. Furthermore, policies aimed at reducing sodium consumption in processed foods and promoting healthier for environments are crucial for preventing hypertension on a broader scale. By fostering a comprehensive understanding of hypertension and addressing its risk factors through multidisciplinary strategies, healthcare systems can empower individuals and communities to take proactive measures in preventing and managing this condition. Ultimately, a concerted effort to integrate advancements in research, technology and public health initiatives will lead to better health outcomes, reduced healthcare costs and improved quality of life for those affected by hypertension solidifying its status as a priority in public health agendas worldwide.

Public awareness and routine screenings are vital for early detection and intervention. By integrating these strategies and fostering a collaborative effort among healthcare providers, patients and communities, we can significantly reduce the burden of hypertension and improve health outcomes for individuals at risk. Ultimately, addressing hypertension not only enhances quality of life but also alleviates the economic impact on healthcare systems worldwide. Empowering individuals with knowledge and resources to manage their health can lead to significant improvements in hypertension outcomes and overall quality of life. Ongoing research into the underlying mechanisms of hypertension and the development of innovative therapies will be key o reducing its burden in the future.

2. Pathophysiology of Hypertension

The pathophysiology of hypertension involves a complex interplay of genetic, environmental and physiological factors that lead to sustained increases in blood pressure. Central to this process is the function of blood vessels, the kidneys and the autonomic nervous system.

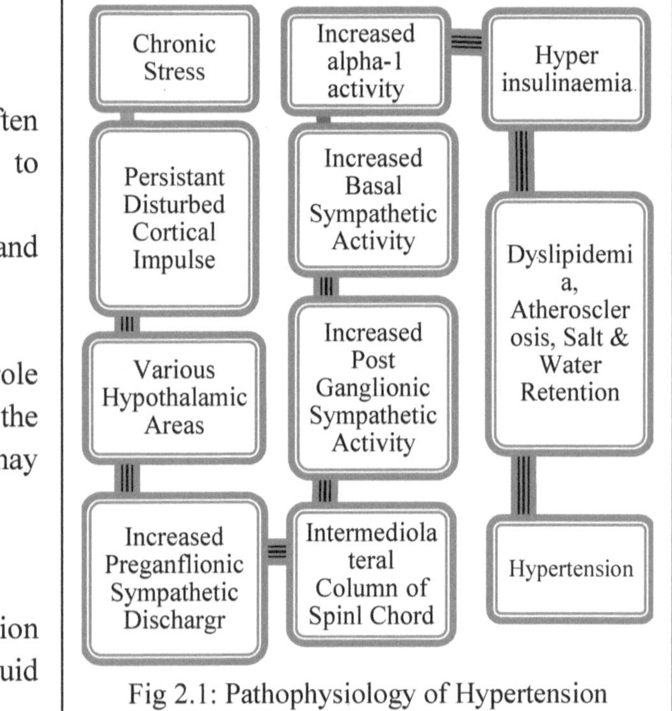

Fig 2.1: Pathophysiology of Hypertension

Increased peripheral resistance, often due to endothelial dysfunction and vascular remodelling, plays a key role while the kidneys may contribute through inappropriate sodium retention and fluid overload. Additionally, hormonal factors, such as overactivity of the renin-angiotensin aldosterone system (RAAS) and increased sympathetic nervous system activity, further elevate blood pressure. These mechanisms can result in a vicious cycle of vascular damage, promoting the development of complications such as heart disease, stroke and renal failure. Understanding these underlying processes is crucial for developing targeted interventions and effective treatment strategies for hypertension. Below is a detailed explanation of the underlying mechanism that contribute to the development of hypertension:

2.1 Renin Angiotensin-Aldosterone System (RAAS) Dysregulation:

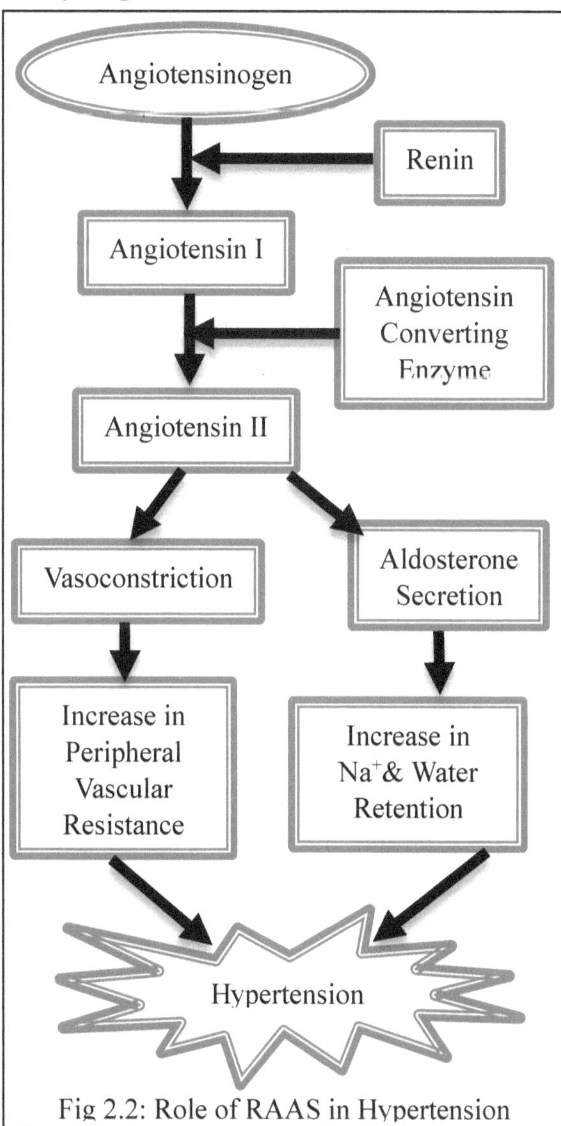

Fig 2.2: Role of RAAS in Hypertension

Dysregulation of RAAS plays a critical role in the pathophysiology of hypertension. In a normally functioning system, the kidneys release renin in response to low blood pressure, leading to the production of angiotensin I, which is the converted to angiotensin II by angiotensin-converting enzyme (ACE). Angiotensin II is a potent vasoconstrictor that raises blood pressure by narrowing blood vessels and stimulating aldosterone secretion from the adrenal glands, promoting sodium and water retention. In hypertension, this regulatory mechanism can become overactive or dysfunctional. Elevated levels of renin and angiotensin II contribute to increased vascular resistance and enhanced fluid volume, resulting in higher blood pressure. This dysregulation may be trigger by factors such as obesity, stress or certain medications that impact kidney function. Chronic activation of the RAAS also leads to structural changes in the blood vessels and heart, further exacerbating hypertension and increasing the risk of cardiovascular events. The RAAS plays a crucial role in regulating blood pressure and fluid balance. When blood pressure or blood volume decreases, the kidneys release renin, which converts angiotensin (produced by the liver) into angiotensin I. This is further converted into angiotensin-converting enzyme (ACE) in the lungs into angiotensin II, a potent vasoconstrictor that raises blood pressure by:

- **Vasoconstriction:** Narrowing of blood vessels increase peripheral resistance.
- **Aldosterone release:** Angiotensin II stimulates the adrenal glands to secrete aldosterone, which promotes sodium and water retention in the kidneys, increasing blood volume and blood pressure.
- **Antidiuretic Hormone (ADH):** Angiotensin II also triggers the release of ADH, which reduces water excretion, further increasing blood volume.

In hypertension, overactivation of the RAAS leads to excessive vasoconstriction and fluid retention, causing chronic elevation of blood pressure. Targeting the RAAS through medications such as ACE inhibitors, angiotensin II receptor blockers (ARBs) and direct renin inhibitors has become a cornerstone of hypertension management, aiming to restore balance within this critical regulatory system and reduce the risk of complications associated with high blood pressure.

2.2 Sympathetic Nervous System (SNS) Hyperactivity:

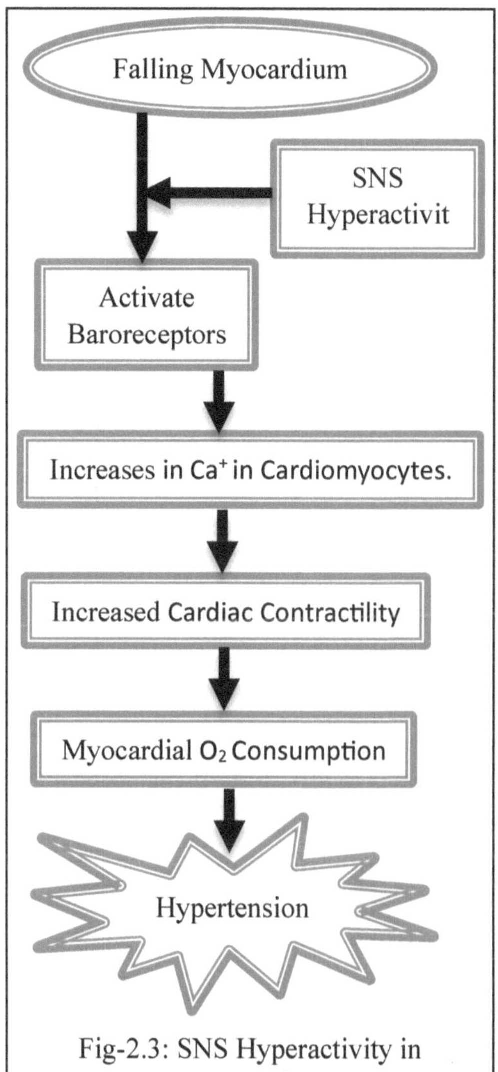

Fig-2.3: SNS Hyperactivity in

The sympathetic nervous system hyperactivity is a significant contributor to development and maintenance of hypertension. This condition is characterized by an overactive sympathetic response, which leads to increased heart rate, heightened vascular tone and elevated levels of norepinephrine cause constriction of blood vessels, resulting in increased peripheral resistance and subsequently high blood pressure. Additionally, sympathetic overactivity can stimulate the kidneys to retain sodium and water, further increasing blood volume and pressure. Factors such as stress, obesity and sleep apnoea can exacerbate sympathetic nervous system activity is often associated with various target organ damages, including left ventricle hypertrophy and renal impairment, which complicate the clinical picture. Understanding the role of sympathetic nervous system hyperactivity in hypertension is crucial for developing effective therapeutic strategies, including lifestyle modifications, pharmacological agents that block adrenergic receptors and interventions aimed at reducing stress and improving overall cardiovascular health. The SNS regulates heart rate, vascular tone, and contractility of the heart. In individuals with hypertension, there may be increases sympathetic nervous activity, which results in:

- **Vasoconstriction:** Increased sympathetic tone leads to constriction of arterioles, raising peripheral resistance.
- **Increased cardiac output:** The heart pumps more blood per minute due to increased heart and force of contraction, leading to elevated blood pressure.

Chronic SNS hyperactivity can contribute to sustained high blood pressure, particularly in stress-related or lifestyle-induced hypertension. In conclusion, hyperactivity of SNS is a significant contributor to the development and persistence of hypertension. Increased sympathetic tone leads to heightened vasoconstriction, elevated heart rate and enhanced cardiac output, all of which contribute to sustained increase in blood pressure. This hyperactivity can result from various factors, including stress, obesity, and genetic predisposition, creating a various cycle that perpetuates hypertension and its associated complications. Understanding the role of the SNS in hypertension underscores the importance of integrative treatment strategies that target both lifestyle modifications and pharmacological interventions aimed at reducing sympathetic overactivity. By addressing this critical aspect of hypertension pathophysiology, healthcare providers can improve patient outcomes and reduce the long-term risk of cardiovascular disease, stroke, and renal dysfunction.

2.3 Endothelial Dysfunction:

Endothelial dysfunction is a pathological feature of hypertension and plays a crucial role in its development and progression. The endothelium, a thin layer of cells lining blood vessel, is essential for maintaining vascular health by regulating vascular tone, inflammation, and blood clotting. In hypertension, factors such

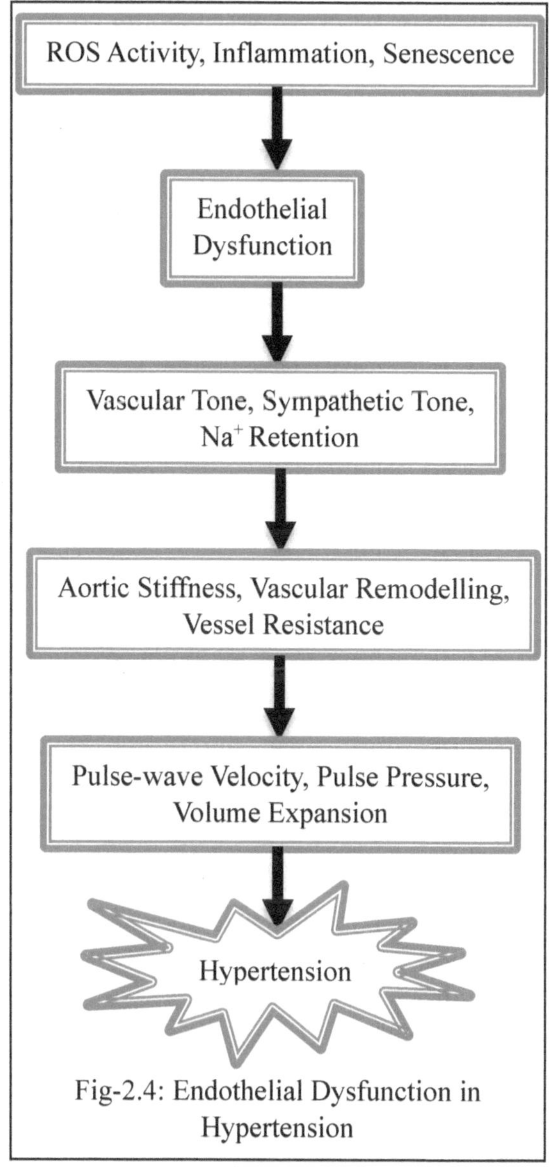

Fig-2.4: Endothelial Dysfunction in Hypertension

as increased sheared stress from elevated blood pressure, oxidative stress and the presence of inflammatory markers can damage endothelial cells, leading to a reduction in the production of nitric oxide (NO), a potent vasodilator. This impaired endothelial function results in decreased vasodilation and increased vascular resistance, contributing to the overall elevation in blood pressure. Additionally, endothelial dysfunction is associated with a pro-inflammatory state and increased expression of adhesion molecules, promoting the recruitment of immune cells and further vascular damage. Over time, these changes can lead to structural remodelling of blood vessels, atherosclerosis and an increased risk of cardiovascular events. Therapeutic strategies that aim to improve endothelial function-such as lifestyle modifications (e.g., diet, exercise), antioxidant therapies and medications like ACE inhibitors or angiotensin receptor blockers are essential components of managing hypertension. Addressing endothelial dysfunction not only helps to control blood pressure but also reduces the risk of associated complications, highlighting the importance of maintaining vascular health in hypertensive patients. In hypertension, endothelial cells often become dysfunctional, leading to:

- **Reduced Nitric Oxide Production:** Decreased availability of NO impairs vasodilation, causing vessels to remain constricted.
- **Increased Endothelin:** Endothelin is a potent vasoconstrictor, and its increased levels contribute to heightened vascular tone.

Endothelial dysfunction is a key factor in the pathophysiology of hypertension, significantly impairing vascular health and contributing to increased blood pressure. This condition is characterized by an imbalance between vasodilatory and vasoconstrictor factors, often resulting from chronic inflammation, oxidative stress and other risk factors such as hyperlipidaemia and diabetes. Endothelial dysfunction leads to reduced production of nitric oxide, a critical mediator of vasodilation and promotes vascular stiffness and remodelling, further exacerbating hypertension. Recognizing the central role of endothelial health in hypertension highlights the importance of interventions aimed at improving endothelial function including lifestyle modifications, dietary changes and pharmacological therapies. Endothelial dysfunction is often linked to oxidative stress, inflammation, and atherosclerosis, all of which are associated with long-term hypertension.

2.4 Vascular Remodelling:

Vascular remodelling in hypertension refers to the structural and functional changes that occur in blood vessels as a response to sustained high blood pressure. This process is characterized by alterations in the composition and organization of the vascular wall including hypertrophy of smooth muscle cells, increased collagen disposition and changes in endothelial cell function. Such remodelling results in reduced vascular compliance and increased stiffness, which

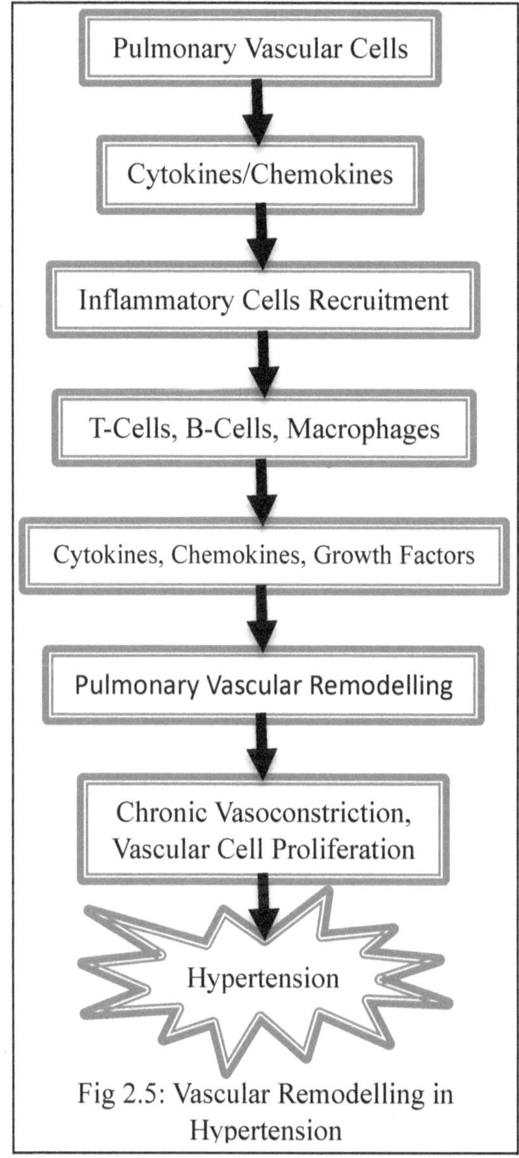

Fig 2.5: Vascular Remodelling in Hypertension

contribute to the persistence of elevated blood pressure. These adaptations can further exacerbate hypertension by increasing peripheral resistance, thereby creating a vicious cycle of elevated blood pressure and ongoing vascular injury. Additionally, vascular remodelling is linked to the development of atherosclerosis and other cardiovascular complications, highlighting its role in the progression of hypertensive disease. Understanding the mechanisms underlying vascular remodelling is crucial for developing targeted therapies that can reverse or prevent these changes, ultimately improving vascular health and reducing the risks associated with chronic hypertension. Chronic high blood pressure causes structural changes in blood vessels, a process known as vascular modelling. This includes:

- **Arteriolar Hypertrophy:** Arteriolar hypertrophy is a significant pathological change observed in hypertension, characterized by the thickening of the arteriolar walls due to increased smooth muscle cell proliferation and extracellular matrix deposition. The smooth muscle cells in the walls of small arteries and arterioles increase in size, leading to thickening and stiffening of vessel walls, which increases vascular resistance.

- **Reduced Vessel Elasticity:** Larger arteries lose their elasticity, which impairs their ability to buffer pressure changes, leading to increased systolic blood pressure and pulse pressure.

Vascular modelling is a critical component of hypertension that involves structural and functional changes in the blood vessels, significantly contributing to the progression of the condition, this process includes alterations such as vessel wall thickening, increased stiffness and lumen narrowing, all of which lead to elevated vascular resistance and sustained high blood pressure. Factors such as chronic inflammation, oxidative stress and excessive mechanical strain play pivotal roles in driving these remodelling processes. Understanding the mechanisms underlying vascular remodelling not only helps in elucidating the pathophysiology of hypertension but also emphasizes the need for targeted therapeutic strategies aimed at reversing or preventing these changes. By addressing vascular remodelling through lifestyle modifications, pharmacological interventions and early detection, healthcare providers can improve vascular health, enhance blood pressure control and ultimately reduce the risk of cardiovascular complications associated with hypertension.

2.5 Kidney Dysfunction and Sodium Retention:

Kidney dysfunction and sodium retention play crucial roles in the development and persistence of hypertension. The kidneys regulate blood pressure by controlling fluid balance and sodium excretion; however, when kidney function is compromised, this regulatory mechanism can become impaired. In the context of hypertension, renal sodium retention leads to increased extracellular fluid volume, which elevates blood pressure through enhanced cardiac output and increased vascular resistance. Factors such as renal artery stenosis, glomerular damage and hormonal imbalances, including activation of the renin-angiotensin-aldosterone system (RAAS), contribute to this sodium retention.

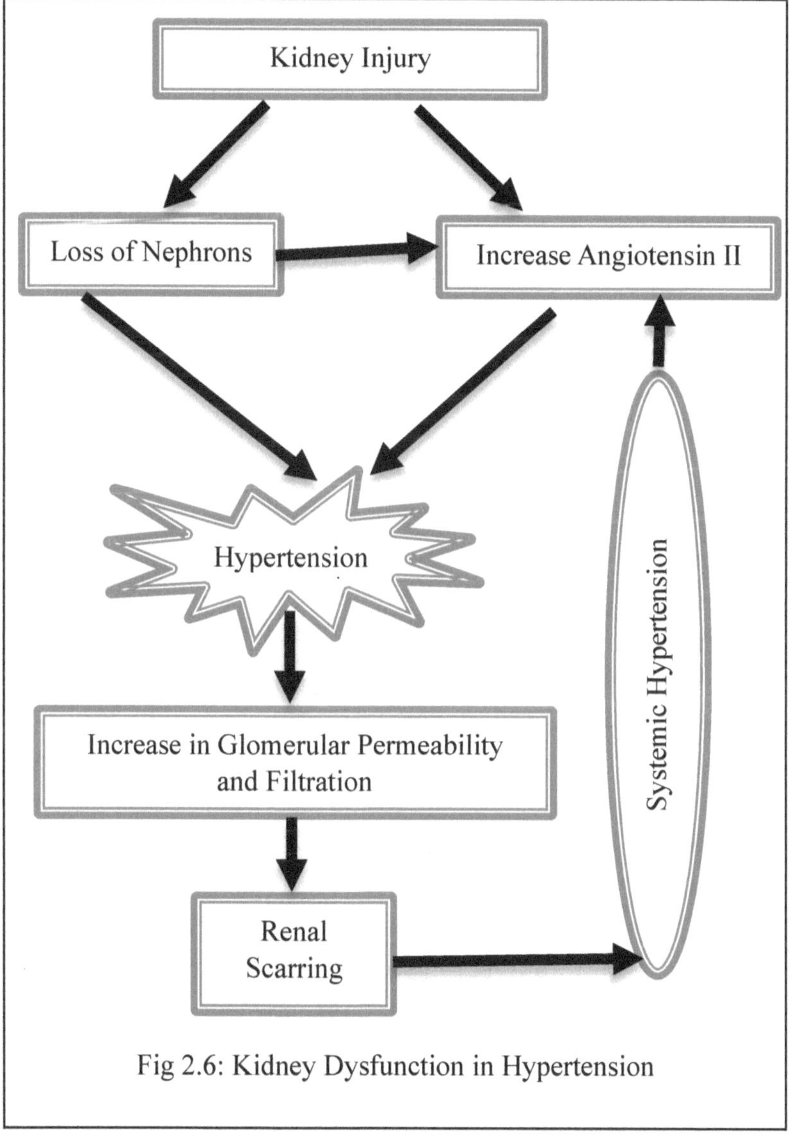

Fig 2.6: Kidney Dysfunction in Hypertension

Furthermore, chronic hypertension can itself cause progressive kidney damage, creating a vicious cycle where hypertension exacerbates kidney dysfunction, leading to further sodium retention and increased blood pressure. Understanding this relationship underscores the importance of targeted interventions aimed at improving renal function and promoting sodium excretion as part of effective hypertension management strategies. The kidneys regulate blood pressure by controlling fluid balance and excreting excess sodium. In hypertensive patients, impaired sodium excretion can lead to:

- **Volume Expansion:** Retention of sodium and water increases blood volume contributing to increased cardiac output and blood pressure.
- **Renal Vasoconstriction:** Decreased renal perfusion further activities the RAAS, leading to even more vasoconstriction and fluid retention.

  Kidney dysfunction is both a cause and consequence of hypertension, and this feedback loop worsens the condition over time.

Kidney dysfunction and sodium retention play a critical role in the development and progression of hypertension, forming a vicious cycle that exacerbates blood pressure elevation. Impaired renal function can lead to reduced sodium excretion, resulting in fluid retention and increased blood volume, which further elevates blood pressure. Conversely, hypertension can cause damage to the renal vasculature and nephron structures, diminishing the kidneys' ability to regulate fluid balance effectively. The interplay between these factors highlights the importance of early detection and management of kidney health in hypertensive patients. Therapeutic strategies that focus on controlling blood pressure and enhancing renal function, including the use of diuretics and lifestyle modifications are essential for breaking this cycle. By addressing kidney dysfunction and sodium retention, healthcare providers can improve overall patient outcomes, reduce cardiovascular risks and enhance the quality of life for individuals affected by hypertension.

2.6 Increased Vascular Resistance:

A hallmark of hypertension is increased total peripheral vascular resistance (TPR). This is due to combinations of:

- Vasoconstriction from RAAS and SNS activity.
- Structural Changes in the blood vessels (vascular remodelling).
- Endothelial dysfunction, which impairs vasodilation.

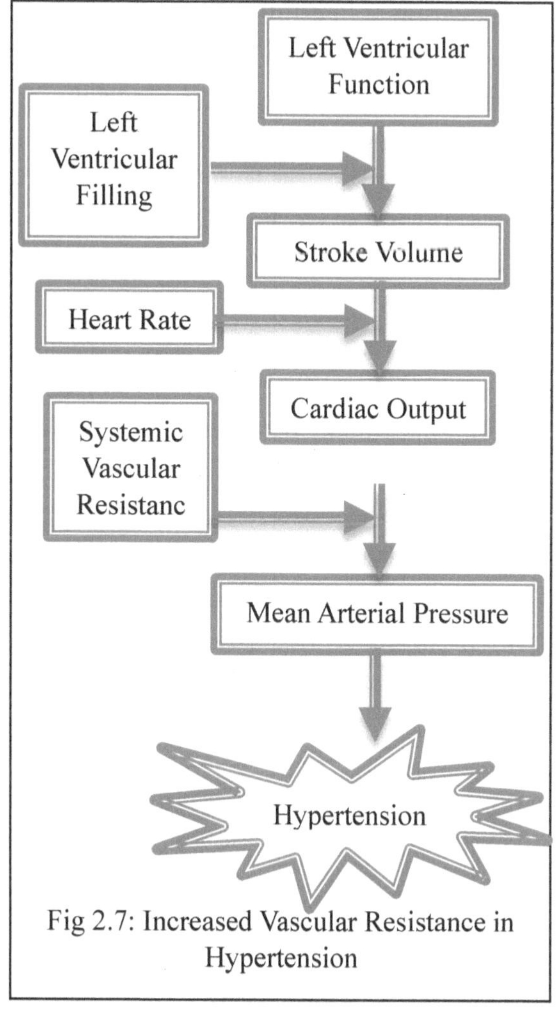

Fig 2.7: Increased Vascular Resistance in Hypertension

Increased vascular resistance is a defining characteristic of hypertension and plays a critical role in the pathophysiology of this condition, leading to sustained elevations in blood pressure. Vascular resistance is primarily determined by the diameter of blood vessels; when the arteries and arterioles constrict or undergo structural changes, resistance increases, making it more difficult for blood to flow through the circulatory system. Several mechanisms contribute to this increased resistance. One of the primary factors is vascular remodelling, which involves hypertrophy of smooth muscle cells and thickening of the arterial walls in response to chronic pressure overload. This remodelling reduces the lumen diameter, thereby increasing resistance. Additionally endothelial dysfunction, characterized by impaired endothelial cell function and reduced production of vasodilators such as nitric oxide, further exacerbates vasoconstriction. Endothelial cells normally help maintain vascular tone and their dysfunction leads to an imbalance favouring constriction over relaxation.

Moreover, the RAAS is often overactive in hypertensive individual. Elevated levels of angiotensin II, a potent vasoconstrictor, directly increase vascular resistance by causing smooth muscle contraction and promoting structural changes in the blood vessels. The RAAS also stimulates aldosterone secretion leading to sodium retention, which increases blood volume and subsequently elevates blood pressure. Increased activity of the sympathetic nervous system also plays a significant role, as heightened norepinephrine levels lead to vasoconstriction and an increase in the heart rate, contributing to elevated vascular resistance. This heightened sympathetic tone is often associated with stress, obesity and other lifestyle factors, further compounding the issue.

The consequences of increased vascular resistance are profound. It not only raises blood pressure but also impress additional workload on the heart potentially leading left ventricular hypertrophy and heart failure over time. Furthermore, chronic high resistance can result in damage to target organs, including the kidneys and brain, increasing the risk of conditions such as chronic kidney disease and stroke. Understanding the mechanism underlying increased vascular resistance is essential for developing targeted therapies for hypertension. Treatments such as ACE inhibitors and calcium channel blockers work to reduce vascular cardiovascular health. By addressing these factors, healthcare providers can more effectively manage hypertension and mitigate its long-term complications.

2.7 Genetic Factors:

Genetic factors play a crucial role in the development and progression of hypertension, influencing both individuals' susceptibility and the heritability of the condition, Numerous studies have identified specific genetic variants associated with blood pressure regulation, highlighting the complex interplay between multiple genes and environmental factors. For instance, polymorphisms in genes related to the RAAS such as the angiotensinogen gene (AGT) and angiotensin II receptor genes (AGTR1 and AGTR2), can affect how the body regulates blood pressure. Additionally, genes involved in vascular function, such as endothelial nitric oxide synthase (ENOS), have been implicated, as variations can lead to altered nitric oxide production, contributing to endothelial dysfunction and increased vascular resistance. Genome-wide association studies (GWAS) have identified numerous loci linked to hypertension, providing insights into the

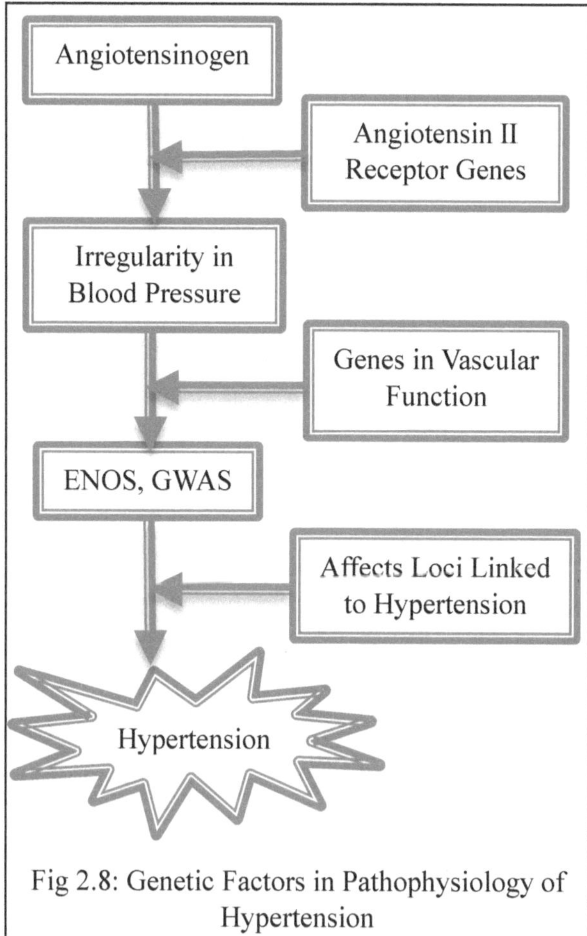

Fig 2.8: Genetic Factors in Pathophysiology of Hypertension

polygenic nature of the condition, where multiple genes contribute small effects that collectively increase risk.

Environmental interactions, such as diet, physical activity and stress can further modify the expression of these genetic predispositions, underscoring the importance of gene-environment interactions in hypertension. Furthermore, familial studies reveal that first-degree relatives of hypertensive individuals have a higher risk of developing hypertension themselves, suggesting a significant genetic component. Epigenetic factors, which involve modifications that affect gene expression without altering DNA sequences, also contribute to hypertension risk, especially in response to environmental stimuli. Overall, understanding the genetic factors in hypertension is vital for identifying at-risk individuals, tailoring prevention strategies and developing targeted therapies that address the underlying genetic contributions to this prevalent condition.

2.8 Insulin Resistance and Metabolic Syndrome:

Insulin resistance and metabolic syndrome are closely linked to hypertension, creating a complex interplay that exacerbates cardiovascular risks. Insulin resistance, a condition where the body's cells become less responsive to insulin, often leads to elevated levels of insulin in the bloodstream, a state known as hyperinsulinemia. This can contribute to increased sympathetic nervous system activity and vascular smooth muscle contraction, both of which elevate blood pressure. Additionally, insulin resistance is frequently associated with obesity, particularly visceral fat accumulation, which further promotes inflammation and the release of pro-inflammatory cytokines that can damage endothelial function. Metabolic syndrome is characterized by a cluster of conditions, including hypertension, dyslipidaemia (elevated triglycerides and low HDL cholesterol), elevated fasting glucose and abdominal obesity. The presence of metabolic syndrome significantly heightens the risk of developing hypertension due to the combined effects of these metabolic derangements. For instance, excess adipose tissue secretes various bioactive substances, including free fatty acids and inflammatory markers, which can impair endothelial function and promote vascular stiffness, thus increasing peripheral resistance. Many hypertensive patients also have insulin resistance or metabolic syndrome, a cluster of conditions that includes obesity, high blood sugar, and dyslipidaemia. Insulin resistance is associated with:

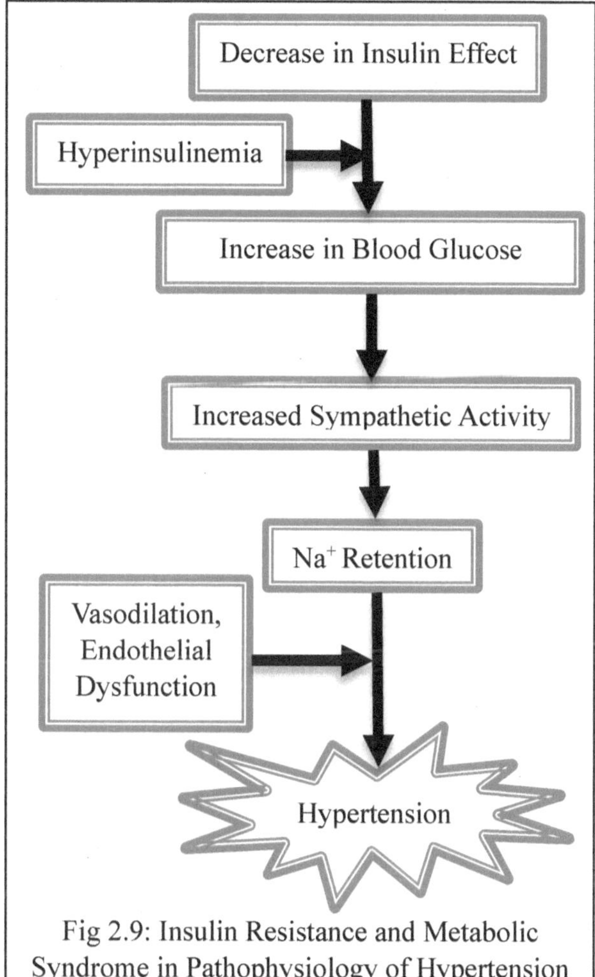

Fig 2.9: Insulin Resistance and Metabolic Syndrome in Pathophysiology of Hypertension

- Increased sympathetic activity.
- Sodium retention.
- Impaired vasodilation due to endothelial dysfunction.

This creates a vicious cycle where metabolic disturbances worsen blood pressure control. Moreover, the insulin resistance seen in metabolic syndrome disrupts normal lipid metabolism, leading to atherogenic dyslipidaemia that contributes to atherosclerosis, further increasing cardiovascular risks. The relationship between insulin resistance, metabolic syndrome and hypertension underscores the importance of lifestyle modifications, such as weight loss, increased physical activity and dietary changes, which can improve insulin sensitivity and help regulate blood pressure. Targeting these interconnected metabolic factors not only aids in managing hypertension but also reduces the overall risk of cardiovascular disease and improves long-term health outcomes. Understanding this triad of insulin resistance, metabolic syndrome and hypertensive treatment strategies aimed at mitigating their combined effects on health.

2.9 Environmental and Lifestyle Factors:

Environmental and lifestyle factors significantly influence the development and management of hypertension, interacting with genetic predispositions to elevate blood pressure levels. A key lifestyle factor is diet, particularly the consumption of high sodium foods, which can lead to increased fluid retention and elevated blood pressure. The western diet, often characterized by excessive salt intake, processed foods and low consumption of fruits and vegetables is associated with higher rates of hypertension. Conversely, dietary patterns such as the DASH (Dietary Approaches to Stop Hypertension) diet, which emphasizes whole grains, lean proteins, fruits and vegetables have been shown to effectively lower blood pressure.

Physical inactivity is another critical lifestyle factor, sedentary behaviour can contribute to weight gain and obesity, both of which are strongly linked to hypertension. Regular aerobic exercise helps improve cardiovascular health, enhance endothelial function and lower blood pressure. Moreover, obesity particularly visceral fat accumulation, is a significant risk factor as it promotes insulin resistance and activates inflammatory pathways that impair vascular function. Alcohol consumption and smoking are also notable lifestyle factors. Excessive alcohol intake can raise blood pressure by affecting the renin-angiotensin-aldosterone system and increasing sympathetic nervous system activity, while smoking causes acute vasoconstriction and chronic damage to the vascular endothelium, contributing to hypertension. Stress in another environmental factor that can influence blood pressure. Chronic psychological stress can lead to increased sympathetic nervous system activity and the release of stress hormones like cortisol, both of which elevate blood pressure over time.

Additionally, socioeconomic factors, such as access to healthcare, education and living conditions play a role in hypertension prevalence. Individuals in lower socioeconomic groups may experience higher stress levels and limited access to healthy foods and healthcare services, further increasing their risk. Addressing these environmental and lifestyle factors through targeted interventions, such as promoting healthier dietary choices, encouraging physical activity and managing stress is essential for preventing and managing hypertension. Comprehensive public health strategies that focus on these aspects can help reduce the overall burden of hypertension in populations and improve cardiovascular health outcomes.

Consequences of Hypertension:

Hypertension, often referred to as the "silent killer", can lead to numerous serious health consequences that affect multiple organ systems. If left untreated, hypertension can lead to severe complications, such as:

- **Atherosclerosis:** High blood pressure damages plaque formation.
- **Heart Failure:** The heart's increased workload can lead to left ventricular hypertrophy and eventual heart failure.
- **Chronic Kidney Diseases:** Hypertension damages the blood vessels in the kidneys, reducing their function over time.
- **Stroke:** High blood pressure can lead to haemorrhagic or ischemic strokes due to the rupture or blockage of cerebral arteries.
- **Retinopathy:** Hypertension can damage the blood vessels in the eyes, leading to vision loss.

Effective management of hypertension is critical to preventing these serious consequences and improving overall health outcomes. Regular monitoring, lifestyle modifications and adherence to treatment can significantly reduce the risk of complications associated with high blood pressure.

In conclusion, the pathophysiology of hypertension is a multifaceted and dynamic process involving a complex interplay of genetic, environmental and physiological factors. Central mechanisms include increased vascular resistance due to structural changes in blood vessels, such as arteriolar hypertrophy and remodelling, alongside endothelial dysfunction that impairs vasodilatory capacity. The overactivation of RAAS and heightened SNS activity further exacerbate these changes, leading to sustained increases in blood pressure. Additionally, factors such as insulin resistance and metabolic syndrome contribute to the hypertensive state, highlighting the significant role of metabolic health in cardiovascular risk. Environmental and lifestyle influences, including dietary habits, physical inactivity, obesity and psychosocial stressors, create a conductive environment for hypertension to develop and persist. Together, these elements culminate in a chronic condition that poses substantial risks for serious health complications, including heart disease, stroke and kidney failure. Understanding the intricate pathophysiological mechanisms underlying hypertension is crucial for developing effective prevention and treatment strategies. By addressing both the biological and lifestyle factors contributing to hypertension, healthcare providers can enhance patient outcomes, reduce the prevalence of hypertension and ultimately improve cardiovascular health on broader scale. This comprehensive approach underscores the importance of a holistic view of hypertension management, integrating medical interventions with lifestyle modifications and public health initiatives to tackle this pervasive health challenge.

3. Risk Factors

Hypertension commonly known as high blood pressure, is a chronic medical condition where the force of blood against the walls of the arteries is consistently too high. Left untreated, hypertension can lead to serious health complications, including heart disease,

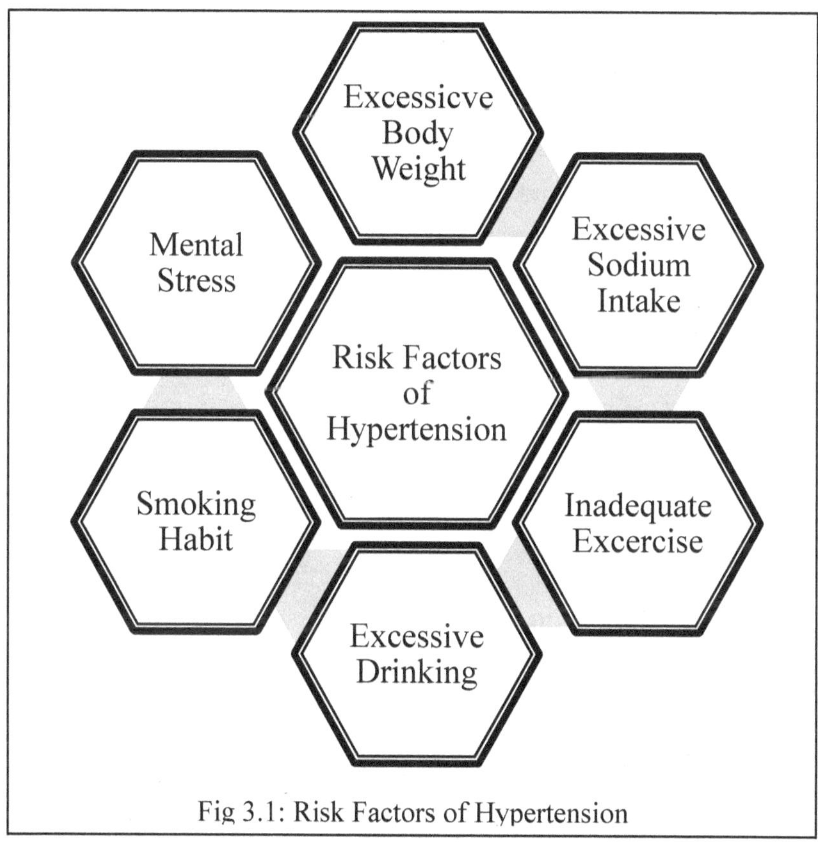

Fig 3.1: Risk Factors of Hypertension

stroke, kidney failure, and more. It is often called "silent killer" because it typically does not present noticeable symptoms until significant damage has occurred. Understanding the risk factors associated with hypertension is critical for prevention, early detection and management. Risk factors can be classified into non-modifiable and modifiable categories, where non-modifiable factors cannot be damaged, but modifiable factors can be adjusted through lifestyle and behavioural changes.

3.1 Non-Modifiable Risk Factors:

Non-modifiable risk factors for hypertension are inherent characteristics that individuals cannot change but significantly influence their susceptibility to developing high blood pressure. These factors include age, such as the risk of hypertension increases with advancing age due to physiological changes in the cardiovascular system and blood vessels. Genetic predisposition and family history also play crucial roles, as individuals with a family history of hypertension are more likely to develop the condition themselves, indicating a hereditary component. Additionally, ethnicity can influence hypertension risk, with certain populations, such as African Americans, experiencing higher rates and more severe forms of hypertension. Recognizing these non-modifiable risk factors is vital for understanding individual risk profiles and guiding preventive strategies, even though they cannot be altered.

a) **Age:** As people age, their risk of developing hypertension increases. This is largely due to changes in the elasticity and function of blood vessels. With age, arteries tend to stiffen, and this contributes to higher blood pressure. The risk is particularly elevated in individuals over 60, although hypertension can develop at any age.

b) **Family History:** A family history of hypertension significantly increase and individual's risk. Genetics play a critical role in blood pressure regulation and having one more first-degree relatives (parents or siblings) with hypertension heightens the likelihood of developing the condition. Specific genetic variants that affect kidney function, salt handling and blood vessel regulation may predispose individuals to high blood pressure.

c) **Gender:** Gender is non-modifiable risk factor where difference in the prevalence of hypertension is seen across age groups. Before the age of 65, men are more likely to develop hypertension than women. However, after the age of 65, women tend to have a higher prevalence of hypertension, often linked to menopause and its hormonal changes.

d) **Race/Ethnicity:** Certain racial and ethnic groups are more predisposed to hypertension than others. For example, African Americans are more likely to develop hypertension at an earlier age and often experience more severe hypertension compared to other populations. They are also at higher risk of complications from hypertension, such as stroke and kidney disease.

e) **Chronic Conditions:** Underlying health conditions, such as chronic kidney disease, diabetes and obstructive sleep apnoea, are strongly linked to the development of hypertension. Kidney disease affects the body's ability to regulate fluid and sodium, while diabetes contributes to blood vessel damage and stiffening, both of which increase blood pressure.

3.2 Modifiable Risk Factors: Modifiable risk factors can be altered through lifestyle changes, behavioural modifications, or medical interventions. Addressing these factors can substantially reduce the risk or hypertension and improve overall cardiovascular health.

a) **Unhealthy Diet High Sodium Intake):** Diet plays a critical role in managing and preventing hypertension. High sodium intake is one of the most significant contributors to elevated blood pressure. Sodium causes the body to retain excess fluid, which increases the volume of the blood and consequently, raises blood pressure. Processed foods, canned goods, fast food, and snacks often contain excessive amounts of sodium. Reducing salt consumption by avoiding these foods and reading labels can help lower blood pressure.

b) **Physical Inactivity:** A sedentary lifestyle is a well-established risk factors for hypertension. Regular physical activity strengthens the heart, improves blood vessel flexibility, and helps maintain healthy levels. Inactivity, on the other hand, contributes to weight gain and increase the risk of other conditions like diabetes, which can also elevate blood pressure. It is recommended that adults engage in at least 150 minutes of moderate intensity exercise each week to maintain cardiovascular health.

c) **Obesity and Overweight:** Excess body weight is a major risk factor for hypertension. Obesity increases the amount of work the heart must do to pump blood throughout the body, thereby increasing blood pressure. Fat deposits around vital organs can also impair normal cardiovascular function. Studies show that even modest weight loss can lead to significant reductions in blood pressure. Maintaining a healthy body mass index (BMI) through a balanced diet and regular physical activity is crucial for hypertension.

d) **Exclusive Alcohol Consumption:** Alcohol can have a direct and substantial effect on blood pressure. Consuming alcohol in excess-defined as more than one drinks per day for women-can raise blood pressure significantly. Over time, heavy drinking weakness the heart muscle and contributes to weight gain, further exacerbating the risk of hypertension. Limiting alcohol intake is essential for blood pressure control.

e) **Smoking and Tobacco Use:** Smoking damages the walls of the arteries, causing them to narrow and harden which increases blood pressure. Additionally, nicotine form smoking causes a temporary but immediate increase in the blood pressure and heart rate. The chemicals in tobacco also promote the buildup of fatty deposits in the arteries, leading to atherosclerosis and increased cardiovascular risk. Quitting smoking has both short- and long-term benefits for blood pressure and overall heart health.

f) **High Stress Levels:** Chronic stress can contribute to temporary spikes in blood pressure, and over time, repeated exposure to stress can lead to sustained hypertension. When stressed, the body releases hormones like cortisol and adrenaline, which temporarily increase blood pressure by constricting blood vessels. Stress management techniques, such as mindfulness, meditation, deep breathing exercises, and adequate rest, can help mitigate this risk factor.

g) **Poor diet (Low in Fruits, Vegetables and Potassium):** A diet low in fruits, vegetables and other potassium rich foods can contribute to hypertension. Potassium helps to balance the sodium levels in the body, and a deficiency in potassium can lead to elevated blood pressure. The DASH (Dietary Approaches to Stop Hypertension) diet, which emphasizes fruits, vegetables, whole grains and lean proteins has been shown to reduce blood pressure in hypertensive individuals.

h) **Exclusive Caffeine Consumption:** Although the long-term effects of caffein on blood pressure are still debated, excessive consumption of caffeine has been shown to cause short term increase in blood pressure, particularly in people sensitive to caffeine. Reducing caffeine intake may help lower blood pressure for some individuals, especially those with high caffeine consumption.

3.3 Additional Factors and Emerging Risks:

In addition to the primary risk factors of hypertension, several additional factors contribute to its development and severity. Chronic stress is significant, as prolonged psychological stress can lead to increased sympathetic nervous system activity, resulting in elevated heart rate and blood pressure. Sleep disorders, particularly obstructive sleep apnoea are also linked to hypertension; the intermittent hypoxia and increased sympathetic activity associated with sleep apnoea can exacerbate blood pressure elevation. Hormonal imbalances, such as those related to conditions like hyperaldosteronism or Cushing's syndrome, can lead to sodium retention and increased vascular resistance.

Furthermore, certain medications, including non-steroidal anti-inflammatory drugs (NSAIDs), corticosteroids and some antidepressants can raise blood pressure as side effect. Environmental factors such as exposure to lead and high levels of air pollution, have also been associated with an increased risk of hypertension. Together, these additional factors highlight the multifaceted nature of hypertension, emphasizing the importance of a comprehensive approach to prevent and management that considers both lifestyle and external influences.

a) **Sleep Deprivation:** Poor or insufficient sleep has been linked to an increased risk of hypertension. Sleep is crucial for regulating stress hormones and maintaining heart health. Chronic sleep deprivation or conditions like sleep apnoea, which disrupt normal sleep patterns, can cause elevated blood pressure. Adequate sleep in necessary for the body's repair and maintenance processes.

b) **Medication and Substance Use:** Certain medications, such as nonsteroidal anti-inflammatory drugs (NSAIDs), oral contraceptives, and certain antidepressants, can increase blood pressure. Illicit drug use, such as cocaine or amphetamines, can also lead to a hypertensive crisis and permanent damage to the cardiovascular system. Individuals should consult their healthcare provider regarding the blood pressure effects of any medications they are taking.

c) **Microbiome:** Emerging studies suggests that gut health and the microbiome may influence blood pressure regulation, metabolic pathways and inflammation. Alterations in gut bacteria composition can affect the production of short-chain fatty acids and other metabolites, which may impact vascular health. This connection highlights the potential for dietary interventions aimed at promoting a healthy microbiome as strategy for managing hypertension.

d) **Socioeconomic Factors:** Lower socioeconomic status can lead to increased stress, poor access to healthcare and healthy lifestyle choices, all contributing to hypertension. These factors contribute to a greater prevalence of risk behaviour such as poor diet, physical inactivity and smoking ultimately leading to elevated blood pressure levels.

e) **Environment Factors:** Environmental factors such as, air pollution, exposure to toxic chemicals and urbanization can

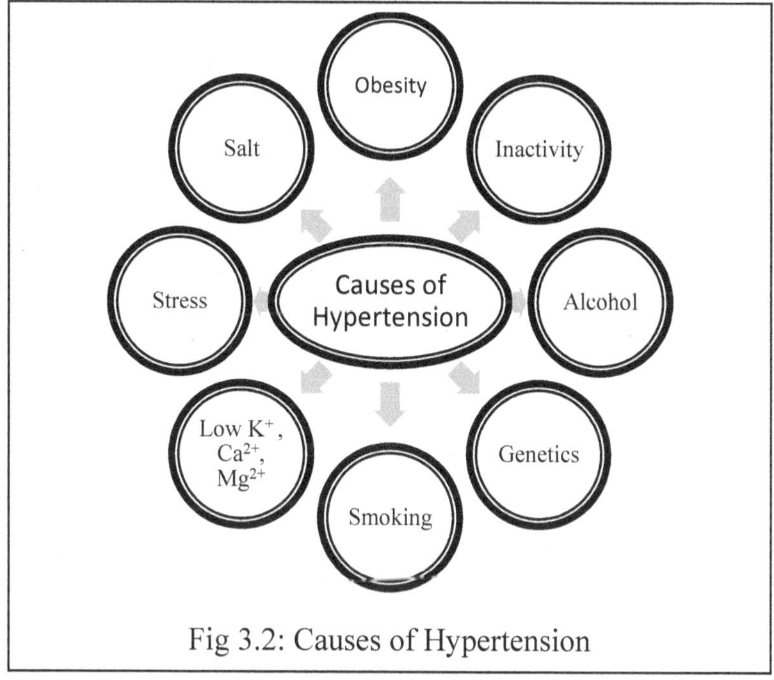

Fig 3.2: Causes of Hypertension

significantly contribute to hypertension. Pollutants like particulate matter and heavy metals can include oxidative stress and inflammation, affecting vascular health. Additionally, living in areas with limited access to green spaces and healthy food options can lead to increasing the risk of elevated blood pressure.

Hypertension is a multifactorial condition influenced by both non-modifiable and modifiable risk factors. While genetics, age and gender cannot be controlled, significant progress can be made in managing modifiable risk factors through lifestyle adjustment, such as a healthier diet, regular physical activity, stress management and smoking cessation. Understanding these risk factors is critical for preventing hypertension and minimizing its complications. Early interventions and proactive measure can help reduce the global burden of hypertension and improve long-term cardiovascular health.

4. Diagnosis of Hypertension

Diagnosing hypertension accurately is essential for preventing long-term complications such as cardiovascular events, kidney disease, and even death. Since hypertension often presents with no symptoms, regular screening and proper diagnostic measures are key to identifying it in its early stages. Moreover, an accurate diagnosis allows for effective treatment plans, reducing the risk of adverse outcomes. Accurate diagnosis typically requires multiple readings taken on separate occasions to account for variability and potential white coat syndrome, where patients exhibit elevated readings in clinical settings. Additional assessments, including patient history, physical examinations and sometimes laboratory tests are essential to rule out secondary causes of hypertension and to evaluate the overall cardiovascular risk. Timely and precise diagnosis is vital, as uncontrolled hypertension can lead to serious complications,

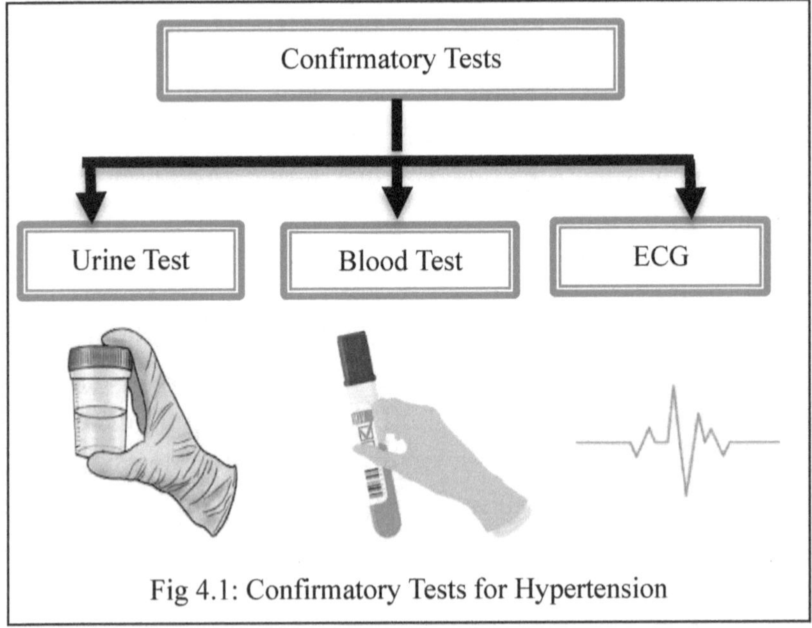

Fig 4.1: Confirmatory Tests for Hypertension

including heart disease, stroke, and kidney damage. Thus,

understanding and implementing proper diagnostic protocols is fundamental in the management and prevention of hypertension.

4.1 Methods of Blood Pressure Measurement:

Blood pressure measurement in hypertension can be conducted through several methods, each with distinct advantages. The most common technique is the auscultatory method, which uses a sphygmomanometer and a stethoscope to detect Korotkoff sounds as the cuff deflates. Automated oscillometric devices are increasingly popular for their ease of use, providing digital readings without the need for manual interpretation. Ambulatory blood pressure monitoring allows for continuous tracking over 24 hours, capturing variations in blood pressure throughout daily activities and reducing the white-coat effect. Home blood pressure monitoring empowers patients to track their own readings, enhancing self-management and adherence to treatment. Each method plays a critical role in accurately diagnosing and managing hypertension, tailored to individual patient needs. There are several methods to measure blood pressure, each with its advantages and limitations.

Sr. No.	Method	Setting
1.	Office Blood Pressure Monitoring (OBPM)	Clinic blood pressure monitoring by Physician
2.	Ambulatory Blood Pressure Monitoring (ABPM)	Fitted at dienic but BP measured while patient does normal daily activities
3.	Home Blood Pressure Monitoring (OBPM)	Twice daily readings for 7 days morning and night

Table 4.1: Methods of Blood Pressure Monitoring

a) Office Blood Pressure Measurement (OBPM):

Office blood pressure measurement is a crucial component in diagnosing and managing hypertension. It involves taking blood pressure readings in clinical setting, where factors such as stress and anxiety may influence results. Accurate measurements require proper technique, including the use of validated sphygmomanometer and ensuring the patient is relaxed and seated comfortably. Multiple readings should be taken over several visits to establish a reliable baseline. This method helps healthcare providers assess the severity of hypertension, monitor treatment efficacy and make informed decisions about medication adjustments and lifestyle interventions. Regular monitoring in the office also plays a vital role in identifying potential complications and ensuring ongoing patient engagement in their health management. This is the most common method used in clinical practice. Blood pressure is measured using a sphygmomanometer (manual or digital) while the patient is seated in relaxed state. The procedure follows a standardized protocol:

- The patient should sit quietly for 5 minutes before the measurement.
- The arm should be supported at heart level.
- The cuff size should be appropriate for the patient's arm circumference.
- At least two readings should be taken, and the average of these readings is considered for diagnosis.

Limitations:

- White coat hypertension (elevated readings in the doctor's office due to anxiety) may result in over-diagnosis.
- Masked hypertension (normal readings in the office but elevated at home) may go undetected.
- Single measurements can be misleading.

b) Ambulatory Blood Pressure Measurement (ABPM):

ABPM is a diagnostic technique that involves wearing a portable device to measure blood pressure at regular intervals over 24 hours. This method provides a comprehensive profile of a patient's blood pressure throughout their daily activities and during sleep. Offering insights into fluctuations that may not be captured during standard office visits. It is particularly useful for diagnosing conditions like white-coat hypertension, where patients exhibit elevated readings in clinical setting but not in everyday life. It also aids in assessing blood pressure variability and the effectiveness of antihypertensive treatments. By providing a more accurate representation of a patient's blood pressure patterns, ABPM helps healthcare providers make informed decisions regarding diagnosis, treatment plans and long-term management strategies for hypertension. This method is considered the gold standard for diagnosing hypertension, particularly in patients with suspected white coat or masked hypertension. ABPM provides valuable information, including:

- Daytime and nighttime blood pressure patterns.
- Blood pressure variability
- Average 24-hour blood pressure

Advantages:

- More accurate reflection of the patient's true blood pressure.
- Allows detection of nocturnal hypertension (elevated blood pressure during sleep), which is a strong predictor of cardiovascular events.
- Reduces the risk of overdiagnosis.

Limitations:

- Expensive and not always readily available.
- Inconvenient for some patients.

c) Home Blood Pressure Monitoring (HBPM):

Human blood pressure monitoring is essential for assessing cardiovascular health and diagnosing conditions like hypertension. It can be performed using various methods, including manual measurements with a sphygmomanometer and automated devices that provides digital readings. Regular monitoring helps identify both elevated and fluctuating blood pressure levels, which can inform treatment decisions and lifestyle modifications. Home monitoring is increasingly encouraged, allowing patients to track their blood pressure in a comfortable environment and share results with healthcare providers. This proactive approach promotes patient engagement and helps manage hypertension more effectively. Accurate blood pressure monitoring is crucial for preventing complications such as heart disease, stroke and kidney damage, making it a key component of routine healthcare. HBPM involves the use of automated devices that patients can use at home to measure their own blood pressure. This method is particularly useful for long-term monitoring and for patients with white coat or masked hypertension.

Advantages:

- Convenient and cost-effective.
- Provides multiple readings over time, leading to a more accurate diagnosis.
- Empowers patients to be actively involved in managing their condition.

Limitations:

- Requires proper training and education for patients to use the device correctly.
- Inconsistent use or incorrect technique may lead to inaccurate readings.

4.2 Diagnostic Criteria and Process:

The diagnostic criteria for hypertension typically involve measuring blood pressure during multiple visits, using standardized methods. The diagnosis of hypertension should never be made based on a single blood pressure measurement. According to the American College of Cardiology/ American Heart Association, hypertension is diagnosed when a patient consistently has a blood pressure reading of 130/80 mmHg or higher. The diagnostic process begins with a thorough patient history and physical examination, followed by at least two or more readings on separate occasions to confirm elevated levels. Additional assessments may include laboratory tests, such as blood tests and urinalysis, to evaluate for underlying causes or complications. Ambulatory blood pressure monitoring may also be utilized to assess blood pressure fluctuations and confirm a diagnosis, especially in cases of suspected white-coat hypertension. Accurate diagnosis is crucial for developing an effective management plan tailored to the individual's health needs. The diagnostic process involves multiple steps:

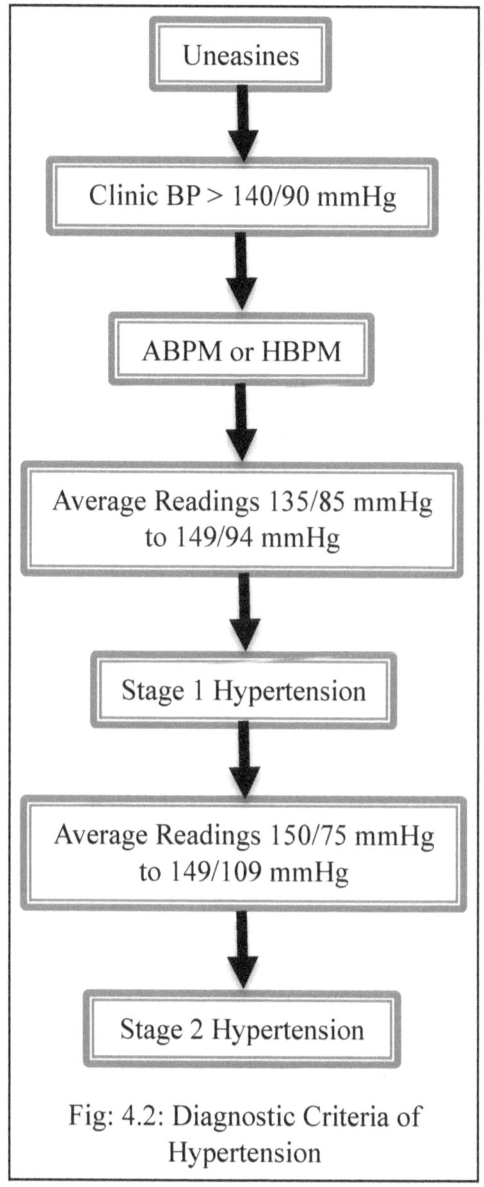

Fig: 4.2: Diagnostic Criteria of Hypertension

a) Initial Screening:

Initial screening for hypertension typically involves measuring blood pressure using sphygmomanometer in a clinical setting. Blood pressure readings are taken at least twice, ideally on separate occasions, to confirm elevated levels. A reading of 130/80 mmHg or higher is generally indicative of hypertension. Alongside blood pressure measurement, healthcare providers often assess risk factors such as age, family history, weight, smoking status and lifestyle factors. Following points should be keep in mind while screening the hypertension initially.

- Blood pressure should be measured in both arms during the first visit. The arm with the higher reading should be used for subsequent measurements.
- Two to three measurements should be taken at least 1 minute apart, and the average of these readings should be recorded.
- If the blood pressure is elevated, follow-up measurements should be scheduled to confirm to diagnosis.

b) Confirmatory Testing:

To confirm a diagnosis of hypertension, at least two elevated readings on separate occasion are needed. The time frame for confirmation varies depending on the initial readings:

- For stage 1 hypertension, a follow-up visit within 1 month is recommended.
- For stage 2 hypertension, confirmatory testing should occur within a shorter period (1-2 weeks).
- For hypertensive urgency or emergency, immediate medical evaluation is necessary.

c) **Use of ABPM or HBPM:**

In patients with suspected white coat or masked hypertension, ABPM or HBPM should be used to confirm the diagnosis. An average daytime blood pressure>135/85 mmHg or 24-hours blood pressure>130/80 mmHg on ABPM confirms the diagnosis of hypertension. ABPM involves continuous blood pressure measurement over 24 hours, providing a comprehensive view of blood pressure fluctuations throughout daily activities and during sleep. HBPM allows patients to monitor their blood pressure at home using a validated device.

❖ **Secondary Hypertension:**

While most cases of hypertension are classified as primary (essential) hypertension, approximately 5-10% of cases have an identifiable underlying cause, known as secondary hypertension. Secondary hypertension is high blood pressure that results from an identifiable underlying condition, as opposes to primary hypertension, which has no specific cause. Common causes of secondary hypertension include kidney disease, hormonal disorders such as hyperaldosteronism or Cushing's syndrome, certain medications and structural abnormalities like coarctation of the aorta. Identifying and treating the underlying condition can often lead to significant improvements in blood pressure control.

Unlike primary hypertension, which typically develops gradually over time, secondary hypertension may appear suddenly or rapidly, making it essential for healthcare providers to conduct thorough evaluations, including blood tests, imaging studies and patient history assessment. Prompt diagnosis and interventions and improve overall health outcomes for affected individuals. Patients suspected of having secondary hypertension should undergo further diagnostic evaluation, including blood tests, imaging, and specialist referral as needed. Common causes of secondary hypertension include:

- **Renal Diseases:** Chronic kidney disease, renal artery stenosis.
- **Endocrine disorders:** Hyperaldosteronism, pheochromocytoma, Cushing's syndrome, hypothyroidism, hyperthyroidism.
- **Medications:** Oral contraceptives, non-steroidal anti-inflammatory drugs (NSAIDs), corticosteroids.
- **Obstructive sleep apnoea:** Linked with resistant hypertension.
- **Coarctation of the aorta:** A congenital condition leading to hypertension in children and young adults.

In conclusion, secondary hypertension represents a significant subset of high blood pressure cases that arise from identifiable underlying conditions, such as endocrine disorders, renal diseases or certain medications. Recognizing and diagnosing secondary hypertension is crucial, as it often responds well to targeted treatments addressing the root cause, potentially leading to improved patient outcomes. Regular monitoring and a thorough evaluation of patients with hypertension are essential to distinguish between primary and secondary forms, ensuring that those affected receive the most effective management strategies. By increasing awareness and understanding of secondary hypertension, healthcare providers can better support patients in achieving optimal blood pressure control and reducing the risk of associated complications.

4.3 Diagnostic Evaluation:

In addition to measuring blood pressure, the diagnostic evaluation for hypertension involves a thorough history, physical examination, and laboratory tests to assess for secondary causes and target organ damage. It is a critical process aimed at accurately identifying elevated blood pressure and its potential underlying causes. This evaluation typically begins with a thorough patient history, including risk factors such as family history, lifestyle habits and any existing medical conditions. Blood pressure measurements are taken using standardized techniques, with multiple readings to ensure accuracy. Additional diagnostic tests, such as laboratory assessments and imaging studies, may be conducted to assess for secondary causes of hypertension and evaluate for related complications. The comprehensive approach not only confirms a diagnosis but also guides appropriate management strategies, ultimately aiming to reduce cardiovascular risk and improve patient outcomes.

a) Medical History:

A detailed medical history should include:

- Duration of elevated blood pressure.
- Family history of hypertension and cardiovascular disease.
- Lifestyle factors: Smoking, alcohol consumption, physical activity, diet.
- Use of medications, including over-the-counter drugs and supplements.
- Symptoms suggesting secondary causes (e.g., headaches, muscle weakness, weight loss, palpitations.)

b) Physical Examination:

The physical exam should include:

- Measurement of blood pressure in both arms.
- Palpation of pulses in both upper and lower extremities.
- Examination for signs of end-organ damage (e.g., hypertensive retinopathy, left ventricular hypertrophy).
- Evaluation of the abdomen for bruits (suggestive of renal artery stenosis) or masses,

c) **Laboratory and Diagnostic Testing:**

Once hypertension is suspected, further tests may be conducted to assess its impact on the body and identify possible secondary causes of hypertension:

- **Blood Tests:** To elevate kidney function (e.g., serum creatinine), blood glucose, lipid profile, and electrolytes.
- **Urine tests:** To check for kidney damage or underlying conditions.
- **Electrocardiography:** In cases of suspected heart failure or structural heart disease, this imagining can help visualize the heart's function and structure.
- **Imaging studies:** Renal ultrasound or CT scan may be performed if secondary causes of hypertension, such as kidney disease, are suspected.

4.4 Special Considerations in Hypertension Diagnosis:

When diagnosing hypertension, several special considerations are essential to ensure accurate assessment and management. Factors such as patient age, ethnicity and comorbidities can influence blood pressure readings and treatment approaches. Additionally, conditions like white-coat syndrome and masked hypertension may complicate diagnosis, necessitating the use of multiple measurement techniques, including home monitoring and ambulatory blood pressure monitoring. Understanding these variables is critical for healthcare providers to deliver personalized care and effectively address the complexities of hypertension in diverse patient populations.

- **Resistant Hypertension:** Resistant hypertension is defined as blood pressure that remains above the target level despite the use of three or more antihypertensive medications, including a diuretic. It requires further evaluation, often with ABPM or additional diagnostic tests to exclude secondary causes.
- **Hypertension in Pregnancy:** Hypertension during pregnancy requires careful monitoring due to the risk of complications like preeclampsia. Blood pressure in pregnant women should be measured with special attention to their physiological changes, and diagnostic criteria differ slightly.

Early and accurate diagnosis of hypertension is key to preventing long-term complications. Regular blood pressure monitoring, either at home or in a clinical setting, along with appropriate diagnostic evaluations, ensures that hypertension is managed effectively. With proper diagnosis, patients can be guided towards lifestyle modifications and medical interventions that significantly reduced the risks associated with elevate blood pressure.

In summary, the diagnosis of hypertension is multifaceted process that requires a careful and systematic approach to ensure accuracy and effective management. Initially, it involves obtaining a comprehensive patient history and performing a thorough physical examination, which helps identify risk factors and potential secondary causes. Consistent blood pressure measurements are crucial; multiple readings taken at different times are necessary to confirm elevated levels, as hypertension can fluctuate due to various factors, including stress and physical activity. The use of validated measurement techniques, such as the auscultatory method or automated devices, is essential for reliable results. Special considerations such as the impact of age, ethnicity and comorbid conditions further complicate the diagnostic landscape, necessitating a tailored approach for each patient. In some cases, additional diagnostic tools like ambulatory blood pressure monitoring may be employed to provide a more comprehensive picture of blood pressure behaviour over time. Furthermore, laboratory tests can help identify underlying conditions that may contribute to secondary hypertension. Ultimately, a thorough and nuanced understanding of the diagnostic criteria and processes not only aids in accurate identification of hypertension but also informs targeted interventions, ultimately improving patient outcomes and reducing the risk of serious cardiovascular complications. As research continuous to evolve, ongoing education and awareness among healthcare providers about the complexities of hypertension diagnosis remain critical to enhancing patient care.

5. Clinical Presentation and Symptoms of Hypertension

The clinical presentation of hypertension, often referred to as the "silent killer", is typically asymptomatic in its early stages, making it difficult to direct without regular monitoring. As blood pressure rises, some individuals may begin to experience symptoms such as headaches, dizziness, blurred vision or shortness of breath, but these signs are often nonspecific and can be attributed to other conditions. Chronic hypertension can lead to serious complications including heart disease, stroke and kidney damage, highlighting the importance of routine blood pressure check. Understanding the clinical manifestation of hypertension is crucial for early detection and effective management ultimately reducing the risk of severe health outcomes.

In addition to the common symptoms, hypertension can also manifest through more severe complications such as hypertensive crises, characterized by significantly elevated blood pressure that may result in organ damage. Patients may also exhibit signs related to secondary conditions, such as chest pain or fatigue, which can signal cardiovascular strain. Furthermore, long-term hypertension may lead to changes in organ function, evident through symptoms like frequent urination, swelling in the legs, or cognitive issues. Because many individuals remain unaware of their condition until complications arise, raising awareness about the importance of regular screenings and lifestyle modifications is vital for effective prevention and management of hypertension.

Hypertension is frequently categorized into two types:

- **Primary (Essential) Hypertension:** Accounts for 90-95% of cases and has no identifiable cause, likely resulting from a combination of genetic predispositions and environmental factors like poor diet and lack of exercise.

- **Secondary Hypertension:** Results from underlying conditions such as kidney disease, hormonal disorders (e.g., hyperaldosteronism, Cushing's syndrome), or the use of medications.

Most individuals with hypertension do not exhibit obvious symptoms, particularly in the early stages of the disease. However, as blood pressure remains elevated over time, target organ damage may occur, leading to a spectrum of clinical presentations.

5.1 Early-Stage Hypertension (Asymptomatic Phase):

Early-stage hypertension, often referred to as prehypertension, is a condition characterized by slightly elevated blood pressure levels that are above the normal range but not yet high enough to be classified as hypertension. Typically defined as systolic blood pressure between 120-129 mmHg and diastolic pressure less than 80 mmHg, this stage serves as a critical warning sign for potential cardiovascular issues. Understanding early-stage hypertension is essential for prevention, as it provides an opportunity for individuals o make lifestyle changes that can effectively lower blood pressure and reduce the risk of developing more severe hypertension and associated health complications.

- **Asymptomatic Presentation:**

  Most hypertensive individuals experience no symptoms in the early stage. Hypertension may remain undiagnosed for years, making routine blood pressure checks crucial for early deduction. Asymptomatic hypertension is often referred to as a silent condition, as individuals may not exhibit any noticeable symptoms despite having elevated blood pressure. This lack of symptoms can lead to a false sense of security, as the underlying health risks associated with uncontrolled hypertension, such as cardiovascular disease and kidney damage, continue to progress unnoticed. Regular blood pressure monitoring is essential for early detection, as many people remain unaware of their condition until it has advanced to a more severe stage, underscoring the importance of proactive health screenings and lifestyle management to mitigate potential complications.

- **Diagnosis:**

The diagnosis of early-stage hypertension involves measuring blood pressure using sphygmomanometer during routine health evaluations. Blood pressure readings of 120-129 mmHg systolic and less than 80 mmHg diastolic indicate this stage. Multiple readings taken on different occasions are essential for an accurate diagnosis, as factors like stress or physical activity can temporarily elevate blood pressure. Additionally, healthcare providers may assess risk factors, including family history, lifestyle habits and other health conditions to determine the best approach for monitoring and potential intervention, emphasizing the importance of early detection in preventing the progression to more severe hypertension.

5.2 Symptoms Associated with severe or Long-Standing Hypertension:

Severe or long-standing hypertension can lead to a range of serious symptoms and complications that may significantly impact an individual's health. Patients may experience persistent headaches, visual disturbances such as blurred vision and episode of dizziness or light-headedness. Other symptoms can include shortness of breath, chest pain and palpitations, often indicating strain on the heart. Additionally, long-term hypertension can result in damage to vital organs, leading to symptoms like fatigue, confusion and frequent urination in cases of kidney impairment. Recognizing these signs is crucial, as they can serve as indicators of advanced cardiovascular issues or other complications, necessitating immediate medical evaluation and intervention. Although hypertension is often asymptomatic, certain clinical symptoms may arise as blood pressure rises to more severe levels or as end-organ damage begins to occur.

These symptoms, though non-specific, may signal uncontrolled or worsening hypertension:

a) **Headaches:**

- **Location:** Commonly occipital or at the back of the head, often worse in the morning.
- **Mechanism:** Increases intracranial pressure due to elevated blood pressure.
- **Presentation:** Throbbing, dull, or pressure-like headaches may become more frequent as hypertension progresses, especially in hypertensive crises.

b) **Dizziness and Light-headedness:**

- Occur because of cerebrovascular disturbances, though more common in individuals with labile (fluctuating) blood pressure.
- **Differential Diagnosis:** Must be differentiated from other causes of dizziness like vestibular disorders or arrhythmias.

c) **Blurred Vision or Visual Disturbances:**

Caused by hypertensive retinopathy, which results from high pressure damaging the small vessels in the retina.

- **Symptoms:** Blurred vision, seeing floaters or flashes, and in severe cases, vision loss.
- **Examination findings:** Fundoscopic exam may reveal arteriovenous nicking, retinal haemorrhages, or papilledema in malignant hypertension.

d) **Chest Pain:**

- **Mechanism:** Elevated blood pressure increases myocardial oxygen demand, potentially resulting in angina or even myocardial infarction.
- **Associated Conditions:** Chronic hypertension may lead to left ventricular hypertrophy (LVH), increasing the risk of ischemic heart disease.
- **Symptoms:** Tightness, pressure, or discomfort in the chest, particularly during exertion.

e) **Shortness of Breath (Dyspnoea):**

- **Causes:** Heart failure due to chronic hypertension leading to left ventricular dysfunction.
- **Associated symptoms:** Paroxysmal nocturnal dyspnoea, orthopnoea (shortness of breath when lying flat), and generalized fatigue.

f) Nosebleeds (Epistaxis):

- Commonly associated with uncontrolled high blood pressure due to fragile blood vessels in the nasal passages.
- **Severity:** Rarely severe but may indicate a hypertensive crisis or need for immediate blood pressure management.

Severe or long-standing hypertension can lead to a range of serious symptoms and complications that reflect its impact on various organs and systems. Patients may experience persistent headaches, severe fatigue, chest pain and shortness of breath, often indicating underlying cardiovascular strain. As the condition progress, symptoms such as vision changes, confusion and difficulty concentrating may arise due to potential brain involvement. Kidney dysfunction can lead to symptoms like increased urination and swelling, while damage to blood vessels heightens the risk of strokes and heart attacks. Recognizing these symptoms is crucial, as they signal the need for immediate medical intervention to prevent life-threatening complications and improve overall health outcomes. Regular monitoring and effective management of blood pressure are essential to mitigate these risks.

5.3 Hypertensive Crises; A Critical Presentation:

A hypertensive crisis is defined by a systolic blood pressure>180 mmHg or diastolic blood pressure>120 mmHg. This condition can be categorized into hypertensive urgency and hypertensive emergency, which involves significant organ impairment and requires immediate intervention. Hypertensive crises can arise from various factors, including poorly managed hypertension, medication non-compliance or acute stressors and lead to serious complications such as stroke, heart failure or renal failure. Prompt recognition and treatment are essential to mitigate risks and improve patient outcome.

- **Hypertensive Urgency:**

  Hypertensive urgency is a condition characterized by a significant increase in blood pressure, typically exceeding 180/120 mmHg, without acute target organ damage. Patients may experience symptoms such as headaches, shortness of breath or nosebleeds, but they often do not present with severe complications like stroke or acute kidney injury. Common causes include non-adherence to antihypertensive medications, excessive salt intake or acute stress. Management typically involves the gradual reduction of blood pressure using oral antihypertensive agents, along with careful monitoring to avoid rapid drops in pressure that could lead to other complications. Follow-up care is essential, focussing on lifestyle modifications, medications adherence and regular blood pressure monitoring to prevent future crises and ensure overall cardiovascular health.

- **Hypertensive emergency:**

  A hypertensive emergency is a critical condition characterized by severely elevated blood pressure, typically defined as systolic blood pressure exceeding 120 mmHg, accompanied by evidence of acute end-organ damage. This can manifest as stroke, myocardial infarction, acute renal failure or aortic dissection. Immediate medical intervention is essential to lower blood pressure rapidly but safely, often using intravenous medications. Prompt treatment is crucial to prevent irreversible damage and reduce morbidity and mortality associated with this life-threatening condition.

  In hypertensive emergency, symptoms may include severe headache, chest pain, shortness of breath, vision changes or confusion, indicating potential organ compromise. Risk factors often include pre-existing hypertension, non-adherence to antihypertensive medications or secondary causes like adrenal tumours or renal artery stenosis. Diagnosis involves thorough clinical assessment and monitoring along with imaging studies to evaluate organ damage. Management typically occurs in an intensive care setting, where blood pressure is carefully titrated to avoid complications associated with rapid reduction such as ischemia or stroke. Long-term treatment strategies may involve lifestyle modifications and ongoing pharmacotherapy to manage underlying hypertension and prevent future emergencies.

Symptoms of Hypertensive Crises: Symptoms of hypertensive crises can manifest suddenly and include severe headache, chest pain, shortness of breath and confusion or altered mental status. Patients may also experience symptoms like vision changes, nausea and palpitations. These signs indicate potentially life-threatening conditions such as stroke, heart attack or acute kidney injury, necessitating immediate medical attention. Recognizing these symptoms promptly is crucial for timely intervention and to prevent severe complications.

- **Severe headache:** Often accompanied by confusion or altered mental status, potentially due to hypertensive encephalopathy.
- **Severe chest pain:** May indicate an acute coronary syndrome or aortic dissection.
- **Shortness of breath:** Due to acute heart failure or pulmonary oedema.
- **Neurological deficits:** Including sudden vision changes, hemiparesis, or difficulty speaking, suggesting a cerebrovascular event such as a stroke.

In conclusion, hypertensive crises are serious medical swift recognition and intervention to prevent life-threatening complications. Effective management involves not only acute treatment but also addressing the underlying cause, such as medication adherence and lifestyle factors. Continuous monitoring and follow-up care are crucial to ensure long-term blood pressure control and to prevent recurrence. By raising awareness and improving management strategies, healthcare providers can significantly reduce the morbidity and mortality associated with these critical events.

5.4 Hypertension and Target Organ Damage:

Prolonged elevated blood pressure can lead to structural and functional changes in the heart such as left ventricular hypertrophy which increase the risk of heart failure and arrhythmias. The kidneys are also vulnerable; hypertension can cause nephrosclerosis, reducing renal function and potentially leading to chronic kidney disease. Additionally, high blood pressure is a major contributor to cardiovascular events including strokes by damaging the blood vessels in the brain and increasing the likelihood of rupture or blockage. The eyes can suffer from hypertensive retinopathy characterized by changes in the retina that may lead to vision loss. Moreover, hypertension can negatively impact peripheral arteries, resulting in peripheral artery disease (PAD), which causes pain and mobility issues. The cumulative effect of these changes underscores the importance of early detection and effective management of hypertension to prevent target organ damage and improve overall health outcomes. Untreated or inadequately managed hypertension leads to damage in critical organs. Symptoms related to target organ damage may indicate long standing disease or poorly controlled hypertension:

a) **Cardiovascular system:** Left ventricular hypertrophy (LVH), coronary artery disease (CAD), and heart failure.

   Symptoms: Chest pain, palpitations, and dyspnoea on exertion.

b) **Kidneys:** Hypertensive nephropathy may present with chronic kidney disease (CKD).

   Symptoms: Fatigue, swelling (due to fluid retention), and changes in urination patterns.

c) **Brain:** Chronic hypertension predisposes to cerebrovascular accidents (strokes) or transient ischemic attacks (TIAs).

Symptoms; Sudden weakness, confusion, slurred speech, or loss of consciousness.

d) **Eyes:** Hypertension retinopathy can progress to visual impairment or blindness.

Symptoms: Blurred vision, visual disturbances or complete vision loss in severe cases.

In conclusion, the relationship between hypertension and target organ damage is critical and multifaceted, underscoring the need for proactive management of high blood pressure. Effective control of hypertension can significantly reduce the risk of complications such as heart failure, kidney disease, stroke and vision loss. Early diagnosis and intervention are essential to mitigate the long-term effects of elevated blood pressure on vital organs. Patients must be educated about the importance of adhering to treatment plans and regularly monitoring their blood pressure. By prioritizing hypertension management, we can not only improve individual health outcomes but also reduce the overall burden on healthcare systems associated with the complications of uncontrolled hypertension.

5.5 Special Population:

Hypertension is a prevalent health concern that effects individuals across various demographics, but certain special populations face unique challenges and risks associated with this condition. These groups include older adults, children, pregnant women and individuals with comorbidities such as diabetes or chronic kidney disease. In order adults, the physiological changes associated with aging along with polypharmacy can complicate hypertension management and increase the likelihood of adverse effects. Children and adolescents, on the other hand may experience hypertension due to obesity or genetic factors, necessitating age-appropriate evaluation and treatment strategies. Pregnant women require careful monitoring and management to prevent complications like preeclampsia, which can pose risks to both mother and foetus.

Additionally, individuals with chronic conditions may have hypertension because of their underlying disease or its treatment requiring a tailored approach to ensure effective management without exacerbating their primary health issues. Understanding the distinct needs and considerations of these special populations is crucial for developing effective treatment plans and improving health outcomes in the management of hypertension.

a) **Elderly Patients:** May present with isolated systolic hypertension and have a higher risk for stroke and heart failure.
b) **Pregnancy:** Hypertension in pregnancy, including preeclampsia, is associated with unique symptoms such as sweeling, proteinuria, and visual disturbances.
c) **Children and Adolescents:** Rare but increasing due to obesity. Symptoms are usually subtle, though children may complain of headaches or fatigue.

In conclusion, addressing hypertension in special populations is crucial for optimizing health outcomes and ensuring effective management. Each group-whether older adults, children, pregnant women or individuals with comorbid conditions requires tailored strategies that consider their unique physiological and medical contexts. A one-size-fits-all approach is insufficient; instead, healthcare providers must focus on individualized treatment plans that consider the specific challenges and risks associated with each population. By enhancing awareness, implementing early screening practices and fostering collaborative care among specialists, we can better manage hypertension and mitigate its complications in these vulnerable groups. Ultimately, a comprehensive understanding of the diverse needs of special populations will lead to more effective interventions and improved quality of life for individuals affected by hypertension. Hypertension is a pervasive, often asymptomatic condition that can progress to severe health complications if left untreated. While most individuals remain unaware of their condition until late stages, clinical symptoms such as headaches, dizziness, visual disturbances, and chest pain may arise as hypertension worsens or target organ damage occurs. Regular and early detection are essential to preventing the log term consequences of uncontrolled high blood pressure, emphasizing the importance of routine blood pressure monitoring and management strategies in at-risk.

The clinical presentation and symptoms of hypertension can vary widely, often making it a silent yet insidious condition. Many individuals may remain asymptomatic until significant complications arise, which underscore the importance of routine screening and monitoring. When symptoms do occur, they can include headaches, dizziness, shortness of breath and blurred vision which may signal acute hypertension or potential target organ damage. Additionally, some patients may experience symptoms related to specific complications, such as pain in the context of cardiovascular issues or kidney dysfunction signs in advanced renal disease. The variability in symptomology emphasizes the need for healthcare providers to maintain a high index of suspicion, especially in high-risk populations. Effective management requires a proactive approach that includes lifestyle modifications, pharmacotherapy and regular follow up to monitor blood pressure and assess for any emerging symptoms or complications. By recognizing and addressing hypertension early, healthcare professionals can significantly reduce the risk of severe health outcomes, ultimately improving the quality of life for affected individuals.

6. Complications of Hypertension

Hypertension is a chronic medical condition characterized by the consistent elevation of pressure within the arteries. Although it frequently presents with few or no symptoms, the long-term consequences of unmanaged hypertension can severe and far-reaching, affecting multiple organ systems and significantly increasing the risk of morbidity and mortality. One of the most critical complications is cardiovascular disease, where the persistent strain on the heart and blood vessels can lead to conditions such as coronary artery disease, heart failure and life-threatening events like heart attacks and strokes. The underlying mechanism often involves the damage and hardening of arteries due to the excessive pressure, which promotes the buildup of plaque and narrows the blood vessels, obstructing blood flow.

In addition to cardiovascular complications, hypertension poses serious risks to renal health. The kidneys play a vital role in regulating blood pressure through fluid and electrolyte balance and chronic high blood pressure can impair their filtering capacity. This impairment may lead to chronic kidney disease (CKD) or even end-stage renal failure, necessitating dialysis or kidney transplantation. The kidney's inability exacerbates hypertension, creating a dangerous cycle. Moreover, hypertension can significantly affect ocular health, leading to hypertensive retinopathy, where elevated blood pressure damages the delicate blood vessels in the retina. This can result in vision impairment or even blindness if felt untreated. Neurologically, the risks associated with hypertension extend to cognitive health, with studies linking high blood pressure to an increase incidence of vascular dementia and cognitive decline. The damage caused to the small blood vessels in the brain can lead to microinfarcts and impair overall cognitive function.

Another serous concern is the formation of aneurysms, particularly in the aorta and other major blood vessels. The weakened arterial walls can balloon out and may eventually rupture, leading to life-threatening internal bleeding. Given these extensive complications, understanding hypertension's far-reaching impacts is essential for effective prevention and management. Regular health check-ups, lifestyle modifications and adherence to prescribed medications are crucial in mitigating these risks and ensuring long term health. Following are the key complications of hypertension:

6.1 Cardiovascular Diseases:

Cardiovascular diseases (CVDs) are among the most significant health threats linked to hypertension, which affects millions of individuals worldwide. Chronic hypertension places excessive strain on the heart and blood vessels, leading to a cascade of detrimental effects that can result in serious conditions such as coronary artery disease, heart failure and arrhythmias. The elevated pressure causes the heart to work harder, leading to a cascade of detrimental effects that can result in serious conditions such as coronary artery disease, heart failure and arrhythmias. The elevated pressure causes the heart to work harder, leading to hypertrophy of the heart muscle and increased risk of ischemic events due to narrowed arteries. Furthermore, hypertension is a major risk factors for stroke, as it can cause damage to the blood vessels in the brain. Understanding the relationship between hypertension and cardiovascular diseases is crucial for prevention and management, highlighting the need for effective monitoring, lifestyle changes and adherence to treatment protocols to mitigate these risks and promotes overall cardiovascular health.

i. Heart Attack:

Hypertension is a critical risk factor for heart attacks, fundamentally altering cardiovascular health over time. Chronic elevation of blood pressure places excessive strain on the arterial walls, leading to a series of pathological changes that significantly increase the risk of myocardial infarction, commonly known as a heart attack. One of the primary mechanisms by which hypertension contributes to heart attacks is through the development of atherosclerosis. High blood pressure accelerates the process of plaque formation in the arteries by damaging the endothelial lining. This damage facilitates the accumulation of lipids, inflammatory cells and fibrous tissues which combine to form plaques that narrow the coronary arteries. Over time, these plaques can harden restricting blood flow to the heart muscles. When blood flow is compromised, the heart does not receive adequate oxygen and nutrients, which can result in ischemia a critical condition that can precede a heart attack.

Moreover, hypertension can lead to the formation of blood clots. When plaques rupture, they expose the underlying material to the blood stream, triggering the coagulation process. A clot can form rapidly at the site of rupture, further obstructing blood flow and potentially leading to a complete blockage of the artery. This scenario is particularly dangerous, as it can result in a sudden heart attack if the blood supply to a significant portion of the heart muscle is interrupted. Additionally, the impact of hypertension on heart structure cannot be overlooked. Chronic high blood pressure often leads to left ventricular hypertrophy (LVH), a condition in which the heart's left ventricle thickens in response to increased workload. This thickening can impair the heart's ability to pump effectively, leading to heart failure and increasing the risk of arrhythmias, which can also precipitate a heart attack.

The overall prevalence of hypertension, combined with its often-asymptomatic nature, makes it a silent but deadly contributor to heart disease. Many individuals remain unaware of their elevated blood pressure, allowing the damaging effects to progress unchecked. Lifestyle factors such as obesity, sedentary behaviour, smoking, and poor dietary choices can exacerbate hypertension, creating a vicious cycle that further elevates cardiovascular risk.

Effective management of hypertension is crucial in preventing heart attacks. This includes lifestyle modifications, such as adopting a heart-healthy diet rich in fruits, vegetables, whole grains, and lean proteins, as well as regular physical activity and weight management. Pharmacological interventions, such as antihypertensive medications, may also be necessary to achieve and maintain target blood pressure levels. Regular monitoring and proactive management can significantly reduce the risk of cardiovascular events, including heart attacks, and improve overall cardiovascular health. Recognizing the connection between hypertension and heart attacks is essential for both patients and healthcare providers to implement effective prevention strategies and interventions.

ii. Heart Failure:

Hypertension is one of the most significant risk factors for the development of heart failure, a progressive condition characterized by the heart's inability to pump blood effectively to meet the body's metabolic demands. Over time, chronic high blood pressure places undue strain on the heart, prompting a series of adaptive responses that, while initially compensatory, ultimately lead to detrimental changes in cardiac structure and function. Initially, the heart attempts to cope with increased workload through a process called left ventricular hypertrophy (LVH), where the walls of the left ventricle thicken to generate more forceful contractions. This thickening, however, also leads to decreased compliance of the heart muscle, causing it to become stiffer. As the left ventricle stiffens, it struggles to fill adequately with blood during diastole (the relaxation phase), resulting in elevated pressures in the heart and pulmonary circulation. This can manifest as heart failure with preserved ejection fraction (HFPEF), where the heart maintains a normal pumping ability but is unable to fill properly due to stiffness.

As hypertension persists, the heart may further adapt by undergoing dilation, leading to heart failure with reduced ejection fraction (HFREF). In this state, the heart's ability to contract effectively diminishes, reducing the amount of blood ejected with each heartbeat. This can be exacerbated by ischemic heart disease, often associated with hypertension, where narrowed coronary arteries limit blood flow to the heart muscle, leading to further deterioration. The hemodynamic changes brought about by hypertension also result in fluid retention, as the kidneys respond to perceived low blood flow by retaining sodium and water. This can lead to increased blood volume and, subsequently, congestion in the lungs and peripheral tissues, causing symptoms such as shortness of breath, fatigue, and swelling (oedema) in the legs and abdomen. The interplay between fluid overload and impaired heart function can create a vicious cycle, where increased workload further aggravates heart failure symptoms.

Additionally, hypertension can contribute to the development of other cardiovascular complications, including arrhythmias, which may further compromise heart function and increase the risk of sudden cardiac events. The inflammatory processes associated with hypertension can also play a role in cardiac remodelling, leading to fibrosis and further deterioration of heart tissue. Management of hypertension is crucial in preventing heart failure. Effective treatment typically involves lifestyle modifications, such as adopting a heart-healthy diet low in sodium, engaging in regular physical activity, achieving and maintaining a healthy weight, and avoiding tobacco and excessive alcohol use. Pharmacological interventions, including antihypertensive medications such as ACE inhibitors, beta-blockers, and diuretics, can help manage blood pressure and mitigate the effects of hypertension on the heart. Regular monitoring and proactive management are essential to slow the progression of heart failure and improve quality of life for affected individuals. Recognizing the strong link between hypertension and heart failure underscores the importance of early detection, intervention, and ongoing care to preserve heart function and overall cardiovascular health.

iii. Coronary Artery Disease:

Coronary artery disease (CAD) is a leading cause of morbidity and mortality worldwide, with hypertension as a major contributing factor. The pathophysiological link between hypertension and CAD is primarily rooted in the process of atherosclerosis, where chronic high blood pressure causes progressive damage to the arterial walls. Elevated blood pressure exerts mechanical stress on the endothelium, the thin layer of cells lining the blood vessels, leading to endothelial dysfunction. This dysfunction is characterized by a decrease in nitric oxide production, a vital molecule that helps maintain vascular health and promotes vasodilation. When the endothelium is compromised, it becomes more permeable, allowing lipoproteins, particularly low-density lipoproteins (LDL), to infiltrate the arterial wall. As these LDL particles accumulate, they become oxidized, triggering an inflammatory response. White blood cells, particularly macrophages, are recruited to the site, engulfing the oxidized LDL and transforming into foam cells, which contribute to plaque formation. Over time, these plaques can grow, narrowing the lumen of the coronary arteries and significantly reducing blood flow to the heart muscle. The resulting ischemia can lead to symptoms such as angina pectoris, which manifests as chest pain or discomfort during physical exertion or stress.

Moreover, hypertension increases the risk of plaque rupture. The continuous mechanical stress on the arterial walls can create micro-tears, exposing the underlying materials of the plaque to the bloodstream. This exposure triggers the coagulation cascade, leading to the formation of a thrombus (blood clot) that can rapidly occlude the artery. Such an event can result in a myocardial infarction, or heart attack, where a portion of the heart muscle is deprived of oxygen and begins to die. Hypertension also contributes to structural changes in the heart itself, including left ventricular hypertrophy (LVH). The thickening of the heart muscle can lead to a decreased ability to pump effectively and increased susceptibility to ischemic events, further exacerbating the risk of CAD. Additionally, the presence of hypertension often coexists with other risk factors such as diabetes, hyperlipidaemia, and smoking, creating a synergistic effect that amplifies the risk of developing CAD.

The clinical implications of CAD due to hypertension are profound. Patients may remain asymptomatic until significant arterial blockage occurs, making regular monitoring of blood pressure and cardiovascular health essential. Diagnosis typically involves non-invasive tests such as stress testing, echocardiography, or imaging techniques like coronary angiography, which can visualize the extent of arterial blockage. Effective management of hypertension is crucial in preventing the onset and progression of CAD. This involves lifestyle modifications, including a diet low in sodium and saturated fats, regular physical activity, smoking cessation, and weight management. Pharmacological treatment may include antihypertensive medications such as ACE inhibitors, angiotensin II receptor blockers, beta-blockers, and statins to control blood pressure and manage cholesterol levels. Regular follow-up and risk assessment can help tailor treatment strategies to individual needs, ultimately reducing the risk of coronary artery disease and its associated complications. Understanding the intricate relationship between hypertension and CAD underscores the importance of early intervention and comprehensive cardiovascular care to improve patient outcomes and quality of life.

iv. Arrhythmias (Irregular Heartbeats):

Arrhythmia, or irregular heartbeats, is a prevalent and serious complication of hypertension, resulting from both structural and electrical alterations within the heart due to prolonged elevated blood pressure. Chronic hypertension exerts excessive mechanical stress on the heart, leading to left ventricular hypertrophy (LVH), a condition where the heart muscle thickens to compensate for increased workload. This thickening not only affects the heart's pumping efficiency but also disrupts normal electrical conduction pathways, making the heart more susceptible to arrhythmias. The structural changes associated with hypertension can cause dilation of the heart chambers, particularly the atria. This atrial enlargement increases the likelihood of atrial fibrillation, a common arrhythmia that involves chaotic electrical activity in the atria. Atrial fibrillation can significantly raise the risk of thromboembolic events, such as stroke, due to the formation of blood clots in the dilated atria. The presence of arrhythmias can complicate the clinical picture in patients with hypertension, leading to symptoms like palpitations, shortness of breath, fatigue, and dizziness. In some cases, arrhythmias can progress to more severe conditions such as ventricular tachycardia or ventricular fibrillation, which can be life-threatening and may result in sudden cardiac arrest.

In addition to the mechanical stress imposed by hypertension, the disease is often accompanied by inflammatory processes that can lead to myocardial fibrosis. This scarring within the heart muscle can interfere with normal electrical conduction, creating pathways for abnormal electrical impulses that can trigger arrhythmias. Furthermore, patients with hypertension frequently have comorbidities such as diabetes and sleep apnea, which can further increase the risk of developing arrhythmias and exacerbate the cardiovascular effects of hypertension. The management of arrhythmias in patients with hypertension requires a multifaceted approach. Control of blood pressure is paramount, as effective management can help mitigate the risk of arrhythmias. Antihypertensive medications, such as beta-blockers, can help reduce heart rate and stabilize electrical conduction. However, it is important to note that some antihypertensive agents can have proarrhythmic effects, necessitating careful selection and monitoring by healthcare providers.

Regular cardiovascular evaluations, including electrocardiograms (ECGs) and Holter monitoring, are essential for detecting arrhythmias early and assessing their impact on overall heart health. Lifestyle modifications, such as maintaining a heart-healthy diet, engaging in regular physical activity, managing stress, and avoiding stimulants like caffeine and nicotine, can also play a critical role in reducing both blood pressure and the likelihood of arrhythmias. In summary, the interplay between hypertension and arrhythmias is complex and multifactorial, requiring vigilant monitoring and comprehensive management to improve patient outcomes. Early identification and appropriate treatment of arrhythmias can significantly enhance the quality of life for individuals with hypertension, while also reducing the risk of severe cardiovascular complications.

6.2 Stroke:

Stroke, a critical medical emergency characterized by the sudden disruption of blood flow to the brain, is one of the most severe complications associated with chronic hypertension, or high blood pressure. Hypertension is a major risk factor for both ischemic and haemorrhagic strokes, with its prevalence leading to significant morbidity globally. In cases of ischemic stroke, hypertension contributes to the development of atherosclerosis, where arteries become narrowed and blocked by plaque, restricting blood flow to brain tissue and resulting in cell death. On the other hand, in haemorrhagic stroke, the elevated blood pressure can weaken blood vessel walls, leading to rupture and subsequent bleeding in or around the brain. The interplay between hypertension and stroke underscores the importance of effective blood pressure management, as uncontrolled hypertension not only increases the likelihood of stroke occurrence but also exacerbates the severity of its consequences. Early recognition of stroke symptoms and prompt medical intervention are vital, as timely treatment can significantly improve outcomes and reduce long-term disability. Understanding this relationship is crucial for healthcare providers and patients alike emphasizing the need for preventive strategies to mitigate the risk associated with hypertension and its potential to trigger life-altering strokes.

i. **Ischemic Stroke:**

Ischemic stroke, which occurs when blood flow to a part of the brain is interrupted, is a critical and often devastating consequence of chronic hypertension. High blood pressure accelerates the process of atherosclerosis, a condition where fatty deposits, cholesterol, and other substances accumulate in the arterial walls, leading to the narrowing and hardening of blood vessels. Over time, this buildup compromises the structural integrity of the arteries, particularly those supplying the brain, such as the carotid and vertebral arteries. Hypertension causes endothelial dysfunction, impairing the ability of blood vessels to regulate blood flow and respond to changes in demand. This dysfunction not only facilitates the formation of plaques but also increases vascular inflammation, making the arteries more susceptible to damage.

The relationship between hypertension and ischemic stroke is multifaceted. Elevated blood pressure increases shear stress on the arterial walls, promoting the rupture of atherosclerotic plaques. When a plaque ruptures, it can expose its contents to the bloodstream, triggering the formation of a thrombus, or blood clot. This clot can migrate and obstruct a cerebral artery, leading to a sudden loss of blood supply to the brain tissue downstream. The lack of oxygen and nutrients causes ischemia, which can result in irreversible neuronal damage within minutes. Depending on the region of the brain affected, this can manifest as various neurological deficits, such as difficulty speaking (aphasia), paralysis or weakness on one side of the body (hemiparesis), impaired coordination, and cognitive dysfunction. Moreover, hypertension is often associated with other risk factors such as diabetes, hyperlipidaemia, and obesity, which compound the risk of ischemic stroke. These factors can lead to a more aggressive form of atherosclerosis and increase the likelihood of acute vascular events. For instance, diabetes can further impair endothelial function and increase inflammation, while high cholesterol levels can contribute to larger and more unstable plaques.

The management of hypertension is crucial in preventing ischemic strokes. Effective strategies include lifestyle modifications such as adopting a heart-healthy diet rich in fruits, vegetables, whole grains, and lean proteins, engaging in regular physical activity, achieving and maintaining a healthy weight, and avoiding tobacco and excessive alcohol use. Pharmacological interventions may include antihypertensive medications such as ACE inhibitors, angiotensin II receptor blockers, beta-blockers, and diuretics, which help lower blood pressure and reduce the strain on the cardiovascular system. Regular monitoring of blood pressure, coupled with routine assessments for other stroke risk factors, is essential for individuals, particularly those with a history of hypertension. Early detection and management of hypertension can significantly reduce the risk of ischemic strokes, improving overall health outcomes and quality of life. Understanding the intricate relationship between hypertension and ischemic stroke highlights the importance of comprehensive cardiovascular care, emphasizing prevention, early intervention, and ongoing management to protect brain health and minimize the long-term consequences of stroke.

ii. Haemorrhagic Stroke:

Haemorrhagic stroke, a critical and often fatal condition, occurs when a blood vessel in the brain ruptures, leading to bleeding that damages brain tissue and disrupts normal brain function. Chronic hypertension is the leading risk factor for this type of stroke, as prolonged elevated blood pressure can weaken the walls of blood vessels, making them more susceptible to rupture. Over time, high blood pressure can lead to structural changes in the arterial walls, including atherosclerosis, which narrows the arteries and can contribute to localized regions of weakness. In particular, the small penetrating arteries that supply deep structures of the brain, such as the basal ganglia and thalamus, are highly vulnerable. When these small vessels rupture, it results in intracerebral haemorrhage, where blood leaks into the surrounding brain tissue, creating a mass effect that increases intracranial pressure. This elevated pressure can compromise cerebral perfusion, leading to ischemia in adjacent brain areas, exacerbating the damage. On the other hand, subarachnoid haemorrhage occurs when bleeding occurs in the subarachnoid space, often due to the rupture of a cerebral aneurysm, which is a weakened area of a blood vessel that bulges under pressure.

The clinical presentation of haemorrhagic stroke can be dramatic and acute. Common symptoms include a sudden, severe headache often described as a "thunderclap headache," along with nausea, vomiting, altered consciousness, and neurological deficits such as weakness or paralysis on one side of the body, difficulty speaking, and seizures. Due to the rapid onset of these symptoms, haemorrhagic strokes typically require immediate medical intervention to control bleeding, relieve pressure on the brain, and stabilize the patient. The prognosis for patients who suffer a haemorrhagic stroke is generally poorer than for those with ischemic strokes. Mortality rates can be high, and many survivors face significant long-term complications, including cognitive impairments, physical disabilities, and emotional disturbances, necessitating extensive rehabilitation and support. The presence of comorbid conditions, such as diabetes, hyperlipidaemia, and obesity, can further complicate recovery and increase the risk of subsequent strokes.

Prevention of haemorrhagic stroke is heavily reliant on the effective management of hypertension. Lifestyle modifications play a critical role, including adhering to a balanced diet low in sodium and rich in fruits, vegetables, and whole grains, maintaining regular physical activity, managing stress, and avoiding smoking and excessive alcohol consumption. Additionally, pharmacological treatment often includes antihypertensive medications such as ACE inhibitors, angiotensin II receptor blockers, calcium channel blockers, and diuretics to achieve and maintain target blood pressure levels. Regular monitoring of blood pressure is crucial, especially for individuals with a history of hypertension or other risk factors. Early identification and treatment of high blood pressure can significantly reduce the risk of vascular complications, including haemorrhagic strokes. This underscores the importance of comprehensive cardiovascular care, including patient education about recognizing stroke symptoms and understanding the critical need for ongoing management of hypertension. Through proactive prevention and early intervention strategies, the risk of haemorrhagic stroke can be effectively minimized, protecting brain health and improving overall quality of life.

6.3 Chronic Kidney Disease:

Chronic kidney disease (CKD) is a progressive and often asymptomatic condition that can develop as a significant complication of long-standing hypertension, or high blood pressure. When blood pressure remains elevated over extended periods, it exerts excessive force on the delicate blood vessels within the kidneys. This pressure can lead to vascular damage and impair the kidneys' ability to filter waste products and excess fluids from the bloodstream effectively. As a result, nephron function deteriorates, leading to a gradual decline in glomerular filtration rate (GFR), which is a critical measure of kidney health. Initially, individuals may experience few symptoms as the kidneys compensate for the loss of function. However, as CKD progresses, signs may emerge, including fatigue, swelling due to fluid retention and changes in urine output.

The accumulation of toxins in the blood can lead to uraemia, characterized by symptoms such as nausea, confusion and itching. Advance CKD may culminate in end-stage renal disease (ESRD), necessitating dialysis or kidney transplantation for survival. The relationship between hypertension and CKD is particularly concerning because it is bidirectional; not only can high blood pressure lead to kidney damage, but compromised kidney function can also contribute to increased blood pressure. The kidneys regulate blood pressure through fluid balance and the production of hormones and when their function declines, it can result in further hypertension, creating a vicious cycle. This interconnection underscores the importance of early detection and management of both hypertension and CKD.

Regular monitoring of blood pressure and kidney function, along with lifestyle modification such as dietary changes, exercise and adherence to medications are essential strategies for preventing the progression of CKD. Ultimately, understanding the intricate relationship between hypertension and chronic kidney disease is vital for developing comprehensive care plans aimed at protecting kidney health and improving overall patient outcomes.

i. **Kidney Damage:**

Hypertension is a major contributor to kidney damage, leading to a progressive decline in renal function that can culminate in chronic kidney disease (CKD) and ultimately end-stage renal disease (ESRD). The kidneys are responsible for filtering waste products from the blood, regulating electrolyte balance, and maintaining fluid homeostasis, all of which are critically affected by elevated blood pressure. Chronic hypertension exerts excessive pressure on the renal vasculature, resulting in a series of pathological changes, including nephrosclerosis, characterized by the hardening and thickening of the small blood vessels within the kidneys. This condition begins with endothelial dysfunction, where the inner lining of blood vessels becomes impaired, reducing its ability to regulate blood flow and maintain vascular tone. Over time, this leads to hyaline arteriosclerosis, where proteinaceous material accumulates in the vessel walls, narrowing the lumen and decreasing perfusion to the nephrons—the functional units of the kidney. As renal blood flow diminishes, the kidneys become less efficient at filtering blood, leading to increased retention of waste products such as urea and creatinine, which can cause systemic toxicity.

Furthermore, the glomeruli—the tiny filters within the kidneys—can undergo hypertrophy and hyperfiltration in response to sustained hypertension. Initially, this might seem adaptive; however, it ultimately leads to glomerular damage, evidenced by the presence of protein in the urine (proteinuria) and a decline in the glomerular filtration rate (GFR). Proteinuria is particularly concerning, as it not only indicates kidney damage but also serves as a predictor of cardiovascular risk. Over time, as nephrons are lost and scarring (fibrosis) occurs within the renal interstitial, kidney function continues to deteriorate, potentially leading to ESRD, where dialysis or kidney transplantation becomes necessary. The relationship between hypertension and kidney damage is often exacerbated by coexisting conditions, such as diabetes mellitus, hyperlipidaemia, and obesity, which can further impair renal function and contribute to the development of CKD. For instance, diabetes can lead to diabetic nephropathy, characterized by increased glomerular pressure and hyperfiltration, compounding the damaging effects of hypertension on renal structures. Additionally, metabolic syndrome, which includes hypertension, obesity, and insulin resistance, presents a significant risk for both cardiovascular and renal complications.

Preventing kidney damage due to hypertension involves a multifaceted approach. Effective blood pressure management is essential, with lifestyle modifications such as adhering to a low-sodium diet, engaging in regular physical activity, achieving and maintaining a healthy weight, and avoiding smoking and excessive alcohol consumption. Pharmacological interventions often include antihypertensive medications like angiotensin-converting enzyme (ACE) inhibitors or angiotensin II receptor blockers (ARBs), which not only lower blood pressure but also provide renal protective effects by reducing intraglomerular pressure. Regular monitoring of blood pressure and renal function, including serum creatinine levels and urine tests for protein, is crucial for early detection of kidney damage. This enables timely intervention to slow the progression of CKD and improve patient outcomes. By recognizing the critical interplay between hypertension and kidney health, healthcare providers can implement comprehensive care strategies that prioritize blood pressure control and renal protection, ultimately reducing the risk of severe complications associated with chronic kidney disease.

ii. End-Stage Renal Failure:

End-stage renal failure (ESRF), or end-stage renal disease (ESRD), is the final stage of chronic kidney disease (CKD), where the kidneys have lost approximately 85-90% of their functional capacity, necessitating renal replacement therapy, such as dialysis or kidney transplantation. Hypertension is a leading cause of ESRD, with chronic high blood pressure leading to significant and progressive damage to the renal vasculature and nephron units. Over time, sustained hypertension results in nephrosclerosis, characterized by the thickening and stiffening of the small arteries in the kidneys. This process diminishes renal perfusion, leading to ischemia, which causes further nephron loss and fibrosis. As nephron damage accumulates, the glomerular filtration rate (GFR) declines, impairing the kidneys' ability to effectively filter waste products and excess fluids from the bloodstream. Consequently, toxic substances like urea and creatinine begin to accumulate in the body, resulting in uraemia. This syndrome manifests with a variety of symptoms, including fatigue, weakness, nausea, vomiting, confusion, and in severe cases, can lead to seizures and coma due to electrolyte imbalances and metabolic disturbances. The kidneys' inability to regulate fluid and electrolyte balance can also cause complications such as hypertension, anaemia, and bone disease, which further complicate the patient's clinical picture.

Patients with ESRD face significant challenges, as they often require dialysis—either haemodialysis or peritoneal dialysis—to perform the essential functions of the kidneys, such as waste removal, fluid balance, and electrolyte management. In haemodialysis, blood is filtered outside the body through a dialysis machine, while peritoneal dialysis uses the lining of the abdomen to filter blood internally. While dialysis can extend life and improve quality of life, it does not cure kidney disease and often comes with its own set of complications, such as infections, vascular access problems, and dietary restrictions. Moreover, the interplay between ESRD and hypertension can lead to a vicious cycle; poorly controlled blood pressure can worsen kidney function, while kidney impairment can contribute to further increases in blood pressure.

Patients with ESRD are at heightened risk for cardiovascular complications, including heart failure, myocardial infarction, and stroke, due to the combined effects of hypertension, fluid overload, and metabolic abnormalities.

Management of ESRD due to hypertension requires a comprehensive approach that includes not only renal replacement therapy but also stringent blood pressure control. Antihypertensive medications, such as ACE inhibitors or ARBs, are often employed to help protect remaining kidney function and manage cardiovascular risk. Lifestyle modifications, including dietary changes (such as sodium restriction), regular physical activity, and weight management, play a crucial role in controlling blood pressure and improving overall health. Additionally, regular monitoring of kidney function, electrolyte levels, and blood pressure is essential for preventing complications and optimizing treatment outcomes. Early detection and intervention are critical in hypertensive patients to delay the progression of CKD to ESRD, emphasizing the need for routine screening and patient education on lifestyle factors that influence both hypertension and kidney health. Ultimately, a multidisciplinary approach involving nephrologists, primary care providers, dietitians, and other healthcare professionals is vital for managing ESRD effectively and enhancing the quality of life for affected individuals.

6.4 Hypertensive Retinopathy:

Hypertensive heart disease is a serious and complex condition that arises as a direct consequence of chronic hypertension, where consistently high blood pressure imposes significant strain on the heart and blood vessels over time. When blood pressure remains elevated, the heart is forced to work harder to pump blood, leading to structural changes that can severely affect its function. One of the most common adaptations is left ventricular hypertrophy (LVH), where the muscle tissue of the heart's left ventricle thickens. Initially, this thickening may help the heart cope with increased workload; however, it eventually reduces the heart's efficiency and can lead to heart failure, characterized by symptoms such as fatigue, shortness of breath and fluid retention.

In addition to LVH, chronic hypertension is a major contributor to coronary artery disease (CAD). Elevated blood pressure accelerates the process of the atherosclerosis, where fatty deposits (plaques) accumulate in the arterial walls, narrowing the arteries and restricting blood flow to the heart muscle. This restriction increases the risk of angina (chest pain) and heart attacks, which can result from a complete blockage of blood flow. Furthermore, hypertension can lead to microvascular damage, affecting the small blood vessels that supply the heart, compounding the risk of ischemic events. Hypertension is also associated with an increased incidence of arrhythmias, which are irregular heartbeats that can disrupt the heart's rhythm and lead to complications such as palpitations, dizziness or even sudden cardiac arrest. The combination of structural changes and electrical disturbances in the heart further complicates the clinical picture, making management more challenging.

The complications of hypertensive heart disease extend beyond the heart itself; it is often linked to other serious health conditions such as heart failure, chronic kidney disease and stroke. As such early recognition and proactive management of hypertension are crucial. This includes lifestyle modifications-such as dietary changes, increased physical activity and weight management as well as pharmacological interventions aimed at controlling blood pressure levels. Understanding the intricate relationship between hypertension and heart disease underscores the need for comprehensive strategies to prevent and treat this multifaceted health issue, ultimately improving patient outcomes and quality of life.

i. Vision Impairment:

Hypertension can have profound effects on ocular health, leading to various forms of vision impairment, particularly through its role in damaging the blood vessels in the eyes. Chronic high blood pressure is known to cause hypertensive retinopathy, a condition characterized by changes in the retinal blood vessels that can lead to vision loss. As blood pressure rises, the small vessels in the retina can become narrowed, leading to reduced blood flow, ischemia, and damage to the retinal tissue. This condition can manifest in several ways, including the development of microaneurysms, haemorrhages, and exudates, which are indicative of fluid leakage from the damaged vessels. One of the earliest signs of hypertensive retinopathy is the appearance of retinal changes visible during a comprehensive eye examination. These changes include cotton wool spots (small white patches on the retina), flame-shaped haemorrhages, and hard exudates, which are yellowish-white lesions that occur due to lipid deposits. As hypertension progresses, more severe changes can occur, such as retinal artery occlusion, which can result in sudden vision loss, and in extreme cases, can lead to more extensive damage like macular oedema or even retinal detachment.

Moreover, hypertension can exacerbate other eye conditions, particularly in individuals with pre-existing conditions like diabetes, which is another major risk factor for vision impairment. Diabetic retinopathy and hypertensive retinopathy can coexist, increasing the risk of significant vision impairment. This co-morbidity can accelerate the progression of retinal damage, leading to quicker and more severe declines in vision. Additionally, high blood pressure can lead to conditions such as papilledema, which is swelling of the optic nerve head due to increased intracranial pressure. This can cause transient visual disturbances, including blurred vision and loss of peripheral vision. In severe cases, it can contribute to permanent vision loss if not addressed promptly.

The risk of vision impairment due to hypertension is further compounded by related conditions such as atherosclerosis, which can affect blood flow to the eyes. Atherosclerosis can lead to the narrowing of the carotid arteries, reducing the blood supply to the eyes and potentially resulting in ischemic optic neuropathy—a condition where the optic nerve is damaged due to insufficient blood flow. To mitigate the risk of vision impairment associated with hypertension, effective management of blood pressure is crucial. This involves regular monitoring, lifestyle modifications such as a heart-healthy diet, regular exercise, weight management, and adherence to antihypertensive medications. Furthermore, regular comprehensive eye examinations are essential for early detection and treatment of any ocular complications arising from hypertension. Early intervention can help manage hypertensive retinopathy and preserve vision, highlighting the importance of an integrated approach to cardiovascular and ocular health. By addressing hypertension proactively, individuals can significantly reduce their risk of vision impairment and maintain overall eye health.

ii. Blindness:

Blindness due to hypertension is a serious and often preventable outcome resulting from the damaging effects of chronically elevated blood pressure on ocular structures. One of the primary conditions associated with hypertension that can lead to blindness is hypertensive retinopathy. This condition develops because of high blood pressure causing changes in the retinal blood vessels, which can lead to significant vision impairment and even total blindness if not effectively managed. Chronic hypertension leads to a series of vascular changes in the retina. These changes include narrowing of retinal vessels, where hypertension causes the small arteries in the retina to narrow, reducing blood flow and oxygen delivery to retinal tissues. This ischemia can damage the retina, leading to visual disturbances. Additionally, elevated blood pressure can cause small bulges in the walls of retinal capillaries, known as microaneurysms, which may rupture and result in retinal haemorrhages. These bleeding events compromise the structural integrity of the retina and can lead to vision loss.

As retinal blood vessels become damaged, they can leak fluid and lipids, resulting in the formation of hard exudates and cotton wool spots, which are indicators of retinal damage that can interfere with normal vision. Macular oedema, swelling in the macula responsible for central vision, can also occur due to hypertensive damage, leading to blurred or distorted vision. Moreover, severe hypertension can lead to the blockage of the central retinal artery or its branches, resulting in sudden and often severe vision loss, a critical condition requiring immediate medical attention. Prolonged high blood pressure can also result in ischemic optic neuropathy, where the optic nerve suffers damage due to insufficient blood supply, leading to sudden vision loss, typically affecting upper or lower fields of vision.

The risk of developing blindness from hypertension is heightened by the presence of other comorbidities, particularly diabetes mellitus. Diabetic retinopathy, characterized by retinal damage due to diabetes, can co-occur with hypertensive retinopathy, leading to a compounded risk of significant visual impairment. Additionally, conditions such as hyperlipidaemia, obesity, and smoking further exacerbate the vascular damage caused by hypertension, increasing the likelihood of vision-threatening complications. Preventing blindness related to hypertension involves several key strategies, including regular blood pressure monitoring, effective management of hypertension through lifestyle changes and medications, routine eye examinations for early detection of hypertensive changes in the retina, and patient education about the importance of managing hypertension and its implications for eye health. Early intervention for those diagnosed with hypertensive retinopathy or other ocular complications, such as laser therapy or intravitreal injections, can help prevent further deterioration of vision.

Ultimately, blindness due to hypertension is a significant public health concern, but it is largely preventable through proactive management of blood pressure and regular eye care. By addressing hypertension early and comprehensively, individuals can reduce their risk of severe ocular complications, preserve their vision, and maintain their overall quality of life. The integration of cardiovascular and ocular health strategies is vital in combating the adverse effects of hypertension on vision.

6.5 Cognitive Impairment:

Cognitive impairment due to hypertension is an increasingly recognized concern in both clinical and public health settings, as high blood pressure can have profound effects on brain health. Chronic hypertension has been linked to structural and functional changes in the brain, including the acceleration of cognitive decline and an increased risk of neurodegenerative disorders such as dementia. The mechanisms behind this relationship involve vascular damage, reduced cerebral blood flow and the promotion of inflammation, all of which contribute to alterations in neuronal health and cognitive processes. As the global prevalence of hypertension rises, understanding its complications for cognitive function becomes crucial, particularly given the aging population and the growing burden of cognitive impairment. Addressing hypertension through effective management and prevention strategies is essential not only for cardiovascular health but also for maintaining cognitive integrity across the lifespan.

i. **Vascular Dementia:**

Vascular dementia is a form of cognitive decline that occurs because of reduced blood flow to the brain, often linked to chronic hypertension. High blood pressure damages blood vessels over time, leading to atherosclerosis, where arteries become narrowed and hardened due to plaque buildup. This condition compromises the delivery of oxygen and nutrients to brain tissues, causing cell death and impairing cognitive function. Vascular dementia can manifest following a series of small strokes or transient ischemic attacks (TIAs), which further disrupt blood flow and contribute to the deterioration of cognitive abilities. Individuals may experience difficulties with memory, reasoning, planning, and problem-solving, alongside other symptoms such as confusion, mood changes, and difficulty with coordination. The impact of hypertension on the brain extends beyond isolated incidents; chronic high blood pressure can lead to a gradual decline in cognitive function, contributing to a more widespread form of vascular cognitive impairment.

Risk factors for vascular dementia include not only hypertension but also diabetes, high cholesterol, obesity, and smoking, all of which can exacerbate vascular damage and increase the likelihood of stroke. The interplay of these factors creates a heightened risk environment for cognitive decline, where the cumulative effects of poor vascular health manifest as diminished cognitive performance. Moreover, vascular dementia can coexist with other forms of dementia, such as Alzheimer's disease, complicating the clinical picture and making diagnosis and management more challenging. Preventive strategies are crucial in mitigating the risk of vascular dementia due to hypertension. Effective blood pressure management through lifestyle modifications, including a balanced diet, regular exercise, weight management, and adherence to prescribed antihypertensive medications, can significantly reduce the risk of developing vascular dementia. Regular monitoring of blood pressure and cardiovascular health, combined with cognitive assessments, is essential for early detection and intervention. By prioritizing vascular health, individuals can help preserve cognitive function and enhance their overall quality of life, highlighting the critical relationship between hypertension and brain health.

ii. Memory Problems:

Hypertension is increasingly recognized as a significant risk factor for cognitive decline and memory problems, particularly as individuals age. Chronic high blood pressure can lead to changes in the brain's structure and function, ultimately affecting cognitive processes such as memory, attention, and executive functioning. One of the primary mechanisms by which hypertension impacts memory is through its detrimental effects on cerebral blood flow. Elevated blood pressure can cause damage to the small blood vessels in the brain, leading to reduced blood supply and oxygen delivery to critical areas involved in memory formation and retrieval. This reduced perfusion can result in ischemia, contributing to the development of small vessel disease, which is characterized by white matter lesions that are often visible on brain imaging. These white matter changes are associated with increased risk of cognitive impairment and have been linked to conditions such as vascular dementia. Additionally, hypertension can promote the formation of atherosclerosis, a condition where fatty deposits build up in the arteries, further limiting blood flow to the brain. As blood vessels become stiffer and narrower due to chronic hypertension, the brain may not receive the necessary nutrients and oxygen, leading to neuronal damage and loss.

Furthermore, hypertension is associated with increased inflammation and oxidative stress, which can exacerbate neurodegenerative processes. Chronic inflammation can disrupt the delicate balance of neurotransmitters involved in cognitive function, potentially leading to deficits in memory and learning. Studies have shown that individuals with untreated hypertension are at a higher risk of developing mild cognitive impairment, a condition that often precedes more severe forms of dementia, including Alzheimer's disease. The impact of hypertension on memory is particularly concerning because it can create a feedback loop: cognitive decline can lead to difficulties in managing health conditions, including hypertension itself. For instance, individuals experiencing memory problems may forget to take their medications, adhere to dietary recommendations, or attend regular check-ups, thereby exacerbating their hypertension and further contributing to cognitive decline.

Addressing hypertension is therefore crucial not only for cardiovascular health but also for maintaining cognitive function and memory. Effective management strategies include lifestyle changes such as adopting a balanced diet rich in fruits, vegetables, and whole grains, engaging in regular physical activity, achieving and maintaining a healthy weight, and avoiding tobacco and excessive alcohol use. Pharmacological treatments may also be necessary to achieve optimal blood pressure control. Additionally, regular monitoring of blood pressure and cognitive health can help identify problems early, allowing for timely interventions to preserve both cardiovascular and cognitive health. Ultimately, understanding the relationship between hypertension and memory problems emphasizes the importance of a holistic approach to health, integrating cardiovascular care with cognitive health strategies to improve overall well-being.

6.6 Aneurysms:

An aneurysm is defined as an abnormal, localized dilation of blood vessel, which can occur in arteries or veins. Among the various factors contributing to aneurysm formation, hypertension chronic elevated blood pressure plays a pivotal role. Over time, persistent high blood pressure exerts undue stress on the vascular walls, leading to structural alterations, including the breakdown of collagen and elastin fibres that provide strength and elasticity to the arteries. The most common types of aneurysms associated with hypertension include aortic aneurysms, which can develop in the thoracic or abdominal aorta and cerebral aneurysms, typically found in the arteries of the brain. In the case of the aorta, hypertension can cause the vessel to balloon outward, significantly increasing the risk of rupture, which can lead to catastrophic internal bleeding and is often fatal without immediate intervention. Cerebral aneurysms can result in subarachnoid haemorrhages if they rupture, leading to severe neurological deficits or death.

Factors such as age, genetics, smoking and the presence of other cardiovascular diseases can exacerbate the risk of developing aneurysms in hypertensive patients. Furthermore, the asymptomatic nature of many aneurysms complicates early detection, making routine monitoring and effective blood pressure management critical. Diagnostic imaging techniques such as ultrasound, CT scans and MRIs are essential for identifying aneurysms particularly in at risk populations. The management of hypertension through lifestyle modifications such as diet and exercise and pharmacological interventions can significantly reduce the risk of aneurysm formation and subsequent complications. Public health initiatives aimed at controlling blood pressure and educating individuals about the risks associated with hypertension are vital in preventing aneurysm related morbidity and mortality. Understanding the intricate relationship between hypertension and aneurysm formation is essential for both patients and healthcare providers in fostering better outcomes through proactive measures and timely intervention.

i. **Aortic Aneurysm:**

An aortic aneurysm, characterized by an abnormal bulging or dilation of the aorta, is a serious condition closely linked to chronic hypertension. Elevated blood pressure significantly increases the mechanical stress on the aortic wall, which can lead to its progressive weakening. Over time, the constant pressure from hypertension causes structural changes within the aortic wall, particularly affecting the middle layer, known as the tunica media. This layer contains smooth muscle cells and elastic fibres, which are crucial for maintaining the aorta's strength and flexibility. When these components become damaged, the aorta loses its ability to withstand normal blood flow pressures, resulting in a bulge or aneurysm.

Aneurysms can occur in either the abdominal aorta (abdominal aortic aneurysm, or AAA) or the thoracic aorta (thoracic aortic aneurysm, or TAA). The most significant concern with an aortic aneurysm is the risk of rupture, which can lead to life-threatening internal bleeding. As the aneurysm enlarges, the walls become increasingly thin and vulnerable; a rupture can occur suddenly and often without warning. The mortality rate associated with a ruptured aortic aneurysm is high, often exceeding 80% if not treated immediately. Hypertension also plays a role in the development of atherosclerosis, where fatty deposits build up within the arterial walls. This condition can further compromise the strength of the aortic wall, creating an environment conducive to aneurysm formation. Risk factors such as advanced age, male gender, family history of aneurysms, smoking, high cholesterol, and connective tissue disorders like Marfan syndrome can exacerbate the likelihood of developing an aortic aneurysm in individuals with high blood pressure.

In many cases, aortic aneurysms may remain asymptomatic until they reach a critical size or rupture. However, some patients may experience nonspecific symptoms such as persistent back or abdominal pain, a pulsating sensation in the abdomen, or even signs of compression on surrounding structures, like hoarseness or difficulty swallowing in the case of a thoracic aneurysm. Imaging techniques, such as ultrasound, CT scans, or MRI, are essential for early detection, allowing for monitoring and timely intervention. Management of an aortic aneurysm typically involves addressing the underlying hypertension. Effective blood pressure control is crucial to reducing the risk of aneurysm progression and rupture. This may include lifestyle modifications, such as a heart-healthy diet low in sodium and saturated fats, regular physical activity, weight management, smoking cessation, and moderation of alcohol intake. Additionally, pharmacological interventions using antihypertensive medications—such as ACE inhibitors, angiotensin receptor blockers, beta-blockers, and diuretics—can help manage blood pressure levels effectively.

In some cases, surgical intervention may be required, particularly for large or symptomatic aneurysms. Surgical options include open surgical repair or endovascular aneurysm repair (EVAR), which is a less invasive procedure that involves placing a stent graft within the aneurysm to reinforce the aortic wall and prevent rupture. Regular follow-up care is crucial for patients with known aneurysms to monitor their size and progression, ensuring timely treatment if necessary. In summary, understanding the connection between hypertension and aortic aneurysm is vital for prevention and management. By effectively controlling blood pressure and recognizing the risk factors associated with aortic aneurysms, individuals can significantly reduce their chances of developing this dangerous condition and its potentially fatal complications. Comprehensive cardiovascular care, including regular monitoring and lifestyle modifications, is essential for maintaining aortic health and preventing aneurysm-related events.

ii. Peripheral Artery Aneurysms:

Peripheral artery aneurysms (PAAs) are abnormal dilations of peripheral arteries, most found in the popliteal and femoral arteries. These aneurysms can arise from several factors, with chronic hypertension being a significant contributor. Elevated blood pressure exerts increased mechanical stress on arterial walls, which can lead to structural changes. Specifically, hypertension can cause hypertrophy of the smooth muscle layer and degradation of the extracellular matrix, particularly the elastin and collagen fibres that provide the artery's tensile strength. Over time, the continuous pressure can induce atherosclerotic changes, promoting plaque formation that further weakens the vessel wall. This weakening predisposes the artery to bulging and the formation of an aneurysm. Patients with hypertension are often also affected by other cardiovascular risk factors, such as diabetes and hyperlipidaemia, which can compound the degenerative processes occurring in the arterial wall.

As the aneurysm enlarges, it poses significant health risks. Complications can include thrombus formation within the aneurysm, which can dislodge and lead to embolic events in distal vessels, potentially causing acute limb ischemia. The risk of rupture, although less common in peripheral aneurysms than in abdominal aortic aneurysms, can lead to catastrophic outcomes, including significant bleeding and limb loss. Diagnosis typically involves imaging techniques such as Doppler ultrasound or magnetic resonance angiography. Management focuses on controlling blood pressure through lifestyle modifications and pharmacotherapy. In cases where aneurysms are large, symptomatic, or at high risk of complications, surgical intervention may be necessary. This could involve techniques such as bypass grafting or endovascular repair, depending on the aneurysm's location and characteristics. Regular monitoring is essential for early detection and management to prevent serious complications associated with PAAs.

6.7 Metabolic Syndrome:

Metabolic syndrome is a multifaceted condition characterized by a cluster of interrelated metabolic risk factors, primarily linked to obesity and insulin resistance. At its core, hypertension plays a pivotal role, acting as both a key component and a critical risk factor for the development of serious health complications, including cardiovascular diseases and type 2 diabetes. Hypertension is often associated with other elements of metabolic syndrome, such as abdominal obesity, which leads to increased visceral fat accumulation. This fat tissue is not merely inert; it secretes various bioactive substances, including inflammatory cytokines and free fatty acids, that disrupt normal metabolic processes. Insulin resistance, a hallmark of metabolic syndrome, results in elevated insulin levels, which can cause sodium retention and increased blood volume, further exacerbating hypertension.

Moreover, dyslipidaemia characterized by elevated triglycerides and reduced levels of high-density lipoprotein (HDL) cholesterol frequently accompanies hypertension in metabolic syndrome. This lipid imbalance can contribute to the development of atherosclerosis, increasing the risk of heart attack and stroke. Hyperglycaemia or elevated blood sugar levels, often emerges due to insulin resistance and can lead to endothelial dysfunction, a precursor to cardiovascular diseases, thereby creating a self-reinforcing cycle of poor health outcomes. The prevalence of metabolic syndrome is escalating globally, driven by lifestyle factors such as sedentary behaviour, poor dietary choices and increased stress levels. As a result, understanding the intricate connections between hypertension and metabolic syndrome is vital for healthcare providers. Early identification and intervention can significantly reduce the risk of developing severe complications, underscoring the importance of integrated management strategies that address lifestyle modifications, pharmacological treatments and regular monitoring of metabolic parameters. This comprehensive approach aims to break the cycle of metabolic dysregulation and hypertension, ultimately promoting better health outcomes for affected individuals.

i. **Increased Risk of Diabetes:**

The connection between hypertension and an increased risk of developing type 2 diabetes is complex and involves various physiological and pathological mechanisms. Chronic high blood pressure can induce significant changes in the body's metabolic pathways, primarily through the promotion of insulin resistance. Insulin resistance occurs when the body's cells become less responsive to insulin, a hormone that plays a critical role in glucose uptake. As blood pressure rises, it often triggers a cascade of inflammatory processes and hormonal imbalances that impair insulin signalling. One of the key players in this relationship is the renin-angiotensin-aldosterone system (RAAS). Chronic activation of RAAS due to hypertension can lead to increased levels of angiotensin II, a potent vasoconstrictor that also promotes inflammatory responses and contributes to insulin resistance. This hormone affects adipose tissue, leading to increased fat accumulation and an inflammatory milieu, which further exacerbates insulin sensitivity issues. Moreover, angiotensin II can directly impair endothelial function, reducing nitric oxide availability and hindering vascular health, which is critical for proper glucose metabolism.

Additionally, the coexistence of obesity with hypertension significantly compounds the risk of developing diabetes. Many individuals with hypertension are overweight or obese, which can lead to excess fat accumulation, particularly visceral fat. This type of fat is metabolically active and secretes various inflammatory cytokines, such as tumour necrosis factor-alpha (TNF-α) and interleukin-6 (IL-6), that further promote insulin resistance and impair glucose homeostasis. Lifestyle factors prevalent in hypertensive populations, such as physical inactivity, poor dietary choices (e.g., high in sugars and saturated fats), and increased stress levels, also play a crucial role. These factors can contribute to weight gain and exacerbate both hypertension and insulin resistance. The synergistic effect of these lifestyle factors creates a feedback loop, where hypertension can lead to increased blood glucose levels and, subsequently, to type 2 diabetes.

Moreover, the prevalence of metabolic syndrome—characterized by a combination of hypertension, abdominal obesity, dyslipidaemia, and insulin resistance—highlights the interconnected nature of these conditions. Individuals with metabolic syndrome face a significantly higher risk of progressing to diabetes compared to those with isolated hypertension. The implications of this relationship are significant, as the coexistence of hypertension and diabetes dramatically increases the risk of cardiovascular diseases, kidney damage, and other complications. Therefore, it is essential for healthcare professionals to screen hypertensive patients for glucose intolerance and diabetes regularly, while also implementing lifestyle interventions such as promoting regular physical activity, balanced nutrition, and weight management. Pharmacological strategies may also be necessary to address both blood pressure and glucose levels, underscoring the importance of a comprehensive approach to managing these interconnected conditions.

ii. Elevated Cholesterol Levels:

Elevated cholesterol levels due to hypertension represent a significant concern in cardiovascular health, as the interplay between these two conditions can lead to a heightened risk of atherosclerosis and other cardiovascular diseases. Chronic hypertension can induce a series of pathological changes that contribute to dyslipidaemia, particularly an increase in low-density lipoprotein (LDL) cholesterol and a decrease in high-density lipoprotein (HDL) cholesterol. The mechanisms underlying this relationship are multifaceted. One major contributor is endothelial dysfunction, which often occurs in the setting of sustained high blood pressure. Elevated pressure can cause mechanical stress on blood vessels, leading to damage of the endothelial lining. This damage promotes a pro-inflammatory state, characterized by the release of cytokines and adhesion molecules that facilitate the infiltration of inflammatory cells and lipids into the arterial wall. The accumulation of LDL cholesterol in the arterial intima leads to the formation of fatty streaks, a precursor to atherosclerotic plaques.

In this context, HDL cholesterol, which normally helps transport cholesterol from peripheral tissues back to the liver for excretion, becomes less effective due to reduced synthesis and functionality, further contributing to elevated total cholesterol levels.

The renin-angiotensin-aldosterone system (RAAS) also plays a crucial role in this relationship. Chronic activation of RAAS due to hypertension results in increased production of angiotensin II, a hormone that not only constricts blood vessels but also stimulates the liver to produce more LDL cholesterol. Angiotensin II can also promote inflammation and oxidative stress, creating a vicious cycle that exacerbates lipid abnormalities. This dysregulation is compounded by the presence of other metabolic conditions frequently found in hypertensive individuals, such as obesity and insulin resistance, which further elevate LDL cholesterol levels while reducing HDL cholesterol. Lifestyle factors prevalent among individuals with hypertension significantly contribute to the elevation of cholesterol levels. Poor dietary choices, including high intakes of saturated fats, trans fats, and simple carbohydrates, can lead to weight gain and metabolic syndrome, increasing the likelihood of elevated LDL and lowered HDL levels. Sedentary lifestyles, often associated with hypertension, further exacerbate dyslipidaemia, as regular physical activity is essential for maintaining healthy cholesterol levels.

The combined effect of hypertension and elevated cholesterol creates a substantial risk for cardiovascular events, such as heart attacks and strokes. The atherosclerotic process can progress more rapidly in individuals with both conditions, leading to significant arterial blockages and compromised blood flow. Therefore, comprehensive management strategies that address both hypertension and cholesterol levels are vital. These strategies typically involve lifestyle modifications, such as adopting a heart-healthy diet (rich in fruits, vegetables, whole grains, and healthy fats), engaging in regular physical activity, and maintaining a healthy weight. Pharmacological interventions, including antihypertensive medications and statins or other lipid-lowering agents, may also be necessary to optimize cardiovascular health and minimize the risk of serious complications. Regular monitoring of blood pressure and lipid levels is essential for effective management and prevention of cardiovascular disease in individuals affected by both hypertension and dyslipidaemia.

6.8 Peripheral Artery Disease (PAD):

Peripheral artery disease is a significant cardiovascular condition that affects millions of individuals, particularly those with risk factors such as hypertension, diabetes, smoking and hyperlipidaemia. The pathophysiology of PAD is primarily rooted in atherosclerosis, where plaque composed of fat, cholesterol and other substances accumulated in the arterial walls, leading to reduced blood flow. Hypertension plays a crucial role in this process as elevated blood pressure contribute to endothelial injury, making arteries more susceptible to plaque formation. When blood pressure is consistently high, it causes mechanical stress on the arterial walls. This stress triggers a cascade of biological responses, including inflammation and the activation of various cellular pathways that promote plaque buildup. Over time, this can lead to significant stenosis (narrowing of the arteries), impeding blood flow to the muscles and tissues, particularly during physical exertion.

The clinical manifestations of PAD are often insidious. Patients may experience intermittent claudication, which presents as muscle pain or cramping in the legs or buttocks during activities such as walking or climbing stairs. This pain is typically relieved by rest, highlighting the disparity between the oxygen demand of the muscles and the reduced supply. As the disease progresses, symptoms may worsen, leading to critical limb ischemia, which can cause severe pain even at rest, non-healing wounds or ulcers and in severe cases may necessitate amputation. The implications of PAD extend beyond the legs; it is also associated with increased cardiovascular morbidity and mortality. Patients with PAD are at a higher risk for heart attack and stroke due to the systemic nature of atherosclerosis. The presence of PAD often indicates widespread vascular disease, promoting healthcare providers to assess and manage other cardiovascular risk factors aggressively.

Management of PAD in patients with hypertension involves a multifaceted approach. Lifestyle modifications, including smoking cessation, dietary changes, regular physical activity and weight management are foundational elements of treatment are foundational elements of treatment. Pharmacological interventions may include antiplatelet agents, statins and medications to manage hypertension and hyperlipidaemia. In certain cases, revascularization procedures such as angioplasty or bypass surgery may be necessary to restore adequate blood flow to the affected limbs. Regular screening for PAD is vital, particularly in high-risk populations as early detection can significantly alter the disease's trajectory. Healthcare providers often use the Ankle-Brachial Index (ABI) test to assess blood flow in the limbs. Education about the signs and symptoms of PAD, along with the importance of controlling blood pressure and other cardiovascular risk factors, is essential to improve patient outcomes and reduce the burden of this debilitating condition.

i. **Reduced Blood Flow to Limbs:**

Chronic hypertension can significantly impair blood flow to the limbs, leading to a condition known as peripheral arterial disease (PAD), which is characterized by narrowed arteries that reduce blood flow to the extremities. The mechanism behind this reduced perfusion involves the structural and functional changes in blood vessels resulting from sustained high blood pressure. Over time, elevated pressure can cause endothelial injury, leading to inflammation and the development of atherosclerosis—a process where fatty plaques build up on arterial walls, further narrowing the vessels. As these plaques accumulate, the arteries become stiffer and less able to dilate, which limits blood flow during physical activity, leading to symptoms such as intermittent claudication, which manifests as pain or cramping in the legs or buttocks during exercise.

Moreover, hypertension is often associated with other risk factors such as diabetes, hyperlipidaemia, and smoking, which can compound vascular damage and exacerbate PAD. Reduced blood flow due to hypertension may lead to ischemia, particularly in the lower limbs, where the demand for oxygen increases during physical exertion. As a result, patients may experience not only pain but also muscle weakness and fatigue, limiting their mobility and quality of life. Prolonged ischemia can lead to more severe complications, including ulcers, gangrene, and in extreme cases, limb loss.

The compromised blood flow also affects the healing capacity of tissues; wounds in the lower extremities may heal more slowly due to insufficient oxygen and nutrient delivery. Furthermore, the combination of reduced blood flow and impaired wound healing increases the risk of infections. Diagnosis of reduced limb blood flow typically involves physical examinations, assessments of pulse quality, and imaging studies such as Doppler ultrasound or angiography to visualize blood flow and identify any blockages. Management strategies focus on controlling hypertension through lifestyle changes (such as a heart-healthy diet and regular exercise) and pharmacological interventions (such as antihypertensives and statins) to improve overall vascular health. Additionally, patients may be encouraged to engage in supervised exercise therapy, which can enhance collateral circulation and improve functional capacity. In severe cases, surgical interventions like angioplasty or bypass grafting may be required to restore adequate blood flow. By addressing hypertension and its consequences on limb circulation, healthcare providers can help reduce the risk of severe complications and enhance patients' quality of life.

ii. Pain and Mobility Issues:

Chronic hypertension can lead to a variety of pain and mobility issues that significantly impact an individual's quality of life. One of the primary mechanisms through which hypertension causes pain is by promoting arterial stiffness and reducing overall blood flow. This reduced perfusion can lead to peripheral artery disease (PAD), a condition in which narrowed arteries limit blood flow to the limbs. Patients with PAD often experience intermittent claudication, which manifests as cramping or aching pain in the legs or buttocks during physical activities such as walking or climbing stairs. The pain typically resolves with rest, but it can discourage physical activity, leading to a sedentary lifestyle that exacerbates hypertension and increases the risk of cardiovascular events. In addition to vascular complications, hypertension is frequently associated with other comorbidities that contribute to pain and mobility limitations. For instance, obesity is common among individuals with hypertension, and the excess weight places additional stress on weight-bearing joints, particularly the knees, hips, and lower back. This added strain can lead to or worsen osteoarthritis, characterized by joint inflammation, stiffness, and pain. As the joints degenerate, individuals may experience reduced range of motion and increased difficulty performing everyday activities, which can further diminish their mobility.

Furthermore, hypertension often coexists with metabolic disorders such as diabetes, which can lead to diabetic neuropathy—nerve damage that may cause pain, tingling, or numbness in the extremities. This neuropathic pain can impair balance and coordination, increasing the risk of falls and subsequent injuries. The chronic pain associated with these conditions can create a cycle of physical inactivity, leading to muscle weakness and deconditioning, which further compounds mobility issues. Psychological factors also play a crucial role in the pain-mobility relationship for individuals with hypertension. Chronic pain can lead to increased anxiety and depression, reducing motivation to engage in physical activity. This psychological distress can be particularly pronounced in individuals who feel limited by their physical condition, contributing to a vicious cycle of pain, inactivity, and worsening health outcomes.

Additionally, medications prescribed for hypertension, such as diuretics, beta-blockers, and some calcium channel blockers, can have side effects that exacerbate pain and mobility issues. Diuretics may lead to electrolyte imbalances, resulting in muscle cramps, while beta-blockers can contribute to fatigue and decreased exercise capacity. These side effects can further discourage individuals from adhering to prescribed physical activity regimens, worsening the overall impact of hypertension on mobility. To address pain and mobility challenges in hypertensive patients, a multifaceted approach is essential. Effective management of hypertension through lifestyle modifications—including weight loss, dietary changes, and regular physical activity—is critical. Engaging in low-impact aerobic exercises, such as walking, swimming, or cycling, can improve cardiovascular health and enhance blood flow, potentially alleviating symptoms of claudication. Strength training and flexibility exercises can also help improve muscle strength, joint function, and overall mobility.

Physical therapy can be beneficial for developing individualized exercise programs that accommodate existing pain and mobility limitations. Pain management strategies, such as the use of nonsteroidal anti-inflammatory drugs (NSAIDs) or alternative therapies like acupuncture, may also provide relief. Furthermore, patient education on self-management techniques, including proper body mechanics and strategies for pacing activities, can empower individuals to take control of their health and improve their functional capabilities. Overall, addressing pain and mobility issues in individuals with hypertension requires an integrated care approach that not only targets blood pressure control but also focuses on enhancing functional capacity, reducing pain, and improving overall well-being. By fostering a proactive approach to health management, patients can experience significant improvements in their quality of life and physical independence.

6.9 Left Ventricular Hypertrophy:

Left ventricular hypertrophy (LVH) is a structural heart condition that results from the adaptive response of the left ventricle to increased workload, primarily due to chronic hypertension. In individuals with sustained high blood pressure, the heart must exert greater force to pump blood through the systemic circulation, leading to an increase in size and mass of the left ventricular muscle fibres. This hypertrophic process involves complex cellular changes, including myocardial cell growth (Hypertrophy), fibrosis and alterations in the extracellular matrix, ultimately thickening the ventricular wall. As hypertension persists, the left ventricle undergoes concentric hypertrophy, where the wall thickness increases without a proportional increase in chamber size. This change is initially beneficial, enabling the heart to maintain cardiac output. However, over time, the increased myocardial mass can lead to detrimental effects. The thickened ventricular walls become stiffer, reducing the heart's ability to relax and fill during diastole, which can result in diastolic dysfunction. This impairment is a precursor to heart failure with preserved ejection fraction (HEPEF).

Moreover, the altered electrical properties of the hypertrophied myocardium increase the risk of arrhythmias, which can have serious implications, including sudden cardiac death. LVH is also a significant predictor of cardiovascular morbidity and mortality, often correlating with a higher incidence of coronary artery disease and stroke. Therefore, recognizing and addressing hypertension early is crucial for preventing the development of LVH and its associated complications. Management strategies may include lifestyle modifications, pharmacotherapy to control blood pressure and regular monitoring to mitigate the long-term risks associated with this condition. The assessment of LVH typically involves imaging techniques such as echocardiography, which can reveal increased left ventricular mass and changes in chamber dimensions.

Additionally, electrocardiograms (ECGs) may show characteristic changes indicative of hypertrophy, such as increased voltage in specific leads. Effective management of LVH centres on controlling blood pressure through a combination of lifestyle changes- such as dietary modifications, regular physical activity, weight management and pharmacological interventions, including antihypertensive medications like ACE inhibitors, angiotensin II receptor blockers and calcium channel blockers. Early intervention not only helps to reverse LVH but also reduces the risk of progression to more severe cardiovascular conditions, highlighting the importance of regular cardiovascular health screenings, particularly in at-risk populations. Understanding the intricate relationship between hypertension and LVH is essential for healthcare providers to develop comprehensive treatment plans aimed at improving patient outcomes and quality of life.

i. **Thickening of Heart Muscle:**

Thickening of the heart muscle, known as left ventricular hypertrophy (LVH), is a prominent complication of chronic hypertension and serves as a critical indicator of cardiovascular health. In the context of sustained high blood pressure, the heart faces increased afterload—the resistance it must overcome to eject blood during systole. This persistent pressure overload stimulates the cardiac myocytes (heart muscle cells) to undergo hypertrophic remodelling, characterized by cellular enlargement, increased protein synthesis, and alterations in the heart's structural components, including collagen deposition and extracellular matrix remodelling. The process begins with mechanical stress on the myocytes, which activates various signalling pathways, including the mitogen-activated protein kinase (MAPK) pathway and the phosphoinositide 3-kinase (PI3K)/Akt pathway. These pathways promote hypertrophy through the activation of specific transcription factors, such as nuclear factor of activated T-cells (NFAT) and myocyte enhancer factor 2 (MEF2), leading to the production of contractile proteins and the thickening of the ventricular walls. Initially, this adaptation allows the heart to maintain adequate cardiac output and meet the demands of the body. However, as LVH progresses, it leads to detrimental changes in cardiac structure and function.

One of the critical consequences of LVH is diastolic dysfunction. As the left ventricle thickens, it becomes less compliant, impairing its ability to relax and fill with blood during diastole. This reduced filling capacity can result in elevated pressures in the left atrium and pulmonary circulation, leading to symptoms such as shortness of breath, particularly during exertion or when lying down, and fatigue. Over time, this can progress to heart failure with preserved ejection fraction (HFpEF), a condition that is increasingly recognized in the context of hypertension. Moreover, LVH is associated with an increased risk of serious cardiovascular events, including arrhythmias, coronary artery disease, and sudden cardiac death. The thickened heart muscle demands more oxygen, making it more susceptible to ischemic episodes, especially if there are concurrent coronary artery lesions. Additionally, the structural and electrical remodelling associated with LVH can predispose patients to atrial fibrillation, a common arrhythmia that further complicates management and increases the risk of stroke.

The diagnosis of LVH is typically made through echocardiography, which can assess the thickness of the left ventricular walls and evaluate overall cardiac function. Electrocardiography (ECG) may also provide clues, showing specific patterns indicative of hypertrophy. Treatment focuses on effectively managing hypertension to prevent or reverse LVH. This may include lifestyle interventions such as weight loss, dietary changes (e.g., reducing sodium intake), and regular physical activity. Pharmacological therapies, particularly those targeting the renin-angiotensin-aldosterone system (RAAS) like ACE inhibitors and angiotensin II receptor blockers (ARBs), have been shown to not only lower blood pressure but also reduce the progression of LVH. Calcium channel blockers and diuretics can also be beneficial in certain patients. Regular monitoring and comprehensive management of hypertension are crucial to mitigate the risks associated with LVH. Through effective control of blood pressure and overall cardiovascular health, patients can significantly improve their quality of life and reduce the long-term complications associated with left ventricular hypertrophy.

ii. Increased Risk of Heart Failure:

Chronic hypertension is a leading cause of heart failure, significantly increasing the risk through a complex interplay of mechanical, structural, and biochemical factors. When blood pressure remains elevated over an extended period, the heart must work harder to overcome increased vascular resistance. This chronic overload leads to left ventricular hypertrophy (LVH), characterized by the thickening of the heart muscle. Initially, this adaptation may seem beneficial, as it helps the heart maintain cardiac output. However, as hypertrophy progresses, it leads to reduced compliance of the left ventricle, impairing the heart's ability to relax and fill adequately during diastole. This condition, known as diastolic dysfunction, is prevalent among patients with hypertension and can progress to heart failure with preserved ejection fraction (HFpEF), where the heart maintains its ability to contract but struggles with filling.

In addition to LVH and diastolic dysfunction, hypertension also contributes to the development of heart failure with reduced ejection fraction (HFrEF). Chronic high blood pressure can lead to ischemic heart disease, where the coronary arteries become narrowed due to atherosclerosis, reducing blood flow to the heart muscle. This ischemia can cause myocardial infarctions (heart attacks), leading to further damage, scar tissue formation, and systolic dysfunction, which are hallmarks of HFrEF. The thickened and less compliant heart muscle, combined with ischemic damage, results in a weakened heart that cannot pump efficiently, culminating in heart failure.

Moreover, the consequences of hypertension extend beyond the heart itself. It is often associated with a cluster of comorbid conditions, including obesity, diabetes, and metabolic syndrome, all of which further increase the risk of heart failure. For example, obesity contributes to inflammation and increased cardiac workload, while diabetes can lead to diabetic cardiomyopathy, characterized by direct damage to heart muscle cells and exacerbated vascular complications. These interconnected conditions can create a vicious cycle, where the presence of one condition accelerates the progression of the others. The neurohormonal responses to chronic hypertension also play a critical role in the development of heart failure. When blood pressure rises, the body activates compensatory mechanisms involving the renin-angiotensin-aldosterone system (RAAS) and sympathetic nervous system. While these systems initially help maintain blood pressure and cardiac output, their prolonged activation leads to fluid retention, further increasing the volume load on the heart and promoting adverse remodelling. Over time, these changes can result in myocardial fibrosis, where scar tissue replaces healthy muscle, further impairing cardiac function and leading to heart failure.

Clinically, patients with heart failure due to hypertension may present with symptoms such as dyspnoea (shortness of breath), orthopnoea (difficulty breathing when lying flat), fatigue, and oedema (swelling), significantly impacting their quality of life. Diagnosis typically involves a combination of patient history, physical examination, echocardiography, and laboratory tests to assess cardiac function and rule out other conditions. Effective management of hypertension is crucial to preventing heart failure. This includes lifestyle interventions such as weight management, a heart-healthy diet (rich in fruits, vegetables, whole grains, and low in sodium), regular physical activity, and avoiding tobacco and excessive alcohol consumption. Pharmacological treatments, including angiotensin-converting enzyme (ACE) inhibitors, angiotensin II receptor blockers (ARBs), beta-blockers, and diuretics, are essential in managing blood pressure and mitigating heart failure risk. Regular monitoring of blood pressure and cardiac function, along with patient education about recognizing early symptoms of heart failure, are vital components of care. By addressing hypertension aggressively, healthcare providers can significantly reduce the incidence and progression of heart failure, ultimately improving patients' health outcomes and quality of life.

6.10 Sexual Dysfunction:

Sexual dysfunction is a multifaceted issue that is increasingly recognized as a significant complication of hypertension, impacting a substantial portion of the population. The physiological mechanisms underlying this relationship are complex. Hypertension can lead to endothelial dysfunction, which impairs the ability of blood vessels to dilate properly, ultimately restricting blood flow to the genital areas. In men, this often manifests as erectile dysfunction, where achieving or maintaining an erection becomes difficult. In women, reduced blood flow can result in decreased arousal, less vaginal lubrication and difficulties reaching orgasm. Beyond the physiological impacts, the psychological ramifications of living with hypertension can further contribute to sexual dysfunction. Chronic health conditions often lead to anxiety, depression and stress, all of which can diminish libido and sexual desire. Furthermore, the stigma surrounding sexual health issues may prevent individuals from discussing these concerns with healthcare providers, leading to a lack of appropriate intervention.

The medications prescribed to manage hypertension can also play a role in sexual dysfunction. While some antihypertensive drugs, like ACE inhibitors, may have neutral or even positive effects on sexual function, others, particularly diuretics and beta-blockers, are commonly associated with adverse sexual side effects. These can include reduced libido, erectile dysfunction and delayed ejaculation in means well as sexual arousal disorders in women. Recognizing and addressing the interplay between hypertension and sexual dysfunction is crucial for healthcare professionals. A comprehensive treatment approach that includes open communication about sexual health, potential adjustments in medication and referrals to specialists, such as sexual health therapists can significantly enhance the quality of life for individuals experiencing these challenges. Ultimately, understanding the connections between hypertension and sexual dysfunction not only aids in patient management but also helps in destigmatizing these conversations, encouraging individuals to seek help and support.

i. Reduced Libido:

Reduced libido or diminished sexual individuals with hypertension impacting both me and women due to a combination of physiological and relational factors. Physiological hypertension can influence hormonal balance leading to lower testosterone levels in men and hormones fluctuation in women, which are crucial for sexual desire. Additionally, high blood pressure can damage blood vessels, impairing circulation and hindering the physiological responses necessary for sexual arousal. Many antihypertensive medications, particularly diuretics and beta-blockers, can also contribute to reduced libido through side effects such as fatigue and erectile dysfunction, creating a discouraging cycle for individuals. Psychological factors play a crucial role as well. The stress of managing a chronic condition like hypertension can lead to anxiety and depression, both of which are closely linked to diminished sexual interest. Individuals may experience concerns about their health status, affecting their self-esteem and body image.

As hypertension can cause physical changes, individuals may become self-conscious, further deterring sexual interest. Relationship dynamics may also suffer as chronic health issued can place strain on intimacy. Partners might feel anxious about engaging in sexual activity due to concerns about discomfort or exacerbating health problems, creating emotional barriers to sexual desire. To effectively address reduced libido associated with hypertension, a multifaceted approach is essential. Open dialogue about sexual health between patients and healthcare providers can help identify specific concerns and potential solutions. Regular assessments of antihypertensive medications can determine if side effects are significant enough to warrant changes in treatment. Therapeutic support from sexual health therapists or counsellors can provide individuals and couples with tools to navigate emotional and relational challenges, enhancing intimacy and desire. Moreover, promoting a healthy lifestyle through regular physical activity, a balanced diet and stress reduction techniques can improve overall well-being and potentially enhance libido.

ii. Erectile Dysfunction:

Erectile dysfunction (ED) is a significant concern for men with hypertension, as the condition is intricately tied to the vascular health that is compromised by high blood pressure. The physiological mechanisms linking hypertension to ED primarily involve endothelial dysfunction, which occurs when the inner lining of blood vessels is damaged due to chronic high blood pressure. This damage reduces the ability of blood vessels to produce nitric oxide, a vital compound that facilitates vasodilation—the relaxation of blood vessels that allows for increased blood flow to the penis. Without sufficient nitric oxide, the physiological process required for achieving and maintaining an erection is severely hindered, leading to difficulties in sexual performance.

Moreover, hypertension often coexists with other metabolic disorders, such as diabetes, obesity, and dyslipidaemia, which further exacerbate the risk of ED. For instance, diabetes can lead to neuropathy and impaired blood flow, compounding the erectile difficulties associated with hypertension. The presence of metabolic syndrome—a cluster of conditions including increased blood pressure, elevated blood sugar, excess body fat around the waist, and abnormal cholesterol levels—can create a compounded risk factor for ED due to its adverse effects on vascular health and insulin sensitivity. The psychological impact of living with hypertension cannot be overlooked either. Men facing chronic health issues often experience anxiety, stress, and depression, which can contribute to or worsen ED. Concerns about sexual performance, particularly in the context of existing health conditions, can create a feedback loop where anxiety about erectile function further impairs sexual performance, leading to lower self-esteem and reduced quality of life.

In addition to the physiological and psychological factors, certain antihypertensive medications can also negatively impact erectile function. Diuretics, which are commonly prescribed to lower blood pressure, may reduce blood flow by decreasing overall blood volume, while some beta-blockers can interfere with the signalling pathways necessary for achieving an erection. While other classes of antihypertensive medications, such as angiotensin-converting enzyme (ACE) inhibitors and calcium channel blockers, are less likely to cause ED, the choice of medication can significantly influence sexual health. To address erectile dysfunction in the context of hypertension, a comprehensive approach is necessary. This may include lifestyle modifications such as weight management, increased physical activity, and dietary changes aimed at improving cardiovascular health. Psychological counselling or sex therapy can be beneficial for addressing the mental health aspects associated with ED.

Additionally, healthcare providers may consider adjusting antihypertensive medications to ones that have a lower risk of impacting erectile function. Treatments specifically targeting ED, such as phosphodiesterase type 5 inhibitors (e.g., sildenafil, tadalafil), can also be effective, provided they are used under medical supervision. By taking an integrative approach that addresses both hypertension and erectile dysfunction, patients can improve their sexual health and overall quality of life.

Complications of hypertension extend far beyond elevated blood pressure readings, profoundly impacting various organ systems and overall health. Chronic hypertension significantly increases the risk of cardiovascular diseases, including heart failure, coronary artery disease, and stroke, primarily through mechanisms such as arterial stiffness, left ventricular hypertrophy, and atherosclerosis. The resultant ischemia and heart muscle damage can lead to life-threatening events like myocardial infarction and arrhythmias. Moreover, hypertension adversely affects the renal system, potentially resulting in chronic kidney disease or kidney failure due to damage to the blood vessels that supply the kidneys, impairing their ability to filter waste effectively. Additionally, hypertension can lead to cerebrovascular complications, including transient ischemic attacks (TIAs) and strokes, by promoting the formation of blood clots or the rupture of weakened blood vessels in the brain. The complications also extend to the eyes, where hypertensive retinopathy can cause vision impairment or loss due to damage to the retinal blood vessels.

Furthermore, the psychological burden of living with a chronic condition like hypertension can contribute to anxiety and depression, compounding the physical health challenges. Therefore, effective management of hypertension is critical not only for lowering blood pressure but also for preventing these serious complications and enhancing overall quality of life. Through lifestyle modifications, regular monitoring, and appropriate pharmacological interventions, patients can mitigate the risks associated with hypertension, promoting better long-term health outcomes and reducing the incidence of these life-altering complications. Ultimately, a comprehensive approach that addresses both the physiological and psychosocial aspects of hypertension is essential for fostering resilience and improving the health and well-being of affected individuals. In addition to the direct physiological complications, hypertension often creates a complex interplay with other health conditions, exacerbating issues like diabetes, obesity, and metabolic syndrome, which can further heighten cardiovascular risks. The cumulative effects of these interconnected conditions underscore the importance of a holistic management approach. Regular health screenings, patient education, and community support systems can empower individuals to take proactive steps toward their health.

7. Management and treatment of Hypertension

The management and treatment of hypertension are paramount in mitigating the risk of serious cardiovascular and systemic complications that arise from this prevalent condition, which affects an estimated one in three adults worldwide. Hypertension, characterized by sustained high blood pressure, poses a significant threat as it contributes to the development of life-altering health issues such as heart disease, stroke, heart failure, and chronic kidney disease. The complexity of hypertension management necessitates a comprehensive, multifaceted approach tailored to individual patient profiles, considering factors such as age, comorbidities, and lifestyle. Effective management begins with accurate assessment and diagnosis. Blood pressure should be measured consistently using standardized techniques to ensure reliable readings, with careful consideration of factors that may affect measurements, such as patient anxiety or improper cuff size. Diagnosis is based on established criteria, typically adhering to guidelines from organizations like the American College of Cardiology and the American Heart Association. The identification of secondary hypertension—caused by underlying conditions such as renal disease or endocrine disorders—also plays a crucial role in treatment decisions.

Once diagnosed, the cornerstone of hypertension management is lifestyle modification, which can significantly lower blood pressure and enhance overall health. Dietary changes, particularly the adoption of the DASH (Dietary Approaches to Stop Hypertension) diet, emphasize the consumption of fruits, vegetables, whole grains, and low-fat dairy while reducing sodium intake. Physical activity, recommended at a minimum of 150 minutes of moderate-intensity exercise per week, further supports blood pressure control and aids in weight management. Reducing alcohol consumption and quitting tobacco are additional critical lifestyle adjustments that contribute to improved cardiovascular health. Pharmacological treatment is often necessary, especially for patients with stage 1 hypertension or higher, and those with comorbid conditions. A range of antihypertensive medications is available, including diuretics, ACE inhibitors, angiotensin II receptor blockers (ARBs), beta-blockers, and calcium channel blockers. The choice of medication should be individualized based on the patient's specific health status, potential side effects, and interactions with other medications. Combination therapy is frequently employed for patients who do not achieve adequate control with a single agent, as it can enhance effectiveness and minimize the risk of side effects.

Monitoring and follow-up are critical components of hypertension management. Regular follow-up appointments allow healthcare providers to assess blood pressure control, evaluate treatment adherence, and adjust medications as necessary. Home blood pressure monitoring can empower patients to engage in their health management actively and provide valuable data for ongoing treatment evaluation. Moreover, addressing the psychological and educational needs of patients is essential for successful hypertension management. Empowering patients through education about their condition, the importance of adherence to treatment, and self-monitoring techniques can enhance their engagement in care and improve outcomes. In summary, the management and treatment of hypertension involve a holistic approach that integrates lifestyle changes, pharmacological interventions, continuous monitoring, and patient education. By understanding the multifactorial nature of hypertension and implementing evidence-based strategies, healthcare providers can significantly reduce the burden of this condition, enhance patient quality of life, and prevent the severe complications that arise from uncontrolled hypertension. As research evolves, ongoing advancements in both pharmacological and non-pharmacological treatments will continue to shape the landscape of hypertension management, paving the way for more effective and personalized care strategies.

7.1 Assessment and Diagnosis:

The assessment and diagnosis of hypertension are critical steps in effectively managing this pervasive health condition, which is often referred to as a "silent killer" due to its typically asymptomatic nature. Accurate diagnosis relies on consistent and standardized blood pressure measurements, typically taken during routine medical visits, to establish whether an individual's blood pressure falls within normal ranges or indicates hypertension. Current guidelines emphasize the importance of multiple readings to confirm elevated levels and the need for careful evaluation of factors that may contribute to hypertension, such as lifestyle, family history, and existing comorbidities. Additionally, assessing for secondary hypertension—caused by identifiable medical conditions—plays a vital role in determining the most appropriate treatment strategy. Through a thorough and systematic approach to assessment and diagnosis, healthcare providers can identify at-risk individuals, tailor interventions effectively, and ultimately reduce the significant health risks associated with uncontrolled hypertension.

i. Guidelines for measuring blood pressure:

Measuring blood pressure accurately is crucial for diagnosing and managing hypertension. To ensure proper measurement, it's important to prepare adequately by creating a quiet and comfortable environment for the patient. The patient should be seated with their back supported and feet flat on the ground, and the arm used for measurement should be at heart level. The right equipment is essential; a calibrated sphygmomanometer should be used, and the correct cuff size selected based on the patient's arm circumference. For example, a standard adult cuff is appropriate for an arm circumference of 22-32 cm. Before measurement, allow the patient to rest for at least five minutes and ensure they have not smoked, exercised, or consumed caffeine within the last 30 minutes.

For manual measurement, place the cuff snugly around the upper arm, palpate the brachial artery, and inflate the cuff rapidly to 20-30 mmHg above the expected systolic pressure. Slowly release the pressure while listening with a stethoscope for Korotkoff sounds: the first sound indicates systolic pressure, while the point where sounds disappear indicates diastolic pressure. In automatic measurement, follow the device instructions for inflation and allow it to measure and display the readings. It's recommended to take at least two measurements, spaced 1-2 minutes apart, and average the last two readings if there is significant variation.

Documentation is essential; record the date, time, arm used, position, and readings, along with any factors that may have influenced the results. For home monitoring, patients should be instructed on proper technique and when to seek medical advice based on their readings. Ambulatory blood pressure monitoring may be considered for more accurate assessments, particularly in cases of white-coat hypertension. Regular review of readings helps determine if lifestyle changes or medications are necessary, and accurate measurement techniques contribute significantly to effective hypertension management. Regular training and calibration of equipment are also vital for maintaining measurement accuracy.

ii. Diagnostic criteria:

The diagnostic criteria for hypertension are primarily based on blood pressure readings obtained through reliable measurement techniques. According to the American College of Cardiology and the American Heart Association, hypertension is classified as having a systolic blood pressure (SBP) of 130 mmHg or higher or a diastolic blood pressure (DBP) of 80 mmHg or higher, based on the average of two or more readings taken on separate occasions. This classification includes various stages: elevated blood pressure is defined as SBP between 120-129 mmHg and DBP less than 80 mmHg, while Stage 1 hypertension ranges from SBP 130-139 mmHg or DBP 80-89 mmHg, and Stage 2 hypertension is characterized by SBP of 140 mmHg or higher or DBP of 90 mmHg or higher.

Accurate diagnosis requires careful measurement in a controlled environment, with considerations for white-coat syndrome, where patients exhibit elevated readings in clinical settings but have normal levels at home. Additional assessments, such as evaluating for secondary causes of hypertension and assessing cardiovascular risk factors, may also be performed to guide management and treatment strategies effectively. These criteria underscore the importance of routine monitoring and consistent methodology to ensure early detection and intervention in hypertension management.

iii. Evaluation of secondary hypertension:

Evaluating secondary hypertension involves a comprehensive assessment to identify underlying causes that may be contributing to elevated blood pressure. Initially, a thorough medical history and physical examination are conducted, focusing on the onset, duration, and severity of hypertension, along with associated symptoms that may suggest specific conditions. Key tests include laboratory evaluations such as serum electrolytes, creatinine, and glucose levels, as well as urinalysis to check for proteinuria or haematuria. Imaging studies like renal ultrasound can help detect renal artery stenosis or other kidney abnormalities. Hormonal assays, including plasma aldosterone concentration and renin activity, may be indicated to assess for conditions like primary aldosteronism or Cushing's syndrome. Additionally, evaluating for pheochromocytoma through 24-hour urine catecholamines or plasma free metanephros's is essential if indicated. Other potential causes, such as sleep apnoea or certain medications, should also be considered. A systematic approach helps in accurately diagnosing secondary hypertension, allowing for targeted treatment of the underlying condition and more effective management of blood pressure.

iv. Role of patient history and physical examination:

The role of patient history and physical examination in hypertension is pivotal for accurate diagnosis and effective management. A comprehensive patient history begins with gathering information about risk factors, including family history of hypertension or cardiovascular disease, lifestyle factors such as diet, physical activity, alcohol consumption, and tobacco use. It is also essential to inquire about the patient's previous blood pressure readings, any history of cardiovascular events, kidney disease, diabetes, or endocrine disorders, which can contribute to secondary hypertension. The review of symptoms, including headaches, visual changes, or chest pain, provides further insight into the potential severity and complications of hypertension. During the physical examination, clinicians assess vital signs, particularly blood pressure measurements in both arms, and perform a thorough cardiovascular assessment, looking for signs of heart failure, such as elevated jugular venous pressure or pulmonary congestion. Additionally, abdominal examination may reveal signs of renal artery stenosis, while neurological evaluation can identify complications related to hypertension, such as hypertensive encephalopathy. The examination often includes an evaluation of the fundus to detect changes in the retinal vessels' indicative of chronic hypertension. Together, the detailed history and physical examination not only aid in diagnosing hypertension but also help identify underlying causes and assess the overall cardiovascular risk, guiding appropriate therapeutic interventions.

7.2 Lifestyle Modifications:

Lifestyle modifications are a cornerstone of hypertension management, playing a crucial role in both preventing and controlling elevated blood pressure. As the first line of defence against hypertension, these changes can significantly reduce the need for medication and lower the risk of associated complications, such as heart disease and stroke. Key modifications include adopting a heart-healthy diet, such as the DASH (Dietary Approaches to Stop Hypertension) diet, which emphasizes the intake of fruits, vegetables, whole grains, and low-fat dairy while minimizing sodium consumption. Regular physical activity is also essential, with recommendations suggesting at least 150 minutes of moderate exercise each week. Additional lifestyle adjustments, including weight management, limiting alcohol intake, and quitting smoking, further contribute to improved blood pressure control. By empowering individuals to make these positive changes, healthcare providers can enhance the overall effectiveness of hypertension treatment and promote better long-term health outcomes.

i. **Dietary changes:**

Dietary changes play a crucial role in managing hypertension and can significantly lower blood pressure levels. One effective approach is adopting the Dietary Approaches to Stop Hypertension (DASH) diet, which emphasizes the consumption of fruits and vegetables, aiming for at least 4-5 servings of each per day, alongside 6-8 servings of whole grains such as brown rice and whole wheat bread. Lean proteins, including fish, poultry, beans, and nuts, should replace red meat and full-fat dairy products, while incorporating 2-3 servings of low-fat or fat-free dairy provides beneficial calcium and vitamin D. Reducing sodium intake is critical; the goal is to limit sodium to less than 2,300 mg per day, ideally to 1,500 mg, by choosing low-sodium options and using herbs and spices for flavour instead of salt. Increasing potassium intake can also aid in lowering blood pressure, with potassium-rich foods including bananas, sweet potatoes, spinach, and beans. Moderating alcohol consumption is important as well, with guidelines suggesting up to one drink per day for women and two for men. Maintaining healthy portion sizes and weight is vital; being mindful of portions and incorporating a balanced variety of food groups can support overall health. Additionally, increasing omega-3 fatty acids through sources like fatty fish and flaxseeds can benefit heart health, while limiting processed foods, which are often high in sodium and unhealthy fats, is crucial. Staying hydrated by drinking adequate amounts of water further supports blood pressure regulation. Together, these dietary strategies not only influence blood pressure but also enhance overall cardiovascular health, potentially reducing the need for medication. Consulting with a healthcare provider or dietitian can help tailor these changes to individual needs and preferences.

ii. **Physical activity recommendations:**

Physical activity is a cornerstone in the management of hypertension, as regular exercise can significantly lower blood pressure and improve overall cardiovascular health. The American Heart Association recommends that adults engage in at least 150 minutes of moderate-intensity aerobic activity each week, or 75 minutes of vigorous-intensity exercise, spread out over the week. This can include activities such as brisk walking, cycling, swimming, or jogging. For those with hypertension, starting with moderate activities like walking or light cycling is ideal, particularly if they have been sedentary. It's essential to incorporate strength training exercises at least two days a week, focusing on all major muscle groups, as this can further enhance blood pressure control and overall fitness. Flexibility and balance exercises, such as yoga or tai chi, can also be beneficial, promoting relaxation and reducing stress, which is important for managing hypertension. Patients should be encouraged to gradually increase their activity level, aiming for a combination of aerobic and resistance training, and to choose activities they enjoy improving adherence. Additionally, engaging in daily physical activity—such as taking the stairs, gardening, or walking instead of driving for short trips—can contribute positively. Before starting any new exercise regimen, especially for individuals with significant hypertension or other health conditions, it's advisable to consult with a healthcare provider to ensure safety and receive personalized recommendations. Regular physical activity not only helps in reducing blood pressure but also aids in weight management, improves mood, and enhances overall quality of life, making it an essential component of hypertension management.

iii. Weight management strategies:

Weight management is a critical component of hypertension management, as excess weight can significantly contribute to elevated blood pressure levels. Effective strategies for weight management include adopting a balanced, calorie-controlled diet combined with regular physical activity. The first step is to assess current weight and set realistic, achievable goals, aiming for a gradual weight loss of 1-2 pounds per week, which is considered safe and sustainable. Implementing the DASH diet, which emphasizes fruits, vegetables, whole grains, lean proteins, and low-fat dairy while reducing sodium intake, can support both weight loss and blood pressure reduction. Portion control is essential; using smaller plates, measuring food portions, and being mindful of serving sizes can help prevent overeating. Additionally, keeping a food diary can increase awareness of eating habits and identify triggers for unhealthy snacking or binge eating.

Regular physical activity should be incorporated into daily routines, with the recommendation of at least 150 minutes of moderate intensity exercise each week, complemented by strength training exercises twice a week. Incorporating lifestyle changes, such as reducing sedentary behaviour by taking breaks from sitting, walking more, and engaging in active hobbies, can also contribute to weight management. It's important to focus on building healthy habits rather than quick fixes, as long-term lifestyle changes yield better results. Support from healthcare providers, dietitians, or weight loss groups can provide motivation and accountability. Ultimately, achieving and maintaining a healthy weight not only helps lower blood pressure but also reduces the risk of cardiovascular diseases and improves overall well-being.

iv. Alcohol and tobacco cessation:

Alcohol and tobacco cessation are crucial components in the management of hypertension, as both substances can significantly elevate blood pressure and increase cardiovascular risk. For individuals with hypertension, reducing alcohol intake is essential; guidelines recommend limiting consumption to no more than one drink per day for women and two drinks per day for men. Excessive alcohol consumption can lead to weight gain, disrupt sleep, and directly affect blood pressure levels. Strategies for reducing alcohol intake include setting clear goals, finding non-alcoholic alternatives, and avoiding triggers that lead to drinking, such as social situations or certain environments. Support groups, counselling, and behavioural therapies can also provide valuable assistance in maintaining these changes.

Tobacco use is a well-established risk factor for hypertension and cardiovascular disease, as it causes blood vessel constriction and damage to the endothelial lining, leading to increased blood pressure. Quitting smoking has immediate benefits for blood pressure and overall health, reducing the risk of heart disease and improving circulation. Cessation strategies include nicotine replacement therapies (such as patches, gums, or inhalers), prescription medications, and behavioural interventions. Support from healthcare providers, smoking cessation programs, and support groups can significantly enhance the chances of successfully quitting. It is also important for individuals to develop coping mechanisms for cravings and stress management techniques to handle withdrawal symptoms. Overall, the cessation of alcohol and tobacco not only aids in controlling hypertension but also promotes long-term health and enhances quality of life, making it a vital focus for anyone managing high blood pressure.

v. Stress management techniques:

Stress management is an essential aspect of hypertension management, as chronic stress can lead to elevated blood pressure and other cardiovascular issues. Effective stress management techniques include a variety of approaches that promote relaxation and emotional well-being. Mindfulness and meditation practices, such as deep breathing exercises, guided imagery, or progressive muscle relaxation, help reduce stress by promoting a state of calm and enhancing awareness of the present moment. Regular physical activity, such as walking, yoga, or tai chi, not only provides cardiovascular benefits but also releases endorphins, which can improve mood and reduce stress levels. Additionally, maintaining a balanced diet rich in fruits, vegetables, and whole grains can have a positive impact on mood and overall well-being. Social support is also vital; engaging with friends and family or participating in support groups can provide emotional outlets and reduce feelings of isolation. Furthermore, time management techniques can help individuals prioritize tasks, set realistic goals, and avoid feeling overwhelmed by daily responsibilities. Cognitive-behavioural therapy (CBT) can be beneficial for those dealing with chronic stress, helping to identify negative thought patterns and develop healthier coping strategies. Lastly, ensuring adequate sleep is crucial, as poor sleep quality can exacerbate stress and contribute to hypertension. By integrating these stress management techniques into daily life, individuals can effectively lower their blood pressure, improve their quality of life, and enhance their overall health.

7.3 Pharmacological Treatments:

Pharmacological treatments for hypertension are essential in managing this prevalent condition, particularly for individuals whose blood pressure remains elevated despite lifestyle modifications. A wide range of antihypertensive medications is available, each with distinct mechanisms of action, efficacy, and side effect profiles. Common classes of drugs include diuretics, which help eliminate excess sodium and fluid; ACE inhibitors and angiotensin II receptor blockers (ARBs), which relax blood vessels; beta-blockers, which reduce heart rate and output; and calcium channel blockers, which prevent calcium from entering heart and blood vessel cells, leading to relaxation of the arteries. The selection of appropriate pharmacotherapy is guided by individual patient factors, including age, comorbidities, and the presence of secondary hypertension. Effective management often involves a combination of medications to achieve optimal blood pressure control while minimizing adverse effects. Through a tailored approach to pharmacological treatment, healthcare providers can significantly reduce the risks associated with hypertension, improving patient outcomes and quality of life.

i. Overview of antihypertensive classes:

Antihypertensive medications are categorized into several classes, each working through different mechanisms to lower blood pressure.

Here's an overview of the main classes:

Sr. No.	Class	Description	Examples
1.	Diuretics	These help the kidneys remove excess sodium and water from the body, reducing blood volume.	Thiazide Diuretics: Hydrochloro-thiazide Loop Diuretics: Furosemide
2.	ACE Inhibitors	Angiotensin-converting enzyme inhibitors block the conversion of angiotensin I to angiotensin II, a substance that narrows blood vessels. This leads to vasodilation and reduced blood pressure.	lisinopril, enalapril
3.	Angiotensin II Receptor Blockers (ARBs)	These medications prevent angiotensin II from binding to its receptors, helping to relax blood vessels.	losartan, valsartan
4.	Calcium Channel Blockers	These drugs inhibit calcium entry into heart and vascular smooth muscle cells, leading to decreased contraction and vasodilation.	amlodipine, diltiazem

5.	Beta Blockers	Beta-adrenergic blockers reduce heart rate and cardiac output by blocking the effects of adrenaline on the heart.	atenolol, metoprolol
6.	Alpha Blockers	These medications work by blocking alpha-adrenergic receptors, leading to vasodilation and decreased blood pressure.	doxazosin, prazosin
7.	Renin Inhibitors	Drugs directly inhibit renin, an enzyme that plays a role in blood pressure regulation.	aliskiren
8.	Central Agonists	These act on the central nervous system to decrease sympathetic outflow, leading to lower heart rate and vascular resistance.	clonidine
9.	Vasodilators	Direct vasodilators relax blood vessel walls, significantly reducing blood pressure.	hydralazine

Each class may be used alone or in combination, depending on the patient's individual needs and response to treatment.

ii. Diuretics:

Diuretics, often referred to as "water pills," are a cornerstone in the management of hypertension and various other conditions, such as heart failure and oedema. They work primarily by promoting the excretion of sodium and water from the kidneys, which helps to reduce blood volume and, consequently, blood pressure.

- **Types of Diuretics**

a) **Thiazide Diuretics:**

- **Examples:** Hydrochlorothiazide, Chlorthalidone, Indapamide.
- **Mechanism:** These diuretics act on the distal convoluted tubule of the nephron, inhibiting sodium reabsorption. This results in increased sodium and water excretion.
- **Indications:** Commonly used for the treatment of hypertension and mild oedema.
- **Side Effects:** Electrolyte imbalances (especially hypokalaemia) increased uric acid levels (which can lead to gout), and potential glucose intolerance.

b) **Loop Diuretics:**

- **Examples:** Furosemide, Bumetanide, Torsemide.
- **Mechanism:** Loop diuretics work on the ascending loop of Henle, where they inhibit the reabsorption of sodium, potassium, and chloride. They are more potent than thiazides and lead to significant diuresis.
- **Indications:** Often prescribed for patients with heart failure, pulmonary oedema, or significant renal impairment.
- **Side Effects:** Risk of hypokalaemia, dehydration, ototoxicity (especially with rapid IV administration), and electrolyte imbalances.

c) **Potassium-Sparing Diuretics:**

- **Examples:** Spironolactone, Eplerenone, Amiloride, Triamterene.
- **Mechanism:** These diuretics act on the collecting ducts and distal convoluted tubules. They either block aldosterone receptors (spironolactone and eplerenone) or directly inhibit sodium channels (amiloride and triamterene), leading to sodium excretion while conserving potassium.
- **Indications:** Often used in conjunction with other diuretics to prevent potassium loss, as well as in heart failure and conditions of hyperaldosteronism.

- **Side Effects:** Hyperkalaemia, hormonal side effects (with spironolactone), and gastrointestinal disturbances.
- **Clinical Considerations:**
- **Monitoring:** Regular monitoring of electrolytes (particularly potassium), renal function, and blood pressure is essential, especially when initiating therapy or adjusting doses.
- **Combination Therapy:** Diuretics are frequently used in combination with other antihypertensive agents (like ACE inhibitors or calcium channel blockers) to enhance efficacy and minimize side effects.
- **Lifestyle Modifications:** Patients are often advised to make dietary changes, such as reducing salt intake, which can further improve the effectiveness of diuretics.

Diuretics are effective in lowering blood pressure and managing fluid overload conditions. Their choice depends on the specific clinical situation, patient tolerance, and the presence of comorbidities. While they are generally safe, attention to side effects and ongoing monitoring is crucial for optimal patient outcomes.

iii. ACE inhibitors:

Angiotensin-Converting Enzyme (ACE) inhibitors are a class of medications primarily used to treat hypertension (high blood pressure) and heart failure. They are also effective in preventing complications in conditions such as diabetes and chronic kidney disease.

➢ **Mechanism of Action:**

ACE inhibitors work by blocking the activity of the angiotensin-converting enzyme, which is responsible for converting angiotensin I (an inactive precursor) into angiotensin II, a potent vasoconstrictor. Angiotensin II has several effects, including:

- **Vasoconstriction:** Narrowing blood vessels, which increases blood pressure.
- **Aldosterone Secretion:** Stimulating the adrenal glands to release aldosterone, leading to sodium and water retention.
- **Increased Sympathetic Activity:** Enhancing the release of norepinephrine, further raising blood pressure.

- **By inhibiting this conversion, ACE inhibitors lead to:**
- **Vasodilation:** Widening of blood vessels, which decreases blood pressure.
- **Reduced Blood Volume:** Due to decreased sodium and water retention.
- **Decreased Cardiac Output:** Reducing the workload on the heart.

- **Common ACE Inhibitors:**

Some commonly prescribed ACE inhibitors include Lisinopril, Enalapril, Ramipril, Captopril, Benazcpril, Quinapril

- **Indications:**

ACE inhibitors are used in a variety of clinical settings, including:

- **Hypertension:** Effective as monotherapy or in combination with other antihypertensives.
- **Heart Failure:** Improves symptoms, reduces hospitalizations, and prolongs survival.
- **Post-Myocardial Infarction:** Reduces mortality and improves outcomes after a heart attack.
- **Diabetic Nephropathy:** Protects kidney function in patients with diabetes.
- **Chronic Kidney Disease:** Slows progression of kidney disease by reducing intraglomerular pressure.
- **Side Effects:**

While generally well-tolerated, ACE inhibitors can cause side effects, including:

- **Cough:** A persistent dry cough occurs in a minority of patients due to increased bradykinin levels.
- **Hyperkalaemia:** Elevated potassium levels due to reduced aldosterone secretion.
- **Angioedema:** A rare but serious allergic reaction characterized by swelling of the face, lips, and airways.
- **Hypotension:** Particularly after the first dose, especially in patients who are volume depleted.

- **Renal Impairment:** Can lead to worsening kidney function, especially in those with renal artery stenosis.

➢ **Contraindications:**

ACE inhibitors are contraindicated in certain situations, including:

- **Pregnancy:** Associated with foetal harm, especially in the second and third trimesters.
- **History of Angioedema:** Previous angioedema related to ACE inhibitors.
- **Bilateral Renal Artery Stenosis:** Can worsen kidney function.

➢ **Clinical Monitoring:**

When prescribing ACE inhibitors, regular monitoring is essential:

- **Blood Pressure:** To ensure effective control of hypertension.
- **Electrolytes:** Especially potassium levels to check for hyperkalaemia.
- **Renal Function:** To monitor for any deterioration in kidney function.

ACE inhibitors play a critical role in managing hypertension and heart failure, providing both symptomatic relief and long-term benefits. Their effectiveness, combined with a relatively favourable side effect profile, makes them a common choice in various patient populations. Careful monitoring and patient education are vital to optimize treatment outcomes and minimize adverse effects.

iv. Angiotensin II receptor blockers (ARBs):

Angiotensin II Receptor Blockers (ARBs) are a class of medications that primarily target the renin-angiotensin-aldosterone system (RAAS) to manage hypertension and various cardiovascular conditions. They work by blocking the effects of angiotensin II, a potent vasoconstrictor, thereby promoting vasodilation and reducing blood pressure.

- **Mechanism of Action:**

ARBs selectively block the type 1 angiotensin II receptors (AT1) found in various tissues, including blood vessels, the heart, and the kidneys. By inhibiting these receptors, ARBs:

- **Promote Vasodilation:** This leads to a decrease in systemic vascular resistance and blood pressure.
- **Reduce Aldosterone Secretion:** Lower levels of aldosterone lead to decreased sodium and water retention, reducing blood volume and pressure.
- **Decrease Sympathetic Nervous System Activity:** This can help lower heart rate and further reduce blood pressure.
- **Common ARBs:** Some widely used ARBs include Losartan, Valsartan, Irbesartan, Candesartan, Olmesartan, Telmisartan
- **Indications:**
  ARBs are indicated for several conditions:
- **Hypertension:** Used as first-line therapy for managing high blood pressure, often in patients who are intolerant to ACE inhibitors due to cough or angioedema.
- **Heart Failure:** ARBs are beneficial in reducing morbidity and mortality in heart failure patients, particularly in those with reduced ejection fraction.
- **Post-Myocardial Infarction:** They help prevent left ventricular remodelling and improve survival rates after a heart attack.
- **Diabetic Nephropathy:** ARBs are effective in slowing the progression of kidney disease in diabetic patients by reducing intraglomerular pressure.
- **Chronic kidney disease:** Used to protect kidney function in patients with chronic kidney disease, particularly in those with diabetes or hypertension.

➢ **Side Effects:**

ARBs are generally well tolerated, but they can cause side effects, including:

- **Hyperkalaemia:** Elevated potassium levels due to decreased aldosterone secretion, which can be serious.
- **Hypotension:** Particularly after the first dose, especially in volume-depleted patients.
- **Renal Impairment:** May worsen kidney function, particularly in patients with renal artery stenosis.
- **Angioedema:** Rare, but possible; less common than with ACE inhibitors.

- **Dizziness or Light-headedness:** Due to blood pressure reduction.
- **Contraindications:**
  ARBs should be used with caution in certain populations:
- **Pregnancy:** Can cause foetal harm, particularly in the second and third trimesters.
- **History of Angioedema:** Previous angioedema related to ARBs or ACE inhibitors is a contraindication.
- **Bilateral Renal Artery Stenosis:** Risk of worsening kidney function.

➢ **Clinical Monitoring:**

When prescribing ARBs, the following monitoring is essential:

- **Blood Pressure:** Regular checks to assess the effectiveness of treatment.
- **Potassium Levels:** To monitor for hyperkalaemia, especially when used with other medications affecting potassium.
- **Renal Function:** Monitoring serum creatinine levels to ensure kidney function remains stable.

Angiotensin II Receptor Blockers are an important class of antihypertensive agents with a range of cardiovascular and renal benefits. They provide an alternative for patients who cannot tolerate ACE inhibitors, with a favourable side effect profile. Individualized treatment plans, regular monitoring, and patient education are crucial for optimizing outcomes while minimizing risks.

v. **Beta-blockers:**

Beta blockers, also known as beta-adrenergic antagonists, are a class of medications that block the effects of adrenaline (epinephrine) on beta-adrenergic receptors. They are commonly used to manage various cardiovascular conditions, including hypertension, heart failure, and arrhythmias.

➢ **Mechanism of Action:**

Beta blockers primarily exert their effects by blocking beta-1 and beta-2 adrenergic receptors:

a) **Beta-1 Receptors:**

a. Primarily located in the heart, their blockade leads to:

- **Decreased Heart Rate:** Reduces the number of impulses generated by the sinoatrial node.
- **Decreased Contractility:** Reduces the force of heart muscle contractions, lowering cardiac output.
- **Decreased Renin Release:** Inhibits renin secretion from the kidneys, reducing angiotensin II production and leading to vasodilation.

b) **Beta-2 Receptors:**

Found in smooth muscles (including the lungs), their blockade can lead to:

- **Bronchoconstriction:** This effect is particularly important in patients with respiratory conditions, as non-selective beta blockers can exacerbate asthma or chronic obstructive pulmonary disease (COPD).

➢ **Common Beta Blockers:**

Beta blockers can be classified as selective or non-selective:

- **Selective Beta-1 Blockers:** Atenolol, Metoprolol, Bisoprolol
- **Non-Selective Beta Blockers:** Propranolol, Nadolol, Timolol
- **Beta Blockers with Additional Properties**: (also known as mixed action) Carvedilol (alpha and beta blockade), Labetalol (alpha and beta blockade)

➢ **Indications:**

Beta blockers are indicated for several conditions:

- **Hypertension:** Effective in lowering blood pressure, particularly in younger patients and those with comorbid conditions such as anxiety or migraines.
- **Heart Failure:** Reduces mortality and improves symptoms in patients with chronic heart failure (particularly beta-1 selective blockers).
- **Post-Myocardial Infarction:** Decreases mortality and the risk of reinfarction.
- **Arrhythmias:** Controls heart rate and rhythm in conditions like atrial fibrillation and ventricular tachycardia.

- **Angina Pectoris:** Relieves chest pain by reducing cardiac workload and oxygen demand.
- **Migraine Prophylaxis:** Effective in preventing migraine headaches.
- **Essential Tremor:** Reduces tremors in conditions like essential tremor and performance anxiety.

➢ **Side Effects:**

While generally well tolerated, beta blockers can cause several side effects:

- **Bradycardia:** Slowed heart rate, which may require dosage adjustment or discontinuation.
- **Fatigue:** Due to reduced heart rate and cardiac output.
- **Cold Extremities:** Reduced blood flow to the hands and feet.
- **Bronchoconstriction:** Particularly with non-selective beta blockers, which can worsen asthma or COPD.
- **Sexual Dysfunction:** Reduced libido or erectile dysfunction.
- **Hypoglycaemia Masking:** Can mask signs of low blood sugar in diabetic patients.

➢ **Contraindications:**

Beta blockers should be avoided or used with caution in certain conditions:

- **Asthma or COPD:** Non-selective beta blockers can exacerbate bronchospasm.
- **Severe Bradycardia:** Can worsen heart rate significantly.
- **Second- or Third-Degree Heart Block:** Without a functioning pacemaker.
- **Acute Heart Failure:** In the absence of appropriate management.

➢ **Clinical Monitoring:**

When prescribing beta blockers, the following monitoring is essential:

- **Heart Rate and Blood Pressure:** Regular assessments to ensure adequate control without excessive bradycardia or hypotension.

- **Signs of Heart Failure:** Monitoring for worsening symptoms in patients with existing heart failure.
- **Blood Glucose Levels:** In diabetic patients, to check for hypoglycaemia.

Beta blockers are a versatile class of medications used for managing various cardiovascular conditions, particularly hypertension, heart failure, and arrhythmias. Their ability to reduce heart rate and myocardial workload makes them beneficial in many clinical scenarios. However, careful selection, monitoring, and patient education are critical to optimize their use and mitigate potential side effects.

vi. Calcium channel blockers:

Calcium channel blockers (CCBs) are a class of medications that inhibit the influx of calcium ions into smooth muscle and cardiac cells, leading to relaxation of vascular smooth muscle and a decrease in heart contractility. They are primarily used to treat hypertension, angina, and certain cardiac arrhythmias.

➢ **Mechanism of Action:**

CCBs work by blocking voltage-gated calcium channels, which are essential for muscle contraction. The main effects of calcium channel blockade include:

a) Vasodilation:

- **Peripheral Vasodilation:** CCBs relax smooth muscle in peripheral arteries, leading to decreased systemic vascular resistance and lower blood pressure.
- **Coronary Vasodilation:** They increase blood flow to the heart muscle, alleviating angina symptoms.

b) Reduced Cardiac Contractility:

By decreasing calcium entry into cardiac myocytes, CCBs reduce the force of contraction of the heart (negative inotropic effect).

c) Decreased Heart Rate:

Some CCBs also slow conduction through the atrioventricular (AV) node, leading to a reduced heart rate (negative chronotropic effect).

- **Types of Calcium Channel Blockers:**

CCBs are typically divided into two main categories based on their primary site of action:

- **Dihydropyridines:** Primarily act on vascular smooth muscle, leading to more significant vasodilation. Examples: Amlodipine, Nifedipine, Felodipine, Isradipine.
- **Non-Dihydropyridines:** Primarily affect the heart and vascular smooth muscle; they have more pronounced effects on heart rate and contractility. Examples: Diltiazem, Verapamil.

- **Indications:**

Calcium channel blockers are indicated for several conditions:

- **Hypertension:** Effective for both systolic and diastolic blood pressure reduction. Often used as first-line therapy or in combination with other antihypertensives.
- **Angina Pectoris:** Used to relieve chest pain by improving blood flow to the heart muscle.
- **Certain Arrhythmias:** Non-dihydropyridines (like diltiazem and verapamil) are effective for controlling heart rate in atrial fibrillation and other tachyarrhythmias.
- **Raynaud's Phenomenon:** Help reduce symptoms by causing vasodilation of peripheral vessels.
- **Migraine Prophylaxis:** Some CCBs, particularly verapamil, may be used to prevent migraines.

- **Side Effects:**

While generally well tolerated, CCBs can cause a range of side effects:

- **Peripheral Oedema:** Commonly associated with dihydropyridines due to vasodilation and increased capillary permeability.
- **Hypotension:** Can occur, especially with excessive dosing or when combined with other antihypertensives.
- **Bradycardia:** More likely with non-dihydropyridines, which can slow heart rate significantly.
- **Constipation:** Particularly with verapamil, due to smooth muscle relaxation in the gastrointestinal tract.

- **Headache and Flushing:** Due to vasodilation effects.

- **Contraindications:**

CCBs should be used with caution or avoided in certain conditions:

- **Severe Aortic Stenosis:** Can worsen cardiac output.
- **Heart Block:** Particularly with non-dihydropyridines, which can exacerbate conduction abnormalities.
- **Heart Failure:** Caution is advised, particularly with negative inotropic effects of non-dihydropyridines.

- **Clinical Monitoring:**

When prescribing CCBs, the following monitoring is essential:

- **Blood Pressure:** Regular checks to ensure effective control without excessive hypotension.
- **Heart Rate:** Particularly with non-dihydropyridines to avoid bradycardia.
- **Peripheral Oedema:** Monitoring for any signs of swelling in the legs or ankles.

Calcium channel blockers are a vital class of antihypertensive agents that provide significant benefits for various cardiovascular conditions, particularly hypertension and angina. Their dual action on vascular smooth muscle and cardiac cells makes them versatile, but careful selection and monitoring are crucial to optimizing their use and minimizing side effects.

vii. Alpha-blockers:

Alpha blockers, also known as alpha-adrenergic antagonists, are a class of medications that primarily block alpha-adrenergic receptors. They are used to treat various conditions, most notably hypertension and symptoms associated with benign prostatic hyperplasia (BPH).

- **Mechanism of Action:**

Alpha blockers work by inhibiting the action of norepinephrine on alpha-adrenergic receptors, which are found in smooth muscle. There are two main types of alpha receptors:

- **Alpha-1 Receptors:** Located in blood vessels, their blockade leads to vasodilation, resulting in a decrease in blood pressure.
- **Alpha-2 Receptors:** Found presynaptically in the central nervous system; their blockade can lead to increased sympathetic outflow. However, alpha-2 blockade is not the primary mechanism of action for most clinical uses of alpha blockers.

➢ **Common Alpha Blockers:**

- **Selective Alpha-1 Blockers:** Doxazosin, Prazosin, Terazosin
- **Non-Selective Alpha Blockers:** Phenoxybenzamine (used primarily for pheochromocytoma), Phentolamine (used in specific situations like acute hypertensive episodes)

➢ **Indications:**

Alpha blockers are indicated for several conditions:

a) **Hypertension:**

Alpha-1 blockers are effective as antihypertensives. They are often used as second-line agents or in combination with other antihypertensives. They are particularly useful in treating patients with coexisting conditions like BPH.

b) **Benign Prostatic Hyperplasia (BPH):**

Alpha-1 blockers are effective in relieving urinary symptoms associated with BPH by relaxing smooth muscle in the prostate and bladder neck, improving urine flow.

c) **Pheochromocytoma:**

- **Non-selective alpha blockers:** (e.g., phenoxybenzamine) are used to manage hypertension in patients with this tumour that secretes catecholamines.
- **Post-Traumatic Stress Disorder (PTSD):** Some alpha blockers (like prazosin) have been used off-label to help manage nightmares and hyperarousal symptoms in PTSD.

➢ **Side Effects:**

While generally well tolerated, alpha blockers can cause side effects, including:

- **Orthostatic Hypotension:** A significant drop in blood pressure upon standing, which can lead to dizziness or fainting.
- **Headache:** Due to vasodilation effects.
- **Nasal Congestion:** As a result of vasodilation in nasal passages.
- **Fatigue:** Some patients may experience tiredness.
- **Palpitations:** Due to compensatory mechanisms following blood pressure changes.

➢ **Contraindications:**

Alpha blockers should be used with caution in certain situations:

- **Severe Heart Failure:** Due to potential hypotension.
- **History of Orthostatic Hypotension:** Patients prone to significant blood pressure drops should be monitored closely.

➢ **Clinical Monitoring:**

When prescribing alpha blockers, the following monitoring is essential:

- **Blood Pressure:** Regular monitoring to assess effectiveness and watch for orthostatic changes.
- **Symptoms of BPH:** Improvement in urinary symptoms should be evaluated.
- **Heart Rate:** Monitoring for potential tachycardia as a compensatory response to blood pressure changes.

Alpha blockers are an important therapeutic option for managing hypertension and BPH. Their ability to relax smooth muscle and improve urinary flow makes them valuable in specific patient populations. While they are generally safe, monitoring for side effects, particularly orthostatic hypotension, is crucial for optimizing patient outcomes.

viii. Direct vasodilators:

Direct vasodilators are a class of antihypertensive medications that work by directly relaxing the smooth muscle in blood vessels, leading to vasodilation and a subsequent decrease in blood pressure. They are typically used in specific clinical situations, especially when rapid blood pressure control is necessary.

➢ **Mechanism of Action:**

Direct vasodilators function by acting on the vascular smooth muscle rather than on the central nervous system or the renin-angiotensin-aldosterone system (RAAS). Their primary mechanisms include:

- **Smooth Muscle Relaxation:** They cause the relaxation of arterial smooth muscle, which decreases systemic vascular resistance (SVR) and lowers blood pressure.
- **Increased Blood Flow:** By dilating blood vessels, they enhance blood flow to various organs.

➢ **Common Direct Vasodilators:**

Following are few examples of direct vasodilator with their mechanism of action:

a) Hydralazine:

- Often used for hypertension, especially in pregnancy (e.g., for gestational hypertension and preeclampsia).
- **Mechanism:** Primarily dilates arterioles; may also have some effect on venous smooth muscle.

b) Minoxidil:

- More potent than hydralazine and used in cases of resistant hypertension.
- **Mechanism:** Causes hyperpolarization of vascular smooth muscle, leading to vasodilation.

c) Nitroprusside:

- Used in hypertensive emergencies and for controlled hypotension during surgery.
- **Mechanism:** Releases nitric oxide (NO), which relaxes both arterial and venous smooth muscle.

d) Diazoxide:

- Utilized for acute hypertension and hypoglycaemia in certain conditions (e.g., insulinoma).
- **Mechanism:** Inhibits insulin release and causes vasodilation.

➢ **Indications:**

Direct vasodilators are indicated for various conditions:

- **Hypertension:** Primarily used in cases of resistant hypertension where other agents have failed. Often used in combination with diuretics and beta blockers to counteract reflex tachycardia and fluid retention.
- **Hypertensive Emergencies:** Nitroprusside is often the drug of choice for rapid blood pressure control in emergencies.
- **Heart Failure:** Used in acute heart failure to reduce afterload and improve cardiac output.
- **Peripheral Vascular Disease:** Helps improve blood flow in conditions like intermittent claudication.

➢ **Side Effects:**

While direct vasodilators can be effective, they also have potential side effects, including:

- **Reflex Tachycardia:** Increased heart rate due to compensatory mechanisms from decreased blood pressure.
- **Fluid Retention:** Often leads to oedema; hence, these medications are typically used with diurctics.
- **Headache:** Due to vasodilation effects.
- **Nausea:** May occur as a side effect.
- **Palpitations:** Resulting from reflex sympathetic activation.
- **Nitroprusside Toxicity**: Prolonged use can lead to cyanide toxicity, especially in patients with renal impairment.

➢ **Contraindications:**

Direct vasodilators should be used with caution in certain conditions:

- **Aortic Dissection:** Rapid changes in blood pressure can worsen the condition.
- **Hypotension:** Not indicated in patients with low baseline blood pressure.
- **Severe Heart Failure:** May lead to excessive vasodilation and worsened cardiac output.

➢ **Clinical Monitoring:**

When prescribing direct vasodilators, careful monitoring is essential:

- **Blood Pressure:** Frequent monitoring is necessary to avoid hypotension and assess the effectiveness of treatment.
- **Heart Rate:** Monitoring for reflex tachycardia is important, especially when starting treatment.
- **Signs of Oedema:** Patients should be monitored for signs of fluid retention, particularly when used with other antihypertensives.

Direct vasodilators are a critical component in the management of hypertension, particularly in resistant cases and acute emergencies. Their ability to rapidly lower blood pressure makes them valuable in specific situations, but they require careful monitoring due to potential side effects. When used appropriately, they can significantly improve patient outcomes in hypertensive crises and other related conditions.

ix. Indications for each class:

Here's a detailed overview of the indications for each class of antihypertensive drugs:

a)Diuretics:

- **Hypertension:** Often used as first-line treatment, especially thiazide diuretics (e.g., hydrochlorothiazide).
- **Heart Failure:** To reduce fluid overload and alleviate symptoms.
- **Oedema:** Due to conditions like liver cirrhosis or kidney disease.
- **Nephrotic Syndrome:** To manage oedema and fluid retention.

b)ACE Inhibitors:

- **Hypertension:** Effective in lowering blood pressure, often used as first-line agents.
- **Heart Failure:** Improves symptoms and reduces mortality.
- **Post-Myocardial Infarction:** Reduces mortality and prevents remodelling of the heart.
- **Diabetic Nephropathy:** Protects kidney function by reducing intraglomerular pressure.
- **Chronic Kidney Disease:** Slows progression, particularly in diabetic patients.

c)Angiotensin II Receptor Blockers (ARBs):

- **Hypertension:** Effective alternatives to ACE inhibitors, especially for patient's intolerant to ACE inhibitors (e.g., cough).
- **Heart Failure:** Similar benefits to ACE inhibitors in managing symptoms and mortality.
- **Diabetic Nephropathy:** Protects kidney function, particularly in diabetic patients.
- **Chronic Kidney Disease:** Slows progression of kidney disease.

d)Calcium Channel Blockers:

- **Hypertension:** Effective for both systolic and diastolic blood pressure reduction; particularly useful in elderly patients.
- **Angina:** Alleviates chest pain by relaxing coronary arteries.
- **Arrhythmias:** Certain CCBs (e.g., verapamil, diltiazem) are used to manage specific arrhythmias.
- **Pulmonary Hypertension:** Some CCBs can be effective in managing this condition.

e)Beta Blockers:

- **Hypertension:** Effective, especially in younger patients or those with comorbidities (e.g., anxiety, migraines).
- **Heart Failure:** Reduces mortality and improves symptoms in chronic heart failure.
- **Post-Myocardial Infarction:** Reduces mortality and prevents further heart attacks.
- **Arrhythmias:** Used to control heart rate in various arrhythmias.
- **Migraine Prophylaxis:** Helps prevent migraine headaches.

f)Alpha Blockers:

- **Hypertension:** Can be used as add-on therapy, particularly in men with benign prostatic hyperplasia (BPH).
- **BPH:** Alleviates urinary symptoms by relaxing smooth muscle in the prostate.

- **Renin Inhibitors:**
- **Hypertension:** Used for treatment in patients who do not respond well to other classes; often as part of combination therapy.

g)Central Agonists:

- **Hypertension:** Effective in cases of resistant hypertension; not typically first-line due to side effects.
- **Attention Deficit Hyperactivity Disorder (ADHD):** Some central agonists are used for managing ADHD.
- **Vasodilators:**
- **Hypertension:** Primarily used in hypertensive emergencies or resistant hypertension.
- **Heart Failure:** Used in acute settings to reduce preload and afterload.

The choice of antihypertensive medication often depends on individual patient characteristics, including the presence of comorbidities, patient age, and potential side effects. Each class has specific indications, and often, a combination of these medications is used to achieve optimal blood pressure control. Regular monitoring and patient education are essential to ensure effective management and adherence to treatment.

x. Dosage and administration:

The management of hypertension often involves a combination of lifestyle modifications and pharmacotherapy. The choice of medication, dosage, and administration schedule is tailored to the individual patient based on several factors, including the severity of hypertension, presence of comorbid conditions, and tolerance of the medication. Below is a detailed overview of various classes of antihypertensive medications, including their typical dosages and administration guidelines.

a) Diuretics:

❖ **Thiazide Diuretics:**
(e.g., Hydrochlorothiazide)

- **Initial Dose:** 12.5 mg to 25 mg once daily.

- **Maintenance Dose:** 25 mg to 50 mg once daily, adjusted based on blood pressure response.
- **Administration:** Can be taken in the morning with or without food.

❖ **Loop Diuretics:**
(e.g., Furosemide)
- **Initial Dose:** 20 mg to 40 mg once or twice daily.
- **Maintenance Dose:** 40 mg to 80 mg, may go up to 600 mg/day in severe cases.
- **Administration:** Oral or intravenous (IV); IV doses should be given slowly to avoid rapid fluid shifts.

❖ **Potassium-Sparing Diuretics:**
(e.g., Spironolactone)
- **Initial Dose:** 25 mg once daily.
- **Maintenance Dose:** 25 mg to 50 mg daily.
- **Administration:** Oral, preferably taken in the morning to avoid nocturia.

b) **ACE Inhibitors:**
(e.g., Lisinopril, Enalapril)

➢ **Initial Dose:**
- **Lisinopril:** 10 mg once daily.
- **Enalapril:** 5 mg once or twice daily.

➢ **Maintenance Dose:**
- **Lisinopril:** 20 mg to 40 mg once daily.
- **Enalapril:** 10 mg to 40 mg daily.
- **Administration:** Oral, with or without food; doses may be adjusted based on renal function and potassium levels.

c) **Angiotensin II Receptor Blockers (ARBs):**
(e.g., Losartan, Valsartan)

➢ **Initial Dose:**
- **Losartan:** 50 mg once daily.
- **Valsartan:** 80 mg once daily.

➢ **Maintenance Dose:**
- **Losartan:** 50 mg to 100 mg daily.

- **Valsartan:** 160 mg to 320 mg daily.
- **Administration:** Oral, can be taken with or without food; renal function should be monitored.

d) Calcium Channel Blockers:

❖ **Dihydropyridines:**
(e.g., Amlodipine, Nifedipine)

➢ **Initial Dose:**
- **Amlodipine:** 5 mg once daily.
- **Nifedipine:** 30 mg extended release once daily.

➢ **Maintenance Dose:**
- **Amlodipine:** 5 mg to 10 mg daily.
- **Nifedipine:** Up to 90 mg daily (in divided doses).
- **Administration:** Oral, with or without food; extended-release formulations should not be crushed.

❖ **Non-Dihydropyridines**:
(e.g., Diltiazem, Verapamil)

➢ **Initial Dose:**
- **Diltiazem:** 120 mg to 240 mg daily (immediate release).
- **Verapamil:** 80 mg to 120 mg daily (immediate release).

➢ **Maintenance Dose:**
- **Diltiazem:** 240 mg to 360 mg daily (extended release).
- **Verapamil:** Up to 480 mg daily (in divided doses).
- **Administration:** Oral; some formulations are extended release and should not be crushed.

e) Beta Blockers:
(e.g., Metoprolol, Atenolol)

➢ **Initial Dose:**
- **Metoprolol:** 25 mg to 100 mg once daily (extended release).
- **Atenolol:** 25 mg to 50 mg once daily.

➢ **Maintenance Dose:**
- **Metoprolol:** 100 mg to 400 mg daily.
- **Atenolol:** Up to 100 mg to 200 mg daily.
- **Administration:** Oral, taken with or without food; extended-release formulations are preferable for once-daily dosing.

f) **Alpha Blockers:**
(e.g., Doxazosin, Prazosin)

➢ **Initial Dose:**

- **Doxazosin:** 1 mg once daily.
- **Prazosin:** 1 mg two to three times daily.

➢ **Maintenance Dose:**

- **Doxazosin:** 2 mg to 8 mg daily.
- **Prazosin:** Up to 20 mg daily in divided doses.
- **Administration:** Oral; may take at bedtime to minimize the risk of orthostatic hypotension.

g) **Direct Vasodilators:**
(e.g., Hydralazine, Minoxidil)

➢ **Initial Dose:**

- **Hydralazine:** 10 mg to 25 mg three times daily.
- **Minoxidil:** 5 mg once daily.

➢ **Maintenance Dose:**

- **Hydralazine:** 50 mg to 100 mg daily (in divided doses).
- **Minoxidil:** Up to 10 mg daily.
- **Administration:** Oral, preferably with food; minoxidil often requires a diuretic to prevent fluid retention.

➢ **General Considerations for Dosage and Administration:**

- **Initial vs. Maintenance Doses:** Start with lower doses, especially in elderly patients or those with renal impairment, and titrate based on blood pressure response and tolerance.
- **Combination Therapy:** Many patients will require a combination of antihypertensive medications to achieve optimal blood pressure control. Common combinations include diuretics with ACE inhibitors or ARBs, or a calcium channel blocker with a beta blocker.
- **Patient Adherence:** Consider using combination pills, when possible, to enhance adherence and simplify dosing regimens.

- **Lifestyle Modifications:** Encourage dietary changes, physical activity, weight management, and smoking cessation alongside medication therapy.

The management of hypertension requires careful consideration of drug selection, dosage, and administration. The specific medication and dosing regimen should be individualized based on the patient's unique clinical profile, including comorbidities and potential side effects. Regular follow-up is crucial to assess treatment effectiveness and adjust therapy as needed.

xi. Side effects and contraindications:

Antihypertensive medications are essential for managing high blood pressure and reducing the risk of cardiovascular events. However, like all medications, they can have side effects and contraindications that need to be considered when prescribing and managing treatment. Below is a detailed overview of the major classes of antihypertensive drugs, including their side effects and contraindications.

a) Diuretics:

- **Common Types:** Thiazide, Loop, and Potassium-Sparing Diuretics

❖ **Side Effects:**

➢ **Thiazide Diuretics** (e.g., Hydrochlorothiazide):

- **Electrolyte Imbalances:** Hypokalaemia (low potassium), hyponatremia (low sodium), hypercalcemia (high calcium).
- **Dehydration:** Can lead to hypotension and dizziness.
- **Gout:** May exacerbate gout attacks due to increased uric acid levels.

➢ **Loop Diuretics** (e.g., Furosemide)

- **Electrolyte Imbalances:** Hypokalaemia, hyponatremia, hypomagnesemia (low magnesium).
- **Ototoxicity:** Especially with high doses or rapid IV administration.
- **Dehydration:** Increased risk of hypotension.

➢ **Potassium-Sparing Diuretics:** (e.g., Spironolactone)

- **Hyperkalaemia:** Risk of high potassium levels, particularly in patients with renal impairment.
- **Gynaecomastia:** Particularly with spironolactone.

❖ **Contraindications:**

- **Thiazide Diuretics:** Anuria, hypersensitivity to sulphonamides.
- **Loop Diuretics:** Anuria, hypersensitivity to sulphonamides.
- **Potassium-Sparing Diuretics:** Hyperkalaemia, significant renal impairment, and Addison's disease.

b) ACE Inhibitors:

- **Common Types:** Lisinopril, Enalapril

➢ **Side Effects:**

- **Cough:** Persistent dry cough due to increased bradykinin levels.
- **Angioedema:** Swelling of the face, lips, or tongue; rare but potentially life-threatening.
- **Hyperkalaemia:** Increased potassium levels, particularly in renal impairment.
- **Hypotension:** Especially after the first dose, particularly in volume-depleted patients.

➢ **Contraindications:**

- **Pregnancy:** Can cause foetal harm.
- **History of Angioedema:** Related to previous ACE inhibitor use.
- **Bilateral Renal Artery Stenosis:** Risk of worsening kidney function.

c) Angiotensin II Receptor Blockers (ARBs)

- **Common Types:** Losartan, Valsartan

➢ **Side Effects:**

- **Hyperkalaemia:** Like ACE inhibitors, particularly in patients with renal impairment.
- **Hypotension:** Especially after the initial dose.

- **Dizziness or Light-headedness:** Due to lowered blood pressure.
- **Contraindications:**
- **Pregnancy:** Contraindicated due to foetal risk.
- **History of Angioedema:** Particularly with ACE inhibitors.
- **Bilateral Renal Artery Stenosis:** Risk of renal failure.

d) **Calcium Channel Blockers:**
- **Common Types:** Amlodipine, Diltiazem, Verapamil

➢ **Side Effects:**
- **Peripheral Oedema:** Particularly with dihydropyridines like amlodipine.
- **Bradycardia:** More common with non-dihydropyridines (diltiazem, verapamil).
- **Hypotension:** Especially with rapid dose titration.
- **Constipation:** Common with verapamil.

➢ **Contraindications:**
- **Severe Heart Failure:** Particularly with non-dihydropyridines due to negative inotropic effects.
- **Second or Third-Degree Heart Block:** Without a pacemaker.
- **Severe Aortic Stenosis:** Can worsen cardiac output.

e) **Beta Blockers:**
- **Common Types:** Metoprolol, Atenolol, Propranolol

➢ **Side Effects:**
- **Bradycardia:** Can lead to symptomatic hypotension.
- **Fatigue:** Due to decreased cardiac output.
- **Cold Extremities:** Due to reduced blood flow.
- **Bronchoconstriction:** Particularly with non-selective beta blockers (e.g., propranolol) in asthmatic patients.
- **Sexual Dysfunction:** Reduced libido or erectile dysfunction.

➢ **Contraindications:**
- **Severe Asthma or COPD:** Particularly with non-selective beta blockers.

- **Second or Third-Degree Heart Block:** Without a functioning pacemaker.
- **Severe Bradycardia:** May worsen heart rate.

f) **Alpha Blockers:**

- **Common Types:** Doxazosin, Prazosin

➢ **Side Effects:**

- **Orthostatic Hypotension:** Especially after the first dose.
- **Fatigue:** Due to vasodilation.
- **Headache:** Common due to vasodilatory effects.
- **Nasal Congestion:** As a result of vasodilation in nasal tissues.

➢ **Contraindications:**

- **Severe Heart Failure:** Risk of worsening symptoms.
- **History of Orthostatic Hypotension:** Increased risk of dizziness and falls.

g) **Direct Vasodilators:**

- **Common Types:** Hydralazine, Minoxidil

➢ **Side Effects:**

- **Reflex Tachycardia:** Compensatory increase in heart rate due to decreased blood pressure.
- **Fluid Retention:** May lead to oedema; often used with diuretics.
- **Headache:** Due to vasodilation.
- **Palpitations:** As a result of reflex sympathetic activation.

➢ **Contraindications:**

- **Aortic Dissection:** Risk of worsening the condition due to rapid blood pressure changes.
- **Severe Hypotension:** Not suitable for patients with low baseline blood pressure.

Antihypertensive medications are crucial for managing hypertension but come with a range of side effects and contraindications that must be carefully considered. Individualized treatment plans, regular monitoring, and patient education are essential to minimize risks and optimize therapeutic outcomes. Regular follow-up allows for the assessment of drug efficacy and tolerance, ensuring that therapy is adjusted as needed for the best patient care.

7.4 Combination Therapy:

Combination therapy for hypertension has emerged as a vital strategy in achieving optimal blood pressure control, particularly for patients whose hypertension is difficult to manage with monotherapy alone. By utilizing two or more antihypertensive agents from different drug classes, healthcare providers can enhance the effectiveness of treatment while reducing the risk of side effects associated with higher doses of a single medication. This approach not only targets multiple pathways involved in regulating blood pressure but also addresses the complex nature of hypertension, which often coexists with other cardiovascular risk factors. Common combinations may include pairing a diuretic with an ACE inhibitor or a calcium channel blocker with an ARB, each designed to improve therapeutic outcomes and promote better adherence. Through careful selection and individualization of combination therapy, healthcare providers can significantly improve management of hypertension, reduce the likelihood of complications, and enhance patients' overall quality of life.

i. Rationale for combination treatment:

The rationale for combination treatment of hypertension stems from the complexity of the disease and the multifactorial nature of its pathophysiology. Hypertension often involves various physiological mechanisms, including increased cardiac output, vascular resistance, and volume overload. Therefore, using a single medication may not effectively target all contributing factors, leading to inadequate blood pressure control.

a) Synergistic Effects:

One of the primary reasons for combination therapy is the potential for synergistic effects, where two or more medications can produce a greater antihypertensive effect than when each drug is used alone. For example, combining a diuretic, which reduces fluid volume and decreases cardiac output, with an ACE inhibitor or an ARB, which helps to relax blood vessels and lower systemic vascular resistance, can result in significant blood pressure reductions. This synergism allows for lower doses of each medication, which can reduce the risk of side effects while maintaining effective blood pressure control.

b) Targeting Different Mechanisms:

Combination therapy allows clinicians to target different underlying mechanisms of hypertension. For instance, a calcium channel blocker can reduce vascular resistance by relaxing arterial smooth muscle, while a beta-blocker can decrease heart rate and contractility. By addressing multiple pathways involved in hypertension, combination treatment can lead to more comprehensive management and improved overall outcomes for patients.

c) Improved Adherence:

Patients often struggle with adherence to medication regimens, particularly when prescribed multiple drugs. However, combination therapies can simplify treatment regimens by reducing the number of medications a patient needs to take. Fixed-dose combination pills, which include two or more antihypertensive agents in a single tablet, can enhance adherence by making it easier for patients to follow their prescribed regimen. Improved adherence is crucial for long-term blood pressure control and reducing the risk of cardiovascular events.

d) Lowering the Risk of Resistant Hypertension:

Combination therapy is particularly beneficial for patients with resistant hypertension—defined as blood pressure that remains uncontrolled despite the use of three or more antihypertensive medications, including a diuretic. By employing multiple agents with different mechanisms of action, clinicians can better address the complexities of resistant hypertension and improve patient outcomes.

e) Individualized Treatment:

Hypertension management often requires a tailored approach, considering patient-specific factors such as age, comorbidities, and individual responses to treatment. Combination therapy allows for greater customization; for example, a patient with both hypertension and heart failure may benefit from a regimen that includes an ACE inhibitor, a diuretic, and a beta-blocker. This individualized approach can enhance efficacy and minimize adverse effects.

f) Long-term Cardiovascular Protection:

Several studies have shown that combination therapy can lead to better long-term cardiovascular outcomes compared to monotherapy. By achieving more significant and sustained reductions in blood pressure, patients may experience lower rates of stroke, heart attack, and other cardiovascular events. This long-term protective effect underscores the importance of addressing hypertension aggressively through combination treatment when necessary.

ii. Common combinations and their benefits:

Combination therapy for hypertension is often necessary to achieve optimal blood pressure control, especially in patients who do not respond adequately to monotherapy. Several common combinations of antihypertensive medications are used, each with specific benefits based on their mechanisms of action, efficacy, and safety profiles. Here are some widely used combinations and their associated benefits:

a) ACE Inhibitors and Diuretics:

- **Common Combinations:** Lisinopril (ACE inhibitor) and Hydrochlorothiazide (thiazide diuretic)
- **Benefits:** This combination effectively targets both blood volume and vascular resistance. The diuretic reduces fluid overload, decreasing cardiac output, while the ACE inhibitor relaxes blood vessels by inhibiting angiotensin II formation, thereby lowering systemic vascular resistance. This dual action is particularly beneficial in patients with heart failure or those at risk of developing heart failure. Additionally, thiazide

diuretics can help counteract the potassium-sparing effects of some ACE inhibitors, enhancing electrolyte balance.

b) **Angiotensin II Receptor Blockers (ARBs) and Diuretics:**

- **Common Combinations:** Losartan (ARB) and Hydrochlorothiazide:
- **Benefits:** Like the ACE inhibitor and diuretic combination, ARBs like losartan block the action of angiotensin II, leading to vasodilation and reduced blood pressure. When paired with a diuretic, this combination can effectively manage hypertension, particularly in patients who may cxperience cough or angioedema with ACE inhibitors. The combination not only improves blood pressure control but also helps mitigate the risk of developing heart failure and renal complications in high-risk patients.

c) **Calcium Channel Blockers and ACE Inhibitors or ARBs:**

- **Common Combinations:** Amlodipine (calcium channel blocker) with Lisinopril or Losartan
- **Benefits:** Calcium channel blockers work by relaxing the smooth muscle in the arterial walls, reducing vascular resistance. When combined with ACE inhibitors or ARBs, which prevent angiotensin II-mediated vasoconstriction, this combination can lead to substantial reductions in blood pressure. This pairing is particularly effective in treating patients with isolated systolic hypertension, common in older adults, as it addresses both systolic and diastolic pressures effectively.

d) **Beta-Blockers and Diuretics:**

- **Common Combinations:** Metoprolol (beta-blocker) and Hydrochlorothiazide
- **Benefits:** Beta-blockers reduce heart rate and myocardial contractility, decreasing cardiac output. When combined with diuretics, this regimen can enhance blood pressure control, especially in patients with coexisting conditions such as coronary artery disease or heart failure. This combination is also effective in managing hypertensive emergencies, where immediate blood pressure reduction is necessary.

e) **Renin Inhibitors and Diuretics:**

- **Common Combinations:** Aliskiren (renin inhibitor) with Hydrochlorothiazide
- **Benefits:** Aliskiren works by inhibiting renin, the enzyme responsible to produce angiotensin I, leading to reduced levels of angiotensin II and subsequent vasodilation. When combined with a diuretic, this approach provides a potent antihypertensive effect. It is particularly useful in patients who have not achieved target blood pressure with other combinations and helps mitigate fluid retention.

f) **Alpha-Blockers and Diuretics:**

- **Common Combinations:** Doxazosin (alpha-blocker) with Hydrochlorothiazide
- **Benefits:** Alpha-blockers reduce vascular resistance by preventing norepinephrine from constricting blood vessels. Pairing them with diuretics can improve blood pressure control, particularly in patients with resistant hypertension. This combination can also benefit men with hypertension and benign prostatic hyperplasia (BPH), as alpha-blockers can help alleviate urinary symptoms.

g) **Fixed-Dose Combinations:**

- **Common Examples:** Lisinopril and Hydrochlorothiazide in a single pill
- **Benefits:** Fixed-dose combinations improve patient adherence by simplifying regimens, reducing pill burden, and ensuring that patients take medications consistently. These combinations often provide synergistic effects, leading to improved blood pressure control. Fixed-dose combinations are especially useful for patients with multiple comorbidities who may require multiple antihypertensive agents.

In summary, various combinations of antihypertensive medications, such as ACE inhibitors with diuretics, ARBs with diuretics, and calcium channel blockers with either ACE inhibitors or ARBs, offer unique benefits that address different pathophysiological aspects of hypertension. These combinations allow for more comprehensive management, optimizing blood pressure control while minimizing the risk of side effects and enhancing patient adherence to treatment regimens. By tailoring combinations to individual patient needs, healthcare providers can significantly improve outcomes and reduce the burden of hypertension-related complications.

iii. Considerations for patient adherence:

Patient adherence to hypertension management is critical for achieving optimal blood pressure control and preventing cardiovascular complications. Several considerations impact adherence, ranging from individual patient factors to the healthcare system's structure. Understanding and addressing these factors can enhance compliance and improve health outcomes.

a) Patient Education and Understanding:

Effective education about hypertension is fundamental. Patients must understand their condition, the importance of managing it, and how medications work. Providing clear information about the potential consequences of uncontrolled hypertension—such as heart disease, stroke, and kidney failure—can motivate patients to adhere to their treatment plans. Educational materials should be tailored to the patient's literacy level and cultural background to ensure comprehension. Engaging patients in discussions about their treatment options also fosters a sense of ownership and responsibility.

b) Complexity of Treatment Regimens:

Complex medication regimens can be a significant barrier to adherence. Patients may struggle to manage multiple medications, especially if they require different dosages or have varying schedules for administration. Simplifying treatment plans, such as using fixed-dose combinations that combine multiple medications into one pill, can significantly improve adherence. Additionally, healthcare providers should encourage the use of medication organizers or blister packs to help patients manage their doses more effectively.

c) Side Effects and Tolerability:

Adverse effects from antihypertensive medications can deter patients from adhering to their regimens. Common side effects, such as dizziness, fatigue, or sexual dysfunction, may lead patients to discontinue their medications without consulting their healthcare providers. It's crucial for healthcare professionals to discuss potential side effects upfront and offer reassurance that adjustments can be made if adverse effects occur. Regular follow-up appointments should include discussions about tolerability and any concerns the patient may have regarding their medications.

d) **Psychosocial Factors:**

Psychosocial factors, including mental health conditions such as depression or anxiety, can significantly impact adherence to treatment. Patients dealing with emotional distress may be less likely to prioritize their health and adhere to medication regimens. Screening for mental health issues and providing appropriate referrals or support can help address these barriers. Social support from family, friends, or support groups also plays a crucial role in motivating patients to adhere to their treatment plans.

e) **Health Literacy and Cognitive Function:**

A patient's health literacy—understanding health-related information—affects their ability to manage their condition effectively. Low health literacy can lead to misunderstandings about medication dosing, timing, or dietary restrictions. Assessing health literacy levels and providing information in accessible formats, using visuals or simplified language, can enhance understanding. Additionally, cognitive impairments, which can occur with aging or neurological conditions, may hinder a patient's ability to remember medication schedules or lifestyle changes. Tailoring communication and using reminders can assist these patients.

f) **Access to Healthcare and Medications:**

Access to healthcare resources and medications is a fundamental consideration for adherence. Patients may struggle with financial constraints, leading to difficulty affording medications or regular healthcare visits. Strategies to mitigate these barriers include discussing generic alternatives, patient assistance programs, and community resources that can provide support. Ensuring that patients have access to healthcare services, including regular follow-ups and lifestyle counselling, is also critical for sustained adherence.

g) **Regular Follow-Up and Monitoring:**

Frequent follow-ups and monitoring are essential to encourage adherence. Regular appointments provide opportunities to assess blood pressure control, address any medication-related concerns, and reinforce the importance of adherence. These visits can serve as motivational checkpoints, where healthcare providers celebrate progress and set new goals. Utilizing telehealth options can also enhance access and convenience for patients, making it easier to maintain regular contact with healthcare providers.

h) **Cultural Considerations:**

Cultural beliefs and practices can influence health behaviours and adherence to treatment. Understanding a patient's cultural background, preferences, and potential barriers can help tailor interventions that resonate more effectively. Engaging in culturally competent care—where providers respect and incorporate a patient's cultural values into their treatment plans—can enhance adherence and trust in the healthcare system.

In summary, improving patient adherence in hypertension management requires a comprehensive understanding of various factors, including education, treatment complexity, side effects, psychosocial influences, health literacy, access to care, and cultural considerations. By addressing these factors through personalized care, effective communication, and supportive interventions, healthcare providers can enhance adherence, leading to better blood pressure control and improved health outcomes for patients with hypertension.

7.5 Monitoring and Follow-Up:

Monitoring and follow-up are critical components in the effective management of hypertension, as they enable healthcare providers to assess treatment efficacy, ensure adherence, and make necessary adjustments to therapy. Regular blood pressure measurements, both in clinical settings and through home monitoring, are essential for tracking changes and evaluating the effectiveness of prescribed interventions. Follow-up visits allow for the identification of potential side effects, the evaluation of comorbid conditions, and the discussion of lifestyle modifications that can further support blood pressure control. Establishing a routine schedule for monitoring helps patients stay engaged in their treatment plan and reinforces the importance of ongoing management. Through diligent monitoring and follow-up, healthcare providers can significantly improve outcomes, minimize the risk of complications, and enhance patients' overall quality of life in their journey toward better cardiovascular health.

i. **Importance of regular blood pressure monitoring:**

Regular blood pressure monitoring is crucial in the management of hypertension, as it provides vital insights into the effectiveness of treatment strategies and the overall cardiovascular health of the patient. Frequent monitoring allows for timely adjustments in antihypertensive medications and lifestyle interventions, helping to maintain blood pressure within target ranges and reduce the risk of complications such as heart disease, stroke, and kidney damage. Self-monitoring at home empowers patients to take an active role in their health management, fostering greater adherence to prescribed treatment plans and lifestyle changes. It also enables individuals to recognize patterns in their blood pressure readings, which can help identify triggers or lifestyle factors that may contribute to fluctuations, such as stress, dietary choices, or physical inactivity.

Moreover, regular monitoring can facilitate early detection of treatment-resistant hypertension, prompting further evaluation for potential underlying causes. This proactive approach encourages better communication between patients and healthcare providers, ensuring that any concerns are addressed promptly and effectively. Additionally, the integration of technology, such as digital blood pressure monitors and mobile health apps, can enhance the ease of tracking readings and sharing them with healthcare professionals, further improving management strategies. Overall, consistent blood pressure monitoring is a cornerstone of effective hypertension management, contributing to better health outcomes and quality of life for patients.

ii. **Follow-up schedules and what to assess:**

Follow-up schedules for patients with hypertension are critical for monitoring blood pressure control, assessing treatment effectiveness, and making necessary adjustments to management strategies. The frequency of follow-up visits typically depends on the severity of hypertension, treatment stability, and the presence of comorbid conditions. For patients with newly diagnosed hypertension or those whose blood pressure is not well controlled, follow-up appointments are often recommended every 1 to 3 months until the blood pressure is stable and within target ranges. Once the blood pressure is well controlled, follow-up visits can be extended to every 6 to 12 months, although patients on complex regimens or with significant health concerns may still require more frequent monitoring.

During follow-up appointments, several key assessments should be made. First and foremost, blood pressure readings should be taken using proper technique to ensure accuracy, ideally measuring both arms and assessing for any discrepancies. Evaluating medication adherence is essential, and healthcare providers should inquire about any challenges the patient may face in following their prescribed regimen, including side effects or financial barriers. Additionally, assessing lifestyle factors—such as dietary habits, physical activity levels, alcohol consumption, and tobacco use—is important to determine if further support or education is needed to promote adherence to lifestyle modifications. Laboratory assessments are also integral during follow-up visits. Routine checks may include monitoring electrolytes, kidney function (such as serum creatinine), and fasting glucose, especially in patients taking certain antihypertensive medications like diuretics or those with diabetes or kidney disease. Regular assessment of lipid profiles is recommended to evaluate cardiovascular risk and guide treatment decisions.

Moreover, it's important to screen for signs of target organ damage, such as heart failure, chronic kidney disease, or retinopathy, through physical examinations and, if necessary, imaging studies or referrals to specialists. Patients should also be educated on recognizing symptoms that may indicate worsening hypertension or complications, such as severe headaches, vision changes, or chest pain. In summary, structured follow-up schedules and comprehensive assessments are crucial components of hypertension management, ensuring that patients receive optimal care and support in their journey towards achieving and maintaining healthy blood pressure levels.

iii. **Adjustments to treatment based on response:**

Adjusting treatment based on a patient's response to hypertension management is essential for achieving optimal blood pressure control and minimizing the risk of cardiovascular complications. This process involves evaluating the effectiveness of current medications, lifestyle modifications, and overall patient adherence to the prescribed regimen.

a) **Assessment of Blood Pressure Control:**

During follow-up visits, healthcare providers should carefully assess the patient's blood pressure readings. If blood pressure remains above target levels—defined as typically less than 130/80 mmHg for most adults with hypertension—providers need to determine whether this lack of control is due to inadequate medication, poor adherence, or other factors such as lifestyle habits or secondary hypertension causes.

b) **Medication Adjustments**

When a patient's blood pressure is not adequately controlled, medication adjustments may be necessary. This could involve increasing the dosage of current antihypertensive medications or adding a new agent from a different class to enhance blood pressure-lowering effects. Common classes of antihypertensive medications include diuretics, ACE inhibitors, angiotensin II receptor blockers (ARBs), calcium channel blockers, and beta-blockers. For instance, if a patient is on a single medication and their blood pressure remains elevated, transitioning to a combination therapy regimen may be effective, as certain combinations have a synergistic effect.

c) **Evaluation of Side Effects:**

When adjusting medications, it is also crucial to consider any side effects the patient may experience. If a particular medication is causing intolerable side effects—such as cough from an ACE inhibitor or oedema from a calcium channel blocker—switching to an alternative medication within the same class or to a different class altogether may improve adherence and patient satisfaction.

d) Lifestyle Modifications:

In conjunction with medication adjustments, providers should reinforce the importance of lifestyle modifications. If a patient's blood pressure is not responding as expected, discussions should focus on dietary changes (like reducing sodium intake and adopting the DASH diet), increasing physical activity, weight management, and smoking cessation. Assessing and addressing barriers to these changes is essential; for example, if a patient struggles with dietary changes due to cultural preferences, tailoring recommendations to be more culturally sensitive can enhance adherence.

e) Monitoring for Secondary Causes:

In cases of persistent hypertension despite optimal treatment, further evaluation for secondary causes may be warranted. Conditions such as renal artery stenosis, primary hyperaldosteronism, or sleep apnoea can contribute to difficult-to-control hypertension. Referring the patient for appropriate diagnostic testing or specialist consultation can help identify these underlying issues and guide targeted interventions.

f) Patient Education and Involvement:

Engaging patients in their treatment plan is critical for long-term success. Providing education about the importance of medication adherence, recognizing symptoms of worsening hypertension, and understanding how lifestyle factors influence blood pressure can empower patients. Involving them in decision-making regarding their treatment adjustments fosters a sense of ownership and responsibility for their health.

7.6 Special Considerations:

When managing hypertension, it is essential to recognize special considerations that may influence treatment decisions and outcomes for specific populations. Factors such as age, sex, ethnicity, and the presence of comorbidities can significantly impact both the pathophysiology of hypertension and the effectiveness of therapeutic interventions. For instance, elderly patients may require different treatment approaches due to age-related physiological changes and the potential for polypharmacy. Similarly, individuals with conditions like diabetes, chronic kidney disease, or heart failure necessitate tailored management strategies to address their unique health profiles. Additionally, pregnant women present a distinct challenge, as hypertension can complicate pregnancy and pose risks to both mother and child. By acknowledging these special considerations, healthcare providers can deliver more personalized and effective care, ultimately improving health outcomes for all patients dealing with hypertension.

i. **Management in specific populations:**

The management of hypertension requires tailored approaches for specific populations, including older adults, racial and ethnic minorities, and individuals with comorbid conditions. For older adults, who often have multiple health issues and varying physiological responses to medications, it's essential to start treatment at lower doses and gradually titrate based on blood pressure responses and tolerance to minimize adverse effects. In racial and ethnic minority groups, such as African Americans, there is often a higher prevalence of hypertension and more severe disease, necessitating the use of specific medication classes, like calcium channel blockers or diuretics, that have proven more effective in these populations.

For individuals with comorbid conditions, such as diabetes or chronic kidney disease, managing hypertension involves a comprehensive approach that addresses both blood pressure and the underlying conditions. This includes selecting antihypertensive medications that are safe and effective in the context of other treatments, and implementing lifestyle modifications that consider dietary restrictions and physical limitations. Additionally, culturally sensitive education and support can enhance adherence to treatment plans and lifestyle changes, recognizing the unique barriers that different populations may face. Overall, a personalized and holistic approach is vital to effectively manage hypertension across diverse populations, improving health outcomes and quality of life.

ii. Addressing treatment-resistant hypertension:

Addressing treatment-resistant hypertension is a complex challenge that requires a comprehensive, systematic approach. Defined as hypertension that remains above target levels despite the use of three or more antihypertensive medications, including a diuretic, this condition necessitates careful evaluation to identify potential underlying causes. A thorough assessment should include reviewing the patient's medication regimen for adherence, possible drug interactions, and the use of medications that may elevate blood pressure, such as nonsteroidal anti-inflammatory drugs (NSAIDs) or certain antidepressants.

Additionally, lifestyle factors, including diet, physical activity, weight, alcohol consumption, and tobacco use, must be scrutinized, as these can significantly impact blood pressure control. Diagnostic evaluations should also consider secondary causes of hypertension, such as renal artery stenosis, hyperaldosteronism, or sleep apnoea, which may require targeted interventions. Once these factors are addressed, treatment strategies may involve escalating medication regimens, such as adding a fourth antihypertensive agent from a different class, utilizing medications like spironolactone or other mineralocorticoid receptor antagonists, or considering newer agents like directly acting vasodilators. Implementing a patient-centred approach that emphasizes shared decision-making is crucial, as it fosters adherence and empowers patients to engage in their treatment plan actively. Moreover, multidisciplinary care involving specialists, such as endocrinologists or nephrologists, may be necessary for managing complex cases. Regular follow-up visits to monitor blood pressure and adjust treatment as needed are essential for optimizing outcomes in patients with treatment-resistant hypertension.

iii. Role of specialists in management:

The role of specialists in the management of hypertension is vital, particularly for patients with complex cases, treatment-resistant hypertension, or those with comorbid conditions. Cardiologists, nephrologists, and endocrinologists often play critical roles in the comprehensive assessment and management of hypertension. For instance, cardiologists may focus on patients with hypertension related to heart disease or those at high risk of cardiovascular events, employing advanced diagnostic tools such as echocardiography to evaluate cardiac function and guide treatment.

Nephrologists are essential when hypertension is linked to kidney disease, helping to address issues such as renal artery stenosis or secondary hypertension due to glomerular diseases. Endocrinologists are crucial in cases where hormonal imbalances, such as primary hyperaldosteronism or pheochromocytoma, contribute to hypertension; they can provide specialized treatments tailored to these conditions. Specialists also play a significant role in the management of lifestyle factors that impact blood pressure, offering resources for dietary modifications, physical activity plans, and behavioural therapies.

Furthermore, they can facilitate access to the latest antihypertensive medications and interventions, including newer agents and devices like renal denervation, which may not be routinely available in primary care settings. Their expertise allows for a more nuanced understanding of the interactions between hypertension and other health issues, leading to more effective and individualized treatment plans. Through collaboration with primary care providers, specialists help ensure a comprehensive approach to managing hypertension, ultimately improving patient outcomes and quality of life. Regular consultations with specialists can also support ongoing education and motivation for patients, reinforcing the importance of adherence to treatment and lifestyle changes.

7.7 Patient Education and Engagement:

Patient education and engagement are fundamental components in the effective management of hypertension, empowering individuals to take an active role in their health and treatment decisions. Understanding hypertension—its causes, risks, and the importance of maintaining healthy blood pressure levels—enables patients to make informed choices about their lifestyle and adhere to prescribed treatment plans. Educational initiatives can include guidance on dietary modifications, the importance of regular physical activity, and techniques for stress reduction, all of which are crucial for blood pressure control. Engaging patients through self-monitoring of blood pressure and fostering open communication with healthcare providers can enhance adherence to medications and lifestyle changes. By prioritizing patient education and involvement, healthcare professionals can significantly improve health outcomes, reduce the burden of hypertension-related complications, and enhance overall quality of life for those affected by this common condition.

i. **Importance of educating patients about their condition:** Educating patients about their condition is vital in the management of hypertension, as it empowers individuals to take an active role in their health and treatment. Understanding hypertension—its causes, consequences, and the importance of blood pressure control—can motivate patients to adhere to prescribed lifestyle changes and medications. When patients are informed about the risks associated with uncontrolled hypertension, such as heart disease, stroke, and kidney damage, they are more likely to appreciate the need for regular monitoring and proactive management. Education also helps patients recognize the significance of lifestyle modifications, including dietary changes, increased physical activity, and stress management techniques, fostering a sense of ownership over their health decisions.

Moreover, when patients understand how to interpret their blood pressure readings and the importance of maintaining a target range, they can better communicate with healthcare providers and contribute to their care plans. This knowledge can reduce feelings of anxiety related to their condition and enhance compliance with follow-up appointments and treatment regimens.

Additionally, education about potential side effects of medications and the importance of adherence can mitigate concerns that may lead to non-compliance. By involving patients in their care through education, healthcare providers can improve health outcomes, enhance quality of life, and potentially reduce healthcare costs associated with complications of uncontrolled hypertension. Ultimately, patient education is a cornerstone of effective hypertension management, fostering a collaborative relationship between patients and providers that promotes sustained engagement in health-promoting behaviours.

ii. **Strategies to improve adherence to lifestyle and medication regimens:** Improving adherence to lifestyle and medication regimens in hypertension is essential for effective management and long-term health outcomes. A multifaceted approach can significantly enhance adherence. First, patient education is crucial; healthcare providers should take the time to explain the importance of lifestyle changes and medication adherence clearly and relatable, helping patients understand how these changes directly impact their health. Setting realistic and achievable goals, both for lifestyle modifications—such as dietary changes, exercise, and weight management—and for medication adherence, can empower patients to take control of their health. Utilizing technology, such as mobile apps that track medication schedules, monitor blood pressure, and provide reminders for both medications and lifestyle activities, can foster engagement and accountability.

Additionally, incorporating behavioural strategies, such as motivational interviewing, can help identify and address barriers to adherence, including misconceptions about medications or the impact of lifestyle changes. Building a strong support system is also vital; involving family members or support groups can create a network of encouragement and accountability. Healthcare providers should regularly check in with patients, reinforcing progress and adjusting the regimen as needed, which helps to sustain motivation and commitment. Financial considerations, such as offering resources for affordable medications or discussing generic options, can alleviate concerns that may impede adherence. Lastly, creating a tailored, patient-centred plan that considers individual preferences, challenges, and lifestyle factors enhances the likelihood of adherence to both lifestyle and medication regimens, ultimately leading to better blood pressure control and improved overall health.

iii. Encouraging self-monitoring and awareness of symptoms:

Encouraging self-monitoring and awareness of symptoms in hypertension is vital for empowering patients to take an active role in their health management. Self-monitoring involves regularly checking blood pressure at home, which can provide immediate feedback and help patients understand how their lifestyle choices, medications, and stress levels affect their blood pressure. Healthcare providers should educate patients on how to use blood pressure monitors correctly, emphasizing the importance of taking readings at consistent times, in a calm environment, and under similar conditions to ensure accuracy. Keeping a detailed log of readings, along with notes on lifestyle factors such as diet, exercise, and stress, can help patients identify patterns and triggers related to their hypertension.

Additionally, raising awareness of hypertension symptoms—such as headaches, dizziness, shortness of breath, or chest pain—can prompt timely medical attention and prevent complications. Patients should be encouraged to recognize these symptoms and understand that while hypertension is often asymptomatic, changes in health can signal the need for adjustments in treatment or lifestyle. Utilizing technology, such as apps that allow tracking of both blood pressure readings and symptoms, can enhance engagement and facilitate communication with healthcare providers. By fostering a sense of ownership over their health through self-monitoring, patients can become more motivated to adhere to treatment plans, make necessary lifestyle changes, and seek help when needed, ultimately leading to better management of hypertension and improved overall health outcomes.

7.8 Future directions in hypertension management and research:

Future directions in hypertension management and research are poised to focus on several key areas aimed at improving patient outcomes and understanding the complexities of this condition. One significant advancement is the move toward personalized medicine, where genomic and biotechnology advancements enable the development of targeted therapies tailored to individual patient profiles, optimizing treatment efficacy and minimizing side effects.

Additionally, the increasing adoption of telehealth and remote monitoring technologies is transforming hypertension management; wearable devices that track blood pressure, heart rate, and physical activity provide real-time data, allowing healthcare providers to adjust treatment plans promptly and enhance patient engagement. The integration of behavioural health interventions, such as stress management and cognitive-behavioural therapy, is also gaining attention, recognizing the crucial role of mental health in managing hypertension. Furthermore, ongoing research is needed to refine dietary guidelines and lifestyle interventions specific to hypertension, exploring the effects of dietary patterns like the Mediterranean or plant-based diets. Discovering new pharmacological agents that target various pathways involved in blood pressure regulation remains essential, with innovations in drug formulation potentially enhancing adherence and improving outcomes.

Additionally, understanding the heterogeneity of hypertension—such as differentiating between resistant hypertension and secondary forms—will allow for more tailored treatment strategies based on underlying causes. Finally, global health initiatives aimed at hypertension prevention and management are critical, especially in low- and middle-income countries where the burden is rising; research that examines cultural, economic, and healthcare system barriers will inform effective public health strategies. By focusing on these directions, the future of hypertension management is set to become more patient-centred, data-driven, and comprehensive, ultimately leading to improved health outcomes and quality of life for those affected by hypertension.

8. Hypertension and Related Conditions

Hypertension is a pervasive health issue that affects millions worldwide and serves as a major risk factor for various cardiovascular and systemic conditions. Characterized by persistent elevation of blood pressure, hypertension not only places significant strain on the heart and blood vessels but also increases the likelihood of developing serious health complications. These related conditions include heart disease, stroke, chronic kidney disease, and metabolic syndrome, all of which can exacerbate the challenges of managing hypertension and contribute to a cycle of declining health. Understanding the intricate relationships between hypertension and these associated conditions is crucial for effective prevention, diagnosis, and management, ultimately aiming to improve patient outcomes and quality of life. Hypertension is a common yet often overlooked health issue that can have far-reaching consequences on overall well-being. Characterized by consistently elevated blood pressure levels, it places added strain on the heart and blood vessels, increasing the likelihood of serious conditions such as coronary artery disease, heart failure, and stroke. The silent nature of hypertension means many individuals remain unaware of their condition until it leads to more severe health problems. Recognizing the interplay between hypertension and its related complications is essential for prevention and effective management, highlighting the importance of regular monitoring, lifestyle changes, and timely medical intervention.

8.1 Cardiovascular Diseases:

Hypertension, often referred to as high blood pressure, is a significant risk factor for various cardiovascular diseases, impacting millions globally. Chronic elevation of blood pressure exerts excessive strain on the heart and blood vessels, leading to structural and functional changes that predispose individuals to conditions such as coronary artery disease, heart failure, and stroke. The relationship between hypertension and cardiovascular health is multifaceted, involving mechanisms such as endothelial dysfunction, atherosclerosis, and increased workload on the heart. Understanding this connection is crucial for prevention and management strategies aimed at reducing cardiovascular morbidity and mortality associated with hypertension. Hypertension plays a critical role in the development of coronary artery disease (CAD) and heart failure through several interconnected mechanisms:

i. **Impact on Blood Vessels:**

Hypertension causes increased pressure within the blood vessels, leading to their thickening and narrowing over time. This can result in reduced blood flow and oxygen delivery to vital organs, heightening the risk of cardiovascular events.

- **Endothelial Damage:** High blood pressure causes damage to the endothelium, the inner lining of blood vessels. This damage promotes inflammation and the formation of plaques, leading to atherosclerosis, which narrows and hardens the arteries.
- **Increased Arterial Stiffness:** Chronic hypertension leads to increased stiffness of the arterial walls, reducing their ability to accommodate blood flow and increasing workload on the heart.

ii. **Increased Cardiac Workload:**

Increased cardiac workload due to hypertension occurs because the heart must pump against elevated blood pressure, leading to hypertrophy of the heart muscle. Over time, this strain can result in decreased cardiac efficiency and increased risk of heart failure and other cardiovascular complications.

- **Left Ventricular Hypertrophy (LVH):** The heart must pump harder to overcome elevated pressure in the arteries, leading to thickening of the left ventricular wall. LVH increases the risk of heart failure as it impairs the heart's ability to relax and fill properly.
- **Increased Oxygen Demand:** As the heart works harder, its oxygen demand rises. If the coronary arteries are narrowed due to atherosclerosis, the heart may not receive adequate oxygen, leading to ischemia and angina.

iii. **Development of Coronary Artery Disease (CAD):**

Hypertension contributes to the development of coronary artery disease by causing damage to the arterial walls, leading to atherosclerosis—a buildup of plaque that narrows and hardens the arteries. This reduced blood flow can result in chest pain, heart attacks, and other serious cardiovascular events.

- **Plaque Formation:** The processes initiated by hypertension, such as endothelial dysfunction and inflammation, contribute to the accumulation of cholesterol and fatty deposits in the arterial walls, forming plaques that can obstruct blood flow.
- **Acute Events:** Ruptured plaques can lead to blood clots, which may cause heart attacks by blocking blood flow to the heart muscle.

iv. Progression to Heart Failure:

Chronic hypertension can lead to heart failure by causing the heart muscle to thicken and stiffen, which reduces its ability to pump blood effectively. Over time, this increased workload can result in weakened heart function, ultimately leading to heart failure.

- **Systolic and Diastolic Dysfunction:** Prolonged hypertension can lead to both systolic (the heart's ability to contract) and diastolic (the heart's ability to relax) dysfunction. This reduces the heart's efficiency in pumping blood, eventually leading to heart failure.
- **Fluid Overload:** Heart failure can cause fluid retention, leading to symptoms such as shortness of breath and swelling, exacerbating the patient's condition.

In summary, hypertension significantly contributes to the development and progression of coronary artery disease and heart failure through mechanisms that involve vascular damage, increased cardiac workload, and impaired blood flow. Effective management of blood pressure is crucial in reducing the risk of these serious cardiovascular conditions and improving overall heart health.

8.2 Chronic Kidney Disease (CKD):

Chronic kidney disease (CKD) is a progressive condition characterized by the gradual loss of kidney function, and hypertension is one of its leading causes. Elevated blood pressure not only damages the kidneys' delicate filtering units but also disrupts the intricate regulatory mechanisms that maintain fluid and electrolyte balance. Over time, the sustained pressure can lead to glomerulosclerosis and reduced renal perfusion, further exacerbating kidney dysfunction. The bidirectional relationship between hypertension and CKD is critical, as each condition can accelerate the progression of the other, highlighting the importance of early detection and effective management. Understanding the impact of hypertension on kidney health is essential for preventing CKD and improving patient outcomes. The relationship between hypertension and chronic kidney disease (CKD) is bidirectional, meaning that each condition can influence the development and progression of the other. Here's a detailed explanation of this complex interplay:

i. **Hypertension Leading to Chronic Kidney Disease:**

Hypertension significantly contributes to the development of chronic kidney disease (CKD) by exerting excessive pressure on the kidney's blood vessels, which can lead to structural and functional impairment. As the kidneys struggle to manage this ongoing strain, their ability to filter waste diminishes, ultimately increasing the risk of kidney failure and necessitating dialysis or transplantation. Hypertension can cause chronic kidney disease (CKD) by damaging the blood vessels in the kidneys, impairing their ability to filter waste and regulate fluids. Over time, sustained high blood pressure can lead to kidney scarring and reduced function, ultimately resulting in CKD and potentially requiring dialysis or transplantation.

- **Increased Pressure on Nephrons:** Elevated blood pressure puts significant stress on the nephrons, the functional units of the kidneys. This can lead to damage over time, impairing kidney function.
- **Glomerulosclerosis:** Chronic hypertension can cause changes in the glomeruli (the filtering units in the kidneys), leading to glomerulosclerosis, where the glomeruli become scarred and less effective at filtering blood.
- **Reduced Renal Perfusion:** High blood pressure can also affect blood flow to the kidneys, leading to ischemia (lack of blood flow), further compromising renal function.

- **Progressive Kidney Damage:** As kidney function declines, waste products build up in the blood, leading to a cycle of worsening kidney health and increasing blood pressure.

ii. **Chronic Kidney Disease Leading to Hypertension:**

Chronic kidney disease (CKD) can lead to hypertension due to the kidneys' impaired ability to regulate fluid and electrolyte balance, resulting in increased blood volume. Additionally, the release of hormones that constrict blood vessels can further elevate blood pressure, creating a vicious cycle that exacerbates both conditions. Managing CKD is crucial to controlling hypertension and preventing further kidney damage.

- **Fluid Retention:** As kidney function declines, the kidneys become less effective at excreting excess sodium and fluid, leading to increased blood volume and elevated blood pressure.
- **Activation of the Renin-Angiotensin-Aldosterone System (RAAS):** CKD often leads to dysregulation of the RAAS, which can increase blood pressure by promoting vasoconstriction and sodium retention.
- **Endothelial Dysfunction:** CKD is associated with changes in the vascular system, including endothelial dysfunction, which can further exacerbate hypertension.
- **Secondary Hyperparathyroidism:** Impaired kidney function can lead to imbalances in calcium and phosphorus levels, triggering hyperparathyroidism, which can contribute to vascular changes and increased blood pressure.

iii. **Consequences of the Bidirectional Relationship:**

The bidirectional relationship between chronic kidney disease (CKD) and hypertension leads to a worsening of both conditions; uncontrolled hypertension can accelerate the progression of CKD, while CKD can make blood pressure more difficult to manage. This interplay increases the risk of cardiovascular complications, organ damage, and a decline in overall health, highlighting the need for integrated management strategies. Addressing one condition effectively is essential to improving outcomes for the other.

- **Worsening Health Outcomes:** The interplay between hypertension and CKD can accelerate the progression of both conditions, leading to more severe cardiovascular risks and complications.
- **Increased Risk of Cardiovascular Events:** Both hypertension and CKD are major risk factors for cardiovascular diseases, making management of both critical in reducing overall morbidity and mortality.

iv. Management Implications:

Managing chronic kidney disease (CKD) resulting from hypertension requires a comprehensive approach that includes strict blood pressure control through lifestyle modifications and antihypertensive medications. Regular monitoring of kidney function and electrolyte levels is essential to prevent further deterioration. Additionally, dietary changes, such as reducing sodium and protein intake, can help mitigate the impact of hypertension on kidney health and improve overall outcomes.

- **Integrated Treatment Approaches:** Effective management of hypertension in patients with CKD is essential. This often includes lifestyle modifications, dietary changes, and the use of antihypertensive medications that also protect kidney function (such as ACE inhibitors and ARBs).
- **Regular Monitoring:** Close monitoring of blood pressure and kidney function is crucial to prevent the deterioration of either condition.

In summary, the bidirectional relationship between hypertension and chronic kidney disease creates a vicious cycle that can significantly impact patient health. Understanding this interplay is vital for developing comprehensive management strategies aimed at preventing progression and improving outcomes for individuals affected by both conditions.

8.3 Diabetes Mellitus:

Hypertension is a prevalent condition that significantly contributes to the development and progression of diabetes mellitus, particularly type 2 diabetes. The relationship between these two disorders is complex and multifaceted, as high blood pressure can induce insulin resistance and impair glucose metabolism, creating a cycle that exacerbates both conditions. Chronic hypertension leads to vascular damage, which can affect insulin signalling pathways and increase the risk of metabolic dysfunction. Conversely, diabetes itself can further elevate blood pressure through mechanisms such as fluid retention and sympathetic nervous system activation. Recognizing the link between hypertension and diabetes is crucial for effective prevention, early intervention, and comprehensive management strategies aimed at reducing the burden of these interconnected health issues. Hypertension is frequently associated with diabetes, particularly type 2 diabetes, due to several interrelated mechanisms and risk factors. Here's a detailed explanation of their association:

i. **Shared Risk Factors:**

Shared risk factors for diabetes mellitus include obesity, physical inactivity, and poor dietary habits, which contribute to insulin resistance and glucose dysregulation. Additionally, hypertension and dyslipidaemia are commonly associated with diabetes, increasing the risk of cardiovascular complications. Addressing these shared risk factors through lifestyle modifications can significantly reduce the incidence of both diabetes and its related health issues.

- **Obesity:** Both hypertension and diabetes are strongly linked to obesity. Excess body fat, especially visceral fat, increases insulin resistance and can raise blood pressure.
- **Physical Inactivity:** Sedentary lifestyles contribute to weight gain and metabolic issues, raising the risk for both conditions.
- **Poor Diet:** Diets high in sodium, saturated fats, and sugars can lead to obesity, hypertension, and impaired glucose metabolism.
- **Genetic Predisposition:** Family history of hypertension or diabetes can elevate individual risk.
- **Dyslipidaemia:** Abnormal lipid levels, such as high triglycerides and low HDL cholesterol are common in both conditions.

ii. **Insulin Resistance:**

Insulin resistance in diabetes mellitus occurs when the body's cells become less responsive to insulin, leading to elevated blood glucose levels. This condition is often associated with type 2 diabetes and can result from factors like obesity, inactivity, and genetic predisposition. Managing insulin resistance is crucial for preventing complications and improving metabolic health through lifestyle changes and medications. Hypertension can contribute to insulin resistance in diabetes mellitus by promoting inflammatory processes and vascular dysfunction, which interfere with insulin signalling. Elevated blood pressure can also increase stress on the pancreas, impairing its ability to produce sufficient insulin. This relationship creates a cycle where hypertension exacerbates insulin resistance, making blood sugar control more challenging.

- **Mechanism of Hypertension:** Insulin resistance, a hallmark of type 2 diabetes, can lead to increased sympathetic nervous system activity and renal sodium retention, both of which elevate blood pressure.
- **Endothelial Dysfunction:** Insulin resistance also contributes to endothelial dysfunction, reducing the ability of blood vessels to dilate and increasing vascular resistance, which can lead to hypertension.

iii. Metabolic Syndrome:

Hypertension is a key component of metabolic syndrome, which is characterized by a cluster of conditions including obesity, dyslipidaemia, and insulin resistance. This syndrome increases the risk of cardiovascular disease and diabetes, as the combination of elevated blood pressure and metabolic abnormalities can lead to significant vascular damage. Effective management of hypertension is crucial for preventing or mitigating the effects of metabolic syndrome.

- **Cluster of Conditions:** Metabolic syndrome, characterized by insulin resistance, obesity, dyslipidaemia, and hypertension, links these two conditions. Individuals with metabolic syndrome have a significantly higher risk of developing both diabetes and hypertension.

iv. Renin-Angiotensin-Aldosterone System (RAAS):

The renin-angiotensin-aldosterone system (RAAS) plays a critical role in hypertension by regulating blood pressure and fluid balance. When blood pressure drops, renin is released from the kidneys, leading to the production of angiotensin II, which constricts blood vessels and stimulates aldosterone release, causing sodium and water retention. This cascade ultimately increases blood volume and pressure, contributing to the development and maintenance of hypertension.

- **Overactivity in Diabetes:** In diabetes, the RAAS can become overactive, leading to increased blood pressure through vasoconstriction and sodium retention, creating a cycle that exacerbates both conditions.

v. Chronic Inflammation:

Chronic inflammation plays a significant role in the interplay between hypertension and diabetes mellitus, exacerbating insulin resistance and metabolic dysfunction. Elevated blood pressure can trigger inflammatory pathways that contribute to vascular damage and the progression of diabetes-related complications. Chronic inflammation is a significant contributor to hypertension, as elevated blood pressure can lead to endothelial dysfunction and promote the release of pro-inflammatory cytokines. This ongoing inflammatory response damages blood vessels and heart tissue, further exacerbating hypertension and increasing the risk of cardiovascular diseases. Targeting inflammation may offer new avenues for managing hypertension and its associated complications.

- **Inflammatory Markers:** Both hypertension and diabetes are associated with chronic low-grade inflammation, which can damage blood vessels and contribute to insulin resistance and elevated blood pressure.

vi. Complications and End-Organ Damage:

Complications from insulin resistance and diabetes mellitus can lead to significant end-organ damage, affecting vital systems such as the cardiovascular, renal, and nervous systems. Chronic high blood sugar levels can result in conditions like cardiovascular disease, diabetic nephropathy, and neuropathy, ultimately compromising overall health and quality of life. Hypertension can lead to severe complications and end-organ damage, affecting vital organs such as the heart, kidneys, and brain. Chronic high blood pressure increases the risk of heart disease, stroke, and chronic kidney disease, as it causes damage to blood vessels and impairs organ function. Early detection and management of hypertension are crucial to preventing these serious health outcomes.

- **Cardiovascular Risk:** The combination of hypertension and diabetes significantly increases the risk of cardiovascular diseases, kidney disease, and other complications. Each condition can accelerate the progression of the other, leading to worse health outcomes.

In summary, hypertension and diabetes are often interconnected through shared risk factors, metabolic changes, and underlying mechanisms such as insulin resistance and inflammation. Addressing both conditions is crucial for improving overall health and reducing the risk of serious complications. Effective management strategies, including lifestyle modifications and appropriate medications, can help mitigate the impact of this association.

8.4 Metabolic Syndrome:

Metabolic syndrome is a cluster of interrelated metabolic risk factors that significantly increase the likelihood of developing cardiovascular disease and type 2 diabetes, and hypertension is a central component of this syndrome. Characterized by a combination of abdominal obesity, insulin resistance, dyslipidaemia, and elevated blood pressure, metabolic syndrome reflects the complex interplay between lifestyle, genetics, and environmental factors. Chronic hypertension not only contributes to the development of insulin resistance and other metabolic abnormalities but also exacerbates the risks associated with the other components of the syndrome.

Understanding the role of hypertension in metabolic syndrome is essential for implementing effective prevention and treatment strategies to mitigate the associated health risks and improve overall health outcomes. Metabolic syndrome is a cluster of conditions that increase the risk of heart disease, stroke, and type 2 diabetes. It is characterized by a combination of metabolic abnormalities that indicate an increased risk for cardiovascular issues and insulin resistance.

i. Components of Metabolic Syndrome:

Metabolic syndrome is a cluster of interrelated health conditions that significantly increases the risk of cardiovascular disease and type 2 diabetes, and hypertension is a key component of this syndrome. It encompasses a combination of factors, including abdominal obesity, insulin resistance, dyslipidaemia (elevated triglycerides and low HDL cholesterol), and elevated blood pressure. The interplay between these components creates a harmful cycle that exacerbates overall health risks, with hypertension often acting both therefore and a contributor to other metabolic disturbances. Understanding the components of metabolic syndrome, particularly in the context of hypertension, is essential for developing effective prevention and treatment strategies.

a) Abdominal Obesity:

Defined as a waist circumference greater than 40 inches in men and 35 inches in women. Excess visceral fat contributes to insulin resistance and increased cardiovascular risk.

b) Increased Blood Pressure:

Hypertension is defined as having blood pressure readings of 130/85 mmHg or higher or being on antihypertensive medication.

c) Elevated Fasting Blood Glucose:

A fasting blood glucose level of 100 mg/dL or higher indicates insulin resistance and increases the risk for type 2 diabetes.

d) Dyslipidaemia:

This typically includes elevated triglycerides (150 mg/dL or higher) and low levels of high-density lipoprotein (HDL) cholesterol (less than 40 mg/dL in men and less than 50 mg/dL in women).

e) Insulin Resistance:

While not always directly measured, insulin resistance is often implied by the presence of elevated fasting glucose and other components.

- **Diagnosis:**

A diagnosis of metabolic syndrome is typically made when a person exhibits at least three of the five components listed above. Recognizing and addressing metabolic syndrome is crucial because it significantly increases the risk of developing serious health conditions, making early intervention and lifestyle modifications essential for management and prevention.

8.5 Peripheral Artery Disease (PAD):

Peripheral artery disease (PAD) is a common vascular condition characterized by narrowed arteries, reducing blood flow to the limbs, and hypertension is a significant contributing factor. Chronic high blood pressure can lead to endothelial dysfunction and atherosclerosis, processes that cause the arteries to harden and narrow over time. This impaired circulation can result in symptoms such as leg pain, cramping, and ultimately, severe complications like non-healing wounds or gangrene. The relationship between hypertension and PAD underscores the importance of early detection and management of high blood pressure, as effective control can help reduce the risk of PAD and its associated morbidity. Understanding this connection is crucial for improving vascular health and preventing the debilitating consequences of reduced blood flow in affected individuals. Hypertension significantly contributes to the development and progression of peripheral artery disease (PAD) through several interconnected mechanisms. Here's an overview of how hypertension impacts PAD:

i. **Endothelial Dysfunction:**

- **Damage to Blood Vessels:** Chronic high blood pressure can lead to endothelial dysfunction, which impairs the ability of blood vessels to dilate properly. This damage can promote inflammation and atherosclerosis, the primary process involved in PAD.

ii. **Atherosclerosis:**

- **Plaque Formation:** Hypertension accelerates the development of atherosclerosis by causing injury to the arterial walls. This leads to the accumulation of cholesterol, fat, and other substances, forming plaques that narrow the arteries, including those in the legs and feet.

iii. **Increased Arterial Stiffness:**

- **Loss of Elasticity:** Persistent hypertension causes structural changes in blood vessels, resulting in increased stiffness. Stiffer arteries are less able to adapt to changes in blood flow, which can further contribute to reduced circulation in the peripheral areas.

iv. **Reduced Blood Flow:**

- **Ischemia:** The combination of narrowed arteries from atherosclerosis and decreased elasticity results in reduced blood flow to the extremities. This can lead to ischemic symptoms, such as pain during walking (claudication) and, in severe cases, ulcers or gangrene.

v. **Increased Risk of Thrombosis:**

- **Clot Formation:** Hypertension can promote a hypercoagulable state, making blood more likely to clot. These clots can further obstruct narrowed arteries, exacerbating ischemia and increasing the risk of acute limb ischemia.

vi. **Compounding Factors:**

- **Interaction with Other Conditions:** Hypertension often coexists with other risk factors for PAD, such as diabetes, smoking, and dyslipidaemia. These factors can synergistically worsen vascular health and increase the likelihood of developing PAD.

In summary, hypertension contributes to peripheral artery disease through mechanisms such as endothelial dysfunction, accelerated atherosclerosis, increased arterial stiffness, and reduced blood flow. Addressing hypertension and associated risk factors is crucial for preventing the onset and progression of PAD, ultimately improving peripheral circulation and reducing the risk of severe complications.

In conclusion, managing hypertension is essential due to its profound impact on public health and its association with life-threatening conditions such as heart disease, stroke, and chronic kidney disease. Effective hypertension management encompasses a multifaceted strategy that includes lifestyle changes, regular monitoring, and, if necessary, pharmacological intervention. Lifestyle modifications are foundational to controlling blood pressure. A heart-healthy diet, often exemplified by the DASH (Dietary Approaches to Stop Hypertension) diet, emphasizes the consumption of fruits, vegetables, whole grains, lean proteins, and low-fat dairy while minimizing sodium intake. Reducing salt to less than 2,300 mg per day—or ideally 1,500 mg—can significantly lower blood pressure levels. Additionally, regular physical activity, such as aerobic exercises for at least 150 minutes per week, contributes to weight management and improved cardiovascular health. Weight management is particularly important, as even a modest reduction in body weight can lead to meaningful decreases in blood pressure. Stress management techniques, including mindfulness, meditation, and breathing exercises, can also help mitigate the physiological impacts of stress on blood pressure. Regular monitoring of blood pressure is crucial for early detection and ongoing management. Home monitoring devices enable individuals to track their readings and share this information with healthcare providers, facilitating timely adjustments to treatment plans.

For many, lifestyle changes alone may not be sufficient, necessitating the use of antihypertensive medications. There are various classes of medications, such as diuretics, ACE inhibitors, calcium channel blockers, and beta-blockers, each with unique mechanisms of action and potential side effects. A healthcare provider can help tailor a regimen that addresses individual health needs and comorbidities, such as diabetes or high cholesterol. Education plays a vital role in hypertension management. Understanding the risk factors—such as family history, age, excessive alcohol consumption, and sedentary lifestyle—empowers individuals to make informed decisions. Regular consultations with healthcare professionals can provide guidance, support, and adjustments to treatment as necessary. Education plays a vital role in hypertension management. Understanding the risk factors—such as family history, age, excessive alcohol consumption, and sedentary lifestyle—empowers individuals to make informed decisions. Regular consultations with healthcare professionals can provide guidance, support, and adjustments to treatment as necessary. In summary, through a combination of lifestyle changes, vigilant monitoring, and appropriate medical intervention, individuals can effectively manage hypertension, significantly reducing their risk of serious complications and enhancing their overall quality of life. Hypertension is a crucial health concern that extends far beyond elevated blood pressure, acting as a significant precursor to various serious conditions such as cardiovascular disease, diabetes, and chronic kidney disease. The persistent strain that high blood pressure places on blood vessels can lead to significant organ damage, contributing to life-threatening complications. For instance, hypertension can accelerate atherosclerosis, increasing the risk of heart attacks and strokes, while also impairing kidney function, leading to chronic kidney disease and potential renal failure.

Moreover, the relationship between hypertension and metabolic disorders like diabetes highlights the need for a holistic approach to health management. Addressing hypertension through lifestyle modifications—such as a balanced diet, regular physical activity, weight management, and stress reduction—can have profound effects on overall health and longevity. Additionally, regular monitoring and early intervention are essential in managing blood pressure effectively and preventing the onset of related conditions. By prioritizing blood pressure control and adopting a proactive approach to health, individuals can not only protect their cardiovascular system but also significantly reduce the risk of developing serious complications. This comprehensive strategy fosters a healthier future, emphasizing the importance of awareness, education, and community support in the fight against hypertension and its associated health risks. Ultimately, investing in hypertension management is an investment in overall well-being and quality of life. Furthermore, public health initiatives that promote awareness of hypertension and its risks are vital in reducing its prevalence. Educating communities about the importance of regular screenings can lead to early detection and better management strategies. Additionally, healthcare providers play a crucial role in guiding patients toward effective treatment options and lifestyle changes tailored to individual needs. Collaborative efforts among patients, healthcare professionals, and policymakers can create a supportive environment that encourages healthier living and enhances the quality of care.

9. Public Health Implications

Public health implications of hypertension extend far beyond individual health concerns, encompassing significant societal, economic, and healthcare system challenges. As a leading risk factor for cardiovascular disease, stroke, and chronic kidney disease, hypertension poses a substantial burden on public health resources and outcomes. Understanding the epidemiology and impact of hypertension is essential for developing effective prevention and management strategies. By addressing the root causes, promoting awareness, and implementing targeted interventions, public health initiatives can reduce the prevalence of hypertension, enhance population health, and ultimately alleviate the associated economic and healthcare burdens. Furthermore, a comprehensive public health approach can foster collaboration among healthcare providers, policymakers, and communities, ensuring equitable access to resources and support for those at risk. By prioritizing hypertension in public health agendas, we can create a healthier society and improve quality of life for countless individuals.

9.1 Importance of Public Health Perspective:

Understanding its significance from a public health perspective is crucial for developing effective interventions, policies, and community awareness strategies. Here are several key aspects highlighting the importance of this perspective:

i. Prevalence and Impact on Population Health:

Hypertension is often referred to as a "silent killer" because it frequently presents without obvious symptoms. Globally, it affects nearly one in four adults, with prevalence rates significantly increasing with age. The widespread nature of hypertension means that it has considerable implications for overall population health. Public health initiatives can help identify at-risk populations and implement strategies to reduce incidence and prevalence, thereby improving community health outcomes.

ii. **Association with Chronic Diseases:**

Hypertension is a major risk factor for various chronic conditions, including heart disease, stroke, and chronic kidney disease. From a public health standpoint, managing hypertension effectively can significantly reduce the burden of these associated diseases. By addressing hypertension, public health efforts can lead to a decrease in morbidity and mortality rates related to cardiovascular events and improve the overall quality of life for individuals.

iii. **Economic Burden:**

The economic implications of hypertension are profound. The condition contributes to increased healthcare costs due to hospitalizations, medications, and management of complications. Public health initiatives focused on prevention and management can alleviate some of these financial burdens on healthcare systems. Cost-effective strategies such as community education, screening programs, and lifestyle intervention initiatives can save substantial healthcare expenditures in the long run.

iv. **Role of Social Determinants of Health:**

Hypertension is influenced by various social determinants of health, including socioeconomic status, access to healthcare, education, and living conditions. A public health perspective emphasizes the importance of addressing these determinants through policies that promote equity. For instance, ensuring access to affordable healthcare, nutritious food, and safe environments for physical activity can help mitigate hypertension rates in disadvantaged communities.

v. **Prevention through Awareness and Education:**

Public health campaigns play a critical role in raising awareness about hypertension, its risk factors, and the importance of regular monitoring. Educational initiatives can empower individuals to take control of their health through lifestyle changes, such as improved diet, increased physical activity, and smoking cessation. By fostering a culture of prevention, public health efforts can significantly reduce the incidence of hypertension and its complications.

vi. **Screening and Early Detection:**

Regular screening for hypertension is essential for early detection and management. Public health systems can implement community-based screening programs that reach underserved populations. By identifying individuals with hypertension early, interventions can be initiated promptly, reducing the likelihood of severe health outcomes and associated healthcare costs.

vii. **Policy Development and Advocacy:**

A public health perspective enables the development of policies aimed at reducing hypertension. This includes advocating for regulations that limit sodium in processed foods, improving urban planning to create walkable neighbourhoods, and supporting programs that promote healthy eating. Engaging policymakers in discussions about hypertension can lead to the implementation of evidence-based strategies that benefit the broader community.

viii. **Interdisciplinary Approaches:**

Addressing hypertension effectively requires collaboration across various sectors, including healthcare, education, urban planning, and social services. A public health framework encourages interdisciplinary partnerships to tackle hypertension holistically. For instance, integrating health education into school curriculums and promoting physical activity in community spaces can create supportive environments for healthier choices.

ix. **Research and Data Collection:**

Public health initiatives can facilitate research on hypertension, identifying trends, risk factors, and effective interventions. Collecting and analysing data on hypertension prevalence and management allows public health officials to tailor programs and allocate resources effectively. Continuous research is vital for understanding the evolving nature of hypertension and its impact on different populations.

vii. **Community Engagement and Empowerment:**

Engaging communities in hypertension awareness and management initiatives fosters a sense of ownership and responsibility for health. Public health campaigns that involve community members in planning and implementation are often more successful. Empowering individuals with knowledge about hypertension and providing resources for self-management can lead to lasting behavioural changes that benefit overall public health.

9.2 Epidemiology of Hypertension:

The epidemiology of hypertension is a crucial area of study that examines the distribution, determinants, and dynamics of high blood pressure within populations. Hypertension is a prevalent condition, affecting nearly one in four adults worldwide, with rates varying by age, gender, ethnicity, and geographic region. Understanding the epidemiological trends helps identify at-risk populations and underlying risk factors, such as obesity, lifestyle choices, and socioeconomic status. This knowledge is essential for developing targeted prevention strategies and public health interventions aimed at reducing the incidence and prevalence of hypertension, ultimately improving overall health outcomes.

i. Global and Local Statistics:

Hypertension is a significant global health concern, with alarming prevalence rates that affect millions of people across various demographics. According to the World Health Organization (WHO), approximately 1.28 billion adults aged 30-79 years worldwide have hypertension, with only about 25% of them adequately controlled. The prevalence of hypertension tends to increase with age, affecting nearly 50% of individuals over the age of 60. Regionally, variations exist; for example, in low- and middle-income countries, the burden of hypertension is rising rapidly due to urbanization, dietary changes, and lifestyle factors. In contrast, high-income countries have witnessed improvements in management and awareness, although challenges persist, particularly among certain populations.

In the United States, the Centres for Disease Control and Prevention (CDC) reports that nearly 47% of adults have hypertension, a significant increase attributed to factors such as obesity and sedentary lifestyles. Disparities in prevalence are also evident at the local level, where certain demographic groups—particularly racial and ethnic minorities—experience higher rates of hypertension due to a combination of genetic, socioeconomic, and environmental factors. For instance, African Americans are more likely to have hypertension compared to other racial groups, often developing it earlier and experiencing more severe complications. Understanding these global and local statistics is vital for public health officials and policymakers to design effective interventions and allocate resources to combat hypertension effectively, ultimately improving health outcomes for diverse populations.

ii. Demographic Trends:

Demographic trends in hypertension reveal significant variations in prevalence and risk factors across different populations, influenced by age, gender, ethnicity, and geographic location. Age is a primary determinant, with hypertension becoming more common as individuals grow older; the risk increases significantly after age 45, peaking among those over 65. This trend is largely attributed to physiological changes in blood vessels and increased prevalence of comorbid conditions. Gender also plays a role, as men typically have higher rates of hypertension in younger age groups, while the prevalence often equalizes or even shifts in favour of women after menopause, likely due to hormonal changes and differences in body composition. Ethnic disparities are notable as well; for instance, African Americans are disproportionately affected by hypertension compared to Caucasians and Hispanics, often experiencing more severe forms of the disease and higher rates of related complications. Geographic variations are also significant, with urban areas typically exhibiting higher rates of hypertension due to lifestyle factors, such as diet and physical inactivity, whereas rural populations may face barriers to healthcare access and education about blood pressure management. Understanding these demographic trends is crucial for public health initiatives aimed at tailoring prevention and intervention strategies that address the specific needs of diverse population groups.

9.3 Health Implications:

Hypertension, often termed the "silent killer," has far-reaching health implications that extend beyond mere elevated blood pressure levels. As a major risk factor for cardiovascular diseases, including heart attack and stroke, hypertension significantly contributes to morbidity and mortality rates worldwide. Chronic high blood pressure can lead to a cascade of complications, such as heart failure, kidney disease, and vision problems, all of which can drastically affect an individual's quality of life. Additionally, hypertension often coexists with other metabolic conditions, such as diabetes and obesity, further complicating health outcomes and increasing the burden on healthcare systems. The systemic effects of hypertension can also lead to damage in vital organs, underscoring the need for early detection and effective management strategies. Given its prevalence and the serious health risks associated with it, hypertension poses not only a personal health challenge but also a significant public health concern, necessitating comprehensive approaches to prevention, education, and treatment to improve population health outcomes.

i. Chronic Diseases

Chronic diseases related to hypertension are intertwined with its pathophysiology and contribute significantly to morbidity and mortality across populations. One of the most pressing concerns is cardiovascular disease (CVD), which encompasses a range of conditions, including coronary artery disease, heart failure, and stroke. Hypertension accelerates the process of atherosclerosis, where elevated blood pressure damages the endothelial lining of blood vessels, leading to the formation of plaques that narrow arteries and restrict blood flow. This can result in angina (chest pain) and increase the risk of acute myocardial infarction (heart attack) and ischemic strokes, making hypertension a leading preventable cause of death worldwide.

In addition to cardiovascular complications, hypertension has a profound impact on renal health. Chronic elevation of blood pressure can cause hypertensive nephropathy, characterized by damage to the renal blood vessels, leading to progressive loss of kidney function. This can result in chronic kidney disease (CKD), which affects millions globally and may require dialysis or kidney transplantation as it progresses to end-stage renal disease. The relationship between hypertension and CKD is particularly concerning, as the two conditions can create a vicious cycle; CKD can further elevate blood pressure due to fluid overload and increased renin production, complicating management efforts.

Moreover, hypertension is frequently associated with metabolic syndrome, a cluster of conditions that includes obesity, dyslipidaemia, and insulin resistance. This syndrome significantly raises the risk for developing type 2 diabetes, where insulin resistance can be exacerbated by high blood pressure. The coexistence of these conditions not only increases the likelihood of cardiovascular events but also contributes to a higher burden of comorbidities, complicating treatment regimens and necessitating a comprehensive, multidisciplinary approach to management. Additionally, hypertension can lead to complications in other organ systems. For instance, it is a major risk factor for vision problems, including hypertensive retinopathy, where high blood pressure damages the retinal blood vessels, potentially leading to vision loss. Similarly, chronic high blood pressure can affect cognitive function and increase the risk of vascular dementia due to reduced blood flow to the brain.

Given these interconnected health issues, addressing hypertension through public health initiatives is essential. Comprehensive strategies that include lifestyle modifications—such as diet, physical activity, and weight management—along with medication adherence and regular health screenings, can significantly reduce the prevalence of hypertension and its associated chronic diseases. Education and awareness campaigns aimed at both healthcare providers and the public are critical in fostering proactive health management, thereby mitigating the extensive burden hypertension imposes on individuals and healthcare systems alike.

ii. Economic Burden

The economic burden of hypertension is substantial, impacting individuals, healthcare systems, and broader economies worldwide. As one of the leading risk factors for cardiovascular disease, stroke, and chronic kidney disease, hypertension contributes to significant healthcare costs associated with treatment, management, and complications. Direct costs include expenditures for antihypertensive medications, routine medical visits, diagnostic tests, and hospitalizations due to hypertension-related complications.

According to various studies, the annual cost of treating hypertension and its related conditions can reach hundreds of billions of dollars in countries like the United States alone. This financial strain is compounded by the indirect costs associated with lost productivity due to illness, disability, and premature death, highlighting the far-reaching implications of uncontrolled hypertension.

Additionally, the burden of hypertension disproportionately affects lower-income populations, where access to preventive care and effective treatment options may be limited. Individuals in these groups often face higher rates of comorbidities, leading to more severe health outcomes and escalating healthcare costs. The lack of access to regular screenings and lifestyle interventions further exacerbates the situation, creating a cycle of poor health and financial instability. Public health initiatives aimed at hypertension prevention and management can therefore play a critical role in reducing healthcare costs by shifting focus from treatment to prevention. By investing in community health programs, educational campaigns, and policies that promote healthier lifestyles, governments can help alleviate the economic burden of hypertension and improve health equity.

Moreover, the economic impact of hypertension extends beyond direct healthcare costs. It influences workforce productivity, as individuals with uncontrolled hypertension may experience absenteeism due to health issues, resulting in decreased work performance and increased burden on employers. Chronic conditions can also lead to long-term disability, necessitating additional support services and impacting social welfare systems. This interplay between health and economic productivity underscores the importance of addressing hypertension as a public health priority, emphasizing the potential for significant economic savings through effective prevention and management strategies. In summary, the economic burden of hypertension is multifaceted, encompassing direct medical costs, indirect costs related to lost productivity, and the disproportionate impact on vulnerable populations. By prioritizing hypertension in public health agendas and implementing targeted interventions, society can not only improve health outcomes but also achieve substantial economic benefits, creating a healthier workforce and reducing the overall financial strain on healthcare systems.

9.4 Risk Factors and Determinants:

Hypertension, or high blood pressure, is influenced by a complex interplay of risk factors and determinants that can be broadly categorized into modifiable and non-modifiable categories. Understanding these factors is crucial for effective prevention and management strategies.

i. **Non-Modifiable Risk Factors:**

Age, genetics, and ethnicity play significant roles in the development of hypertension. As individuals age, the elasticity of blood vessels decreases, which often leads to increased blood pressure. Genetic predisposition also contributes to hypertension; family history of high blood pressure can indicate an inherited risk, making certain individuals more susceptible. Ethnic background is another important determinant, with studies showing that African Americans have higher rates of hypertension and tend to experience more severe forms of the condition compared to other racial groups. This disparity highlights the need for tailored public health interventions that consider these demographic factors.

ii. **Modifiable Risk Factors:**

Lifestyle choices significantly influence the risk of developing hypertension. A diet high in sodium, saturated fats, and low in fruits and vegetables can lead to increased blood pressure. Excessive salt intake is particularly concerning, as it causes the body to retain water, raising blood volume and pressure. Physical inactivity is another key modifiable risk factor; sedentary lifestyles contribute to obesity and metabolic syndrome, both of which are strongly linked to hypertension. Obesity itself is a major risk factor, as excess body weight increases the workload on the heart and raises blood pressure. Alcohol consumption and tobacco use are also critical lifestyle factors; excessive alcohol intake can raise blood pressure, while smoking damages blood vessels and contributes to atherosclerosis.

iii. Social Determinants of Health:

Beyond individual lifestyle choices, social determinants of health significantly influence hypertension risk. Socioeconomic status is a key determinant, as individuals with lower income levels often face barriers to accessing healthy foods, regular healthcare, and wellness programs. Additionally, education plays a role in health literacy, impacting an individual's ability to make informed decisions about diet and lifestyle. Living conditions, including neighbourhood safety and access to recreational spaces, can also affect physical activity levels and overall health. Stress, whether from economic hardship, social instability, or other environmental factors, has been linked to hypertension; chronic stress can lead to hormonal changes that increase blood pressure.

iv. Psychosocial Factors:

Mental health and psychosocial stressors are increasingly recognized as contributing factors to hypertension. Chronic stress, anxiety, and depression can lead to unhealthy coping mechanisms, such as poor dietary choices and physical inactivity, exacerbating blood pressure issues. Moreover, the cumulative effects of stress over time can lead to sustained elevations in blood pressure, making psychosocial support an essential component of hypertension management.

9.4.1 Lifestyle Factors:

Lifestyle risk factors play a crucial role in the development and management of hypertension. Understanding these factors is essential for effective prevention strategies and interventions aimed at reducing blood pressure and improving overall health.

i. Dietary Habits:

One of the most significant lifestyle risk factors for hypertension is diet, particularly the intake of sodium. High sodium consumption leads to fluid retention, which increases blood volume and, consequently, blood pressure. The typical Western diet, often rich in processed foods, contributes to excessive sodium intake, far exceeding the recommended limits. In contrast, diets high in potassium, found in fruits and vegetables, can help counteract the effects of sodium and promote lower blood pressure. The DASH (Dietary Approaches to Stop Hypertension) diet emphasizes a balance of nutrients and encourages the consumption of whole foods, including whole grains, lean proteins, and plenty of fruits and vegetables, which have been shown to lower blood pressure effectively.

ii. Physical Inactivity:

Sedentary behaviour is another major lifestyle risk factor contributing to hypertension. Regular physical activity helps maintain a healthy weight, reduces stress, and promotes overall cardiovascular health. Exercise improves heart function and increases blood flow, which can help lower blood pressure levels. Inactive individuals are more likely to become overweight or obese, further elevating their risk for hypertension. The American Heart Association recommends at least 150 minutes of moderate-intensity aerobic exercise per week, which can significantly reduce blood pressure and enhance overall cardiovascular health.

iii. Obesity and Body Weight:

Obesity is closely linked to hypertension, as excess body weight increases the workload on the heart and raises blood pressure. Fat tissue produces hormones and inflammatory substances that can disrupt the normal functioning of blood vessels, further contributing to high blood pressure. Maintaining a healthy weight through a balanced diet and regular physical activity is critical in managing and preventing hypertension. For individuals who are already hypertensive, weight loss can lead to significant reductions in blood pressure, often requiring less medication or even eliminating the need for it altogether.

iv. Alcohol Consumption:

The relationship between alcohol consumption and hypertension is well-documented. While moderate alcohol intake may have some protective cardiovascular effects, excessive drinking can lead to elevated blood pressure. Heavy drinking can damage the heart muscle, cause arrhythmias, and contribute to weight gain, all of which increase hypertension risk. Public health guidelines generally recommend limiting alcohol intake to moderate levels—defined as up to one drink per day for women and up to two drinks per day for men—to mitigate these risks.

v. Tobacco Use:

Smoking is another critical lifestyle risk factor for hypertension. The chemicals in tobacco can damage blood vessels and lead to atherosclerosis, the narrowing and hardening of arteries. This damage increases the resistance against which the heart must pump, raising blood pressure. Moreover, the temporary rise in blood pressure that occurs with smoking can become a chronic issue for regular smokers. Quitting smoking is essential for improving overall cardiovascular health and reducing hypertension risk. Evidence shows that blood pressure decreases within weeks of cessation, and the long-term benefits extend well beyond hypertension.

vi. Stress Management:

Chronic stress is increasingly recognized as a contributor to hypertension. Stress can trigger the release of hormones like cortisol and adrenaline, which temporarily elevate blood pressure. Moreover, individuals under stress may resort to unhealthy coping mechanisms, such as overeating, smoking, or drinking alcohol, which can exacerbate hypertension. Developing effective stress management techniques, such as mindfulness, yoga, meditation, and regular physical activity, can help mitigate these effects and contribute to better blood pressure control.

In summary, lifestyle risk factors significantly influence the development and management of hypertension. By addressing dietary habits, physical inactivity, obesity, alcohol consumption, tobacco use, and stress, individuals can take proactive steps to reduce their risk of hypertension and improve their overall health. Public health initiatives that promote healthy lifestyle choices and provide education on the impacts of these risk factors are essential for reducing the prevalence of hypertension and its associated health complications.

9.4.2 Social determinants:

Social determinants of hypertension are the conditions in which individuals are born, grow, live, work, and age. These factors significantly influence health outcomes, including the prevalence and management of hypertension. Understanding these determinants is critical for developing effective public health strategies aimed at reducing hypertension rates and improving overall population health.

i. Socioeconomic Status:

Socioeconomic status (SES) is one of the most significant social determinants affecting hypertension. Individuals with lower income and education levels often have limited access to healthcare, healthy food options, and resources for physical activity. This lack of access contributes to poorer health outcomes, including higher rates of hypertension. Lower SES is associated with increased stress, both financial and social, which can exacerbate health issues. Moreover, individuals in lower-income neighbourhoods may live in environments that lack safe spaces for exercise or access to fresh produce, leading to dietary habits high in sodium and unhealthy fats.

ii. Access to Healthcare:

Access to quality healthcare services is a critical determinant of hypertension management. Individuals without health insurance or those in underserved areas may face barriers to receiving regular check-ups, screenings, and necessary medications for hypertension. This lack of access can lead to late diagnoses and inadequate management of the condition, increasing the risk of complications. Additionally, cultural and linguistic barriers can hinder effective communication between healthcare providers and patients, affecting adherence to treatment plans.

iii. Education and Health Literacy:

Education is another crucial social determinant influencing hypertension. Higher levels of education are often correlated with better health literacy, which refers to an individual's ability to understand health information and make informed decisions about their health. Individuals with lower educational attainment may lack the knowledge necessary to recognize the risks of hypertension or the importance of lifestyle changes and medication adherence. Public health campaigns focused on improving health literacy can empower individuals to take control of their health, encouraging healthier behaviours and more effective management of hypertension.

iv. Built Environment:

The built environment—the physical surroundings where people live, work, and play—plays a significant role in influencing lifestyle behaviours that affect hypertension. Neighbourhoods with limited access to parks, recreational facilities, and safe walking paths can discourage physical activity. Additionally, areas with a high concentration of fast-food restaurants and convenience stores often provide limited access to healthy food options, leading to diets high in sodium and unhealthy fats. Urban planning and policies that promote the development of green spaces, safe pedestrian pathways, and access to supermarkets with healthy food choices are essential for creating environments that support heart health and reduce hypertension risk.

v. Social Support and Community Networks:

Social support networks and community engagement are also significant determinants of hypertension. Individuals who have strong social connections and support systems tend to have better health outcomes, including lower blood pressure levels. Conversely, social isolation and lack of community engagement can contribute to stress and unhealthy coping mechanisms, which can elevate blood pressure. Programs that foster community involvement and support, such as group exercise classes or health education workshops, can enhance social cohesion and provide individuals with the resources and motivation needed to manage their hypertension effectively.

vi. Cultural Factors:

Cultural beliefs and practices also influence health behaviours related to hypertension. Different cultures may have varying perceptions of health, diet, and the importance of seeking medical care, which can affect hypertension management. For example, some communities may have traditional dietary practices that include high sodium foods, while others may emphasize herbal remedies over pharmaceutical treatments. Understanding and respecting cultural perspectives while providing culturally competent care can improve patient engagement and adherence to hypertension management strategies.

In conclusion, social determinants of hypertension encompass a wide range of factors, including socioeconomic status, access to healthcare, education, the built environment, social support, and cultural influences. Addressing these determinants through comprehensive public health strategies is essential for reducing the prevalence of hypertension and improving health outcomes for vulnerable populations. By creating environments that support healthy choices and ensuring equitable access to healthcare and education, we can significantly mitigate the impact of hypertension on individuals and communities.

9.5 Prevention and Management Strategies:

Prevention and management strategies for hypertension are essential components of public health initiatives aimed at reducing the prevalence and impact of this widespread condition. With hypertension affecting nearly one in four adults globally, comprehensive approaches are critical to mitigate its associated health risks, including cardiovascular disease, stroke, and chronic kidney disease. Effective strategies encompass both lifestyle modifications and medical interventions. On the lifestyle front, promoting a balanced diet low in sodium and rich in fruits and vegetables, encouraging regular physical activity, maintaining a healthy weight, and limiting alcohol consumption and tobacco use are foundational elements of hypertension prevention. Additionally, community-based education and awareness campaigns play a pivotal role in informing individuals about the risks of high blood pressure and the importance of regular monitoring. On the clinical side, timely diagnosis and personalized treatment plans, including the appropriate use of antihypertensive medications, are vital for managing hypertension and minimizing complications. Integrated care approaches that address the social determinants of health, enhance access to healthcare services, and foster supportive environments for healthy behaviours are crucial for effective hypertension management. By combining these multifaceted strategies, public health efforts can significantly reduce the burden of hypertension and improve overall health outcomes for individuals and communities.

9.5.1 Public Health Interventions:

Public health interventions for hypertension are vital in addressing the prevalence and impact of this condition, which affects millions globally. These interventions encompass a range of strategies aimed at prevention, early detection, management, and education to mitigate the risks associated with high blood pressure. A comprehensive approach that integrates community engagement, policy advocacy, and healthcare access is essential for effective hypertension control.

i. **Community-Based Programs:**

One of the most effective public health interventions is the implementation of community-based programs that promote healthy lifestyles. These initiatives often focus on educating individuals about the importance of maintaining a balanced diet, engaging in regular physical activity, and avoiding harmful habits such as excessive alcohol consumption and smoking. Programs may include cooking classes, nutrition workshops, and exercise groups that not only provide practical skills but also foster a sense of community. For example, community gardens can promote access to fresh produce while encouraging physical activity among participants. These programs can be tailored to meet the specific needs of diverse populations, ensuring that cultural considerations are integrated into health promotion efforts.

ii. Screening and Early Detection:

Another critical intervention is the promotion of regular blood pressure screening and early detection of hypertension. Public health campaigns can encourage individuals to have their blood pressure checked at routine medical visits or through community health fairs. Targeting high-risk populations, such as those with a family history of hypertension or individuals over the age of 40, can facilitate timely diagnosis and intervention. Mobile health units or partnerships with local organizations can further expand access to screening in underserved areas, ensuring that those most at risk receive appropriate attention. Early detection is essential, as it allows for prompt lifestyle modifications and medical management, significantly reducing the risk of complications.

iii. Policy and Environmental Changes:

Public health interventions also involve advocating for policy changes that create supportive environments for healthy living. This includes implementing regulations to reduce sodium levels in processed foods, promoting clear food labelling, and encouraging the availability of healthier food options in schools, workplaces, and communities. Urban planning initiatives that create walkable neighbourhoods, increase access to parks, and provide safe spaces for physical activity can further promote healthier lifestyles. Policies aimed at reducing tobacco use and alcohol consumption, such as increased taxes on cigarettes and alcohol, can significantly contribute to lowering hypertension rates.

iv. Healthcare Access and Quality Improvement:

Improving access to healthcare services is another essential aspect of public health interventions for hypertension. Ensuring that individuals have access to primary care providers who can offer comprehensive blood pressure management, including lifestyle counselling and medication management, is crucial. This may involve expanding insurance coverage, reducing financial barriers, and increasing the availability of healthcare services in underserved areas. Training healthcare providers in culturally competent care can also enhance patient engagement and adherence to treatment plans. Furthermore, integrated care models that involve collaboration between primary care providers, nutritionists, and mental health professionals can provide a holistic approach to hypertension management, addressing both physiological and psychosocial factors.

v. Public Awareness Campaigns:

Finally, public awareness campaigns are vital in educating the community about hypertension, its risks, and prevention strategies. These campaigns can utilize various media platforms, including social media, television, and print materials, to disseminate information widely. Targeted messaging can reach specific populations, raising awareness about the importance of regular blood pressure monitoring and healthy lifestyle choices. Engaging community leaders and influencers can further amplify these messages, making them more relatable and impactful. By fostering a culture of health literacy, these campaigns empower individuals to take proactive steps in managing their blood pressure and seeking medical care when necessary.

In conclusion, public health interventions for hypertension encompass a multifaceted approach that includes community-based programs, screening initiatives, policy advocacy, improved healthcare access, and public awareness campaigns. By addressing both the individual and systemic factors contributing to hypertension, these interventions can significantly reduce its prevalence and associated health risks, ultimately leading to improved health outcomes for communities and populations at large.

9.5.2 Screening and Early Detection:

Screening and early detection of hypertension are essential components of effective public health strategies aimed at reducing the prevalence of high blood pressure and its associated complications. By identifying individuals with elevated blood pressure early, healthcare providers can implement timely interventions that can significantly mitigate the risks of cardiovascular disease, stroke, and kidney damage. The process of screening involves measuring blood pressure at regular intervals and utilizing standardized guidelines to interpret the results, ensuring that those who are at risk receive appropriate follow-up care.

i. Importance of Regular Screening:

Regular blood pressure screening is crucial, particularly because hypertension often presents with no symptoms, earning it the moniker "silent killer." Many individuals remain unaware of their condition until serious health complications arise, underscoring the need for proactive monitoring. Public health organizations, including the American Heart Association and the World Health Organization, recommend that adults begin routine blood pressure checks at age 40, or earlier if they have risk factors such as obesity, a family history of hypertension, or pre-existing conditions like diabetes. Early detection allows for lifestyle modifications and medical treatments to be initiated before the condition progresses, leading to better health outcomes and reduced healthcare costs over time.

ii. Community-Based Screening Initiatives:

Community-based screening programs play a vital role in increasing access to blood pressure measurements, particularly in underserved populations. Health fairs, community clinics, and workplace wellness programs can provide free or low-cost blood pressure screenings, ensuring that individuals who may not regularly visit healthcare providers receive necessary assessments. Mobile health units can further extend the reach of these services, bringing screening directly to communities with limited healthcare access. By fostering partnerships with local organizations, healthcare systems can enhance the visibility and accessibility of screening initiatives, encouraging more individuals to participate.

iii. Utilizing Technology for Early Detection:

Advances in technology also support the screening and early detection of hypertension. Home blood pressure monitoring devices have become increasingly popular, allowing individuals to check their blood pressure regularly in the comfort of their own homes. These devices can provide valuable data that patients can share with their healthcare providers during appointments, facilitating better-informed decisions regarding management. Additionally, telehealth platforms enable remote monitoring and consultations, making it easier for individuals to receive timely guidance and interventions, particularly during times when in-person visits may be challenging.

iv. Integrating Screening into Routine Care:

Integrating blood pressure screening into routine healthcare visits is another critical strategy for early detection. Primary care providers can implement standardized protocols that include blood pressure checks during annual physical exams and regular follow-ups. Training healthcare professionals to understand the importance of screening and how to effectively communicate results to patients can enhance the likelihood of follow-up action. Furthermore, electronic health records can flag patients who are due for screening based on age and risk factors, ensuring that no individuals fall through the cracks.

v. Education and Follow-Up:

Alongside screening, education about hypertension is paramount. Patients should be informed about the significance of knowing their blood pressure numbers and the lifestyle changes that can help manage or prevent hypertension. If an individual's blood pressure is found to be elevated, appropriate follow-up care must be arranged. This may include referrals to specialists, lifestyle counselling, and medication management as necessary. Ensuring that patients understand their blood pressure readings, the implications of elevated readings, and the importance of adhering to treatment plans can lead to better management of hypertension.

In conclusion, screening and early detection of hypertension are fundamental to preventing the serious health consequences associated with this condition. By implementing community-based initiatives, utilizing technology, integrating screening into routine care, and providing education, public health systems can enhance the detection of hypertension and facilitate timely interventions. These efforts ultimately lead to improved health outcomes and a reduction in the burden of hypertension-related diseases across populations.

9.6 Policy Implications:

The policy implications of hypertension are critical in shaping public health initiatives aimed at reducing the prevalence and burden of this pervasive condition. Hypertension is a major contributor to cardiovascular diseases, stroke, and chronic kidney disease, making it imperative for policymakers to address its root causes and implement effective interventions. This involves creating a comprehensive framework that includes strategies for prevention, early detection, and management of hypertension at both individual and community levels. Policies can facilitate access to healthcare services, promote healthy lifestyle choices, and regulate environmental factors that contribute to high blood pressure, such as dietary sodium intake and tobacco use. Additionally, integrating hypertension management into broader health care policies can improve health equity by ensuring that underserved populations receive adequate resources and support. By leveraging evidence-based strategies and fostering collaboration among stakeholders—such as healthcare providers, community organizations, and government agencies—policymakers can effectively address the multifaceted nature of hypertension, ultimately leading to improved health outcomes and reduced healthcare costs.

9.6.1 Legislation and Regulation:

Legislation and regulation surrounding hypertension play a crucial role in shaping public health outcomes and reducing the burden of this prevalent condition. Effective policies can create environments conducive to healthier lifestyles, ensure access to necessary healthcare services, and promote early detection and management of hypertension. These legislative measures can encompass a variety of strategies, including the regulation of food and beverage industries, tobacco control policies, healthcare access improvements, and funding for public health initiatives.

i. Food and Nutrition Regulations:

One of the most impactful areas of legislation regarding hypertension is the regulation of dietary sodium. High sodium intake is a well-established risk factor for developing hypertension, and many governments are taking steps to address this through public policy. For instance, countries like the United Kingdom and initiatives like the World Health Organization's "Global Action Plan for the Prevention and Control of Noncommunicable Diseases" advocate for sodium reduction in processed foods. Legislation may mandate clearer labelling of sodium content on food packaging, enabling consumers to make informed choices. Additionally, regulations can encourage or require food manufacturers to reduce sodium levels in their products, significantly impacting population-level sodium consumption and, consequently, hypertension rates.

ii. Tobacco Control Policies:

Smoking is another significant risk factor for hypertension, and robust tobacco control legislation is essential for mitigating its impact on public health. Policies that increase tobacco taxes, restrict advertising, and promote smoke-free environments can significantly reduce smoking rates. Smoke-free laws not only protect non-smokers from second hand smoke but also create a supportive environment for smokers who wish to quit. Comprehensive cessation programs funded by legislation can provide resources and support for individuals trying to quit, thereby reducing hypertension rates linked to tobacco use. Countries with strict tobacco control measures have observed reductions in cardiovascular disease rates, demonstrating the effectiveness of such policies.

iii. Access to Healthcare:

Legislation aimed at improving access to healthcare services is critical for effective hypertension management. Policies that expand health insurance coverage, such as those implemented under the Affordable Care Act in the United States, ensure that more individuals can receive regular blood pressure screenings, necessary medications, and lifestyle counselling. Additionally, legislation that funds community health centres can help bring services to underserved populations, ensuring that those most at risk for hypertension receive appropriate care. By addressing financial and geographic barriers to healthcare, these policies contribute to early detection and effective management of hypertension.

iv. Funding for Public Health Initiatives:

Government funding for public health programs targeting hypertension is vital for sustained intervention efforts. Legislation that allocates resources for community-based education campaigns can enhance awareness about hypertension risks and promote healthy lifestyle choices. Programs that offer free blood pressure screenings, nutritional education, and physical activity initiatives can effectively reduce hypertension prevalence in communities. Additionally, funding research on hypertension can inform evidence-based policies and interventions, ensuring that public health strategies are grounded in the latest scientific findings.

v. Workplace Regulations:

Another important aspect of hypertension regulation involves workplace health policies. Legislation that encourages or mandates health promotion programs within the workplace can help employees manage their blood pressure effectively. Programs that focus on stress management, healthy eating, and physical activity can foster a healthier workforce. Employers may also be encouraged to provide access to health screenings, making it easier for employees to monitor their blood pressure. Such workplace interventions not only benefit individual health but can also lead to reduced healthcare costs for employers, creating a win-win situation.

In conclusion, legislation and regulation play a pivotal role in addressing hypertension at multiple levels. By implementing policies that target dietary habits, tobacco use, healthcare access, public health funding, and workplace wellness, governments can create a comprehensive approach to prevent and manage hypertension. These regulatory measures are essential not only for improving individual health outcomes but also for reducing the overall burden of hypertension on healthcare systems and society. By prioritizing hypertension in public health legislation, policymakers can contribute to healthier populations and sustainable health improvements.

9.6.2 Healthcare Access:

Access to healthcare is a critical determinant in the effective management and prevention of hypertension. Ensuring that individuals can obtain timely and appropriate care is essential for reducing the prevalence of high blood pressure and its associated health complications. Several factors influence healthcare access, including geographic location, economic status, insurance coverage, and the availability of healthcare providers.

i. Geographic Barriers:

Geographic location significantly impacts access to healthcare services for hypertension management. Individuals living in rural or underserved urban areas often face challenges in accessing medical care, including limited availability of healthcare facilities and specialists. This can lead to delays in diagnosis and treatment, ultimately worsening health outcomes. For example, many rural communities lack primary care providers who can regularly monitor blood pressure and provide lifestyle counselling. To address these disparities, innovative solutions such as telehealth services and mobile health clinics are being implemented to reach individuals in remote areas. By leveraging technology, healthcare providers can offer consultations, monitoring, and education, thereby increasing access for those who might otherwise go untreated.

ii. Economic Barriers:

Economic status is another crucial factor affecting healthcare access. Individuals with lower incomes are often less likely to have health insurance, which can limit their ability to afford necessary medical care, including regular blood pressure screenings and medications. The cost of antihypertensive drugs can be a significant barrier, leading some individuals to forgo treatment or medications due to financial constraints. Additionally, low-income populations may prioritize immediate needs over preventive health care, exacerbating health disparities. Policies that expand Medicaid eligibility or provide subsidies for low-income individuals can improve access to necessary healthcare services. Implementing sliding scale fees at community health centres can also make care more affordable for low-income patients.

iii. Insurance Coverage:

Access to healthcare for hypertension management is heavily influenced by insurance coverage. Inadequate or lack of insurance often results in delayed diagnosis and treatment of hypertension. Insurance policies that cover regular screenings, preventive services, and lifestyle counselling are crucial in facilitating access to care. The Affordable Care Act (ACA) in the United States has made strides in improving access by expanding Medicaid and requiring insurance plans to cover preventive services without cost-sharing. However, gaps remain, particularly in states that have not expanded Medicaid, leading to continued disparities in hypertension management for uninsured and underinsured populations. Advocacy for comprehensive insurance reforms that prioritize coverage for hypertension-related services is essential to bridge these gaps.

iv. Availability of Healthcare Providers:

The availability of qualified healthcare providers directly impacts access to hypertension care. A shortage of healthcare professionals, particularly in primary care, can limit patients' ability to receive timely evaluations and ongoing management for hypertension. Many regions face challenges in attracting and retaining healthcare providers, particularly in rural areas. Strategies to increase the number of healthcare professionals, such as loan repayment programs for those who practice in underserved areas and training initiatives to expand the workforce, can enhance access to care.

v. Education and Awareness:

Beyond physical access to healthcare services, education and health literacy are vital components of effective hypertension management. Many individuals may be unaware of their blood pressure status or the importance of regular monitoring and lifestyle changes. Public health campaigns aimed at increasing awareness of hypertension, its risks, and the need for regular check-ups can empower individuals to seek care. Educational programs in community settings can help individuals understand their blood pressure readings and the lifestyle changes needed to manage or prevent hypertension effectively. By enhancing health literacy, communities can promote proactive healthcare-seeking behaviour, leading to earlier detection and better management of hypertension.

In conclusion, access to healthcare is a fundamental aspect of hypertension prevention and management. Geographic, economic, and systemic barriers must be addressed to ensure that all individuals can receive timely and effective care. By expanding insurance coverage, enhancing the availability of healthcare providers, and promoting education and awareness, policymakers and healthcare systems can create an environment that supports better blood pressure management and ultimately improves health outcomes for individuals affected by hypertension.

9.7 Challenges and Barriers:

Hypertension poses significant challenges and barriers that hinder effective prevention, diagnosis, and management. One of the foremost challenges is the widespread lack of awareness; many individuals with hypertension remain asymptomatic, leading them to underestimate the importance of regular screenings. This is compounded by socioeconomic barriers, as individuals in low-income communities often lack access to healthcare services due to inadequate insurance coverage, high costs of medications, and limited availability of healthcare providers. Geographic disparities further exacerbate the issue, particularly in rural areas where healthcare facilities are sparse, and transportation can be a significant obstacle. Additionally, cultural factors and health literacy play a role; individuals from diverse backgrounds may have differing perceptions of health and may not fully understand hypertension or the lifestyle changes required for management. Stigma around chronic illnesses can discourage individuals from seeking help, while misinformation about blood pressure and its risks can lead to ineffective self-management. Moreover, systemic issues such as fragmented healthcare systems and lack of coordinated care can hinder comprehensive management strategies, leaving many without the support needed to effectively control their blood pressure. Addressing these multifaceted challenges requires a coordinated approach that includes improving healthcare access, increasing awareness and education, and fostering supportive environments that empower individuals to take charge of their health.

9.7.1 Implementation Issues:

Implementing effective strategies for the prevention and management of hypertension presents several critical issues that can hinder success at both the individual and population levels. These implementation issues encompass healthcare system challenges, resource allocation, community engagement, and the integration of evidence-based practices into routine care.

i. Healthcare System Challenges:

One of the primary implementation issues lies within the healthcare system itself. Fragmentation of care is a significant barrier; many patients receive treatment from multiple providers without adequate coordination between them. This can result in inconsistent management plans, ineffective communication, and missed opportunities for patient education. Additionally, primary care providers often face high patient volumes, leaving them with limited time to focus on preventive care and comprehensive management of chronic conditions like hypertension. Without adequate support systems, such as care managers or health coaches, patients may struggle to adhere to treatment plans or lifestyle changes, leading to poor health outcomes.

ii. Resource Allocation:

Adequate resource allocation is another critical issue in the implementation of hypertension management strategies. Public health initiatives aimed at addressing hypertension often require significant funding for screening programs, educational campaigns, and community-based interventions. However, budget constraints can limit the availability of these resources, particularly in underserved areas where the burden of hypertension is often greatest. Furthermore, healthcare providers may lack access to essential tools, such as blood pressure monitors and educational materials, which are necessary for effective patient management. Policymakers must prioritize hypertension within health budgets and ensure that funding is directed towards initiatives that will have the most significant impact on public health outcomes.

iii. Community Engagement:

Engaging communities is essential for the successful implementation of hypertension prevention and management strategies. Many public health interventions fail to resonate with target populations due to a lack of cultural sensitivity or awareness of community needs. Effective implementation requires the involvement of community leaders and stakeholders in the development of programs that are tailored to local contexts. For example, culturally appropriate educational materials and outreach efforts can help ensure that information about hypertension is accessible and relatable. Additionally, fostering community partnerships can enhance the reach and effectiveness of interventions. Programs that involve local organizations, schools, and businesses can create a supportive environment that encourages healthy behaviours and facilitates access to care.

iv. Integration of Evidence-Based Practices:

The integration of evidence-based practices into routine healthcare is essential for effective hypertension management but presents its own set of challenges. Despite the availability of guidelines and best practices, many healthcare providers may not consistently implement these recommendations due to time constraints, lack of awareness, or insufficient training. For instance, providers may struggle to incorporate lifestyle counselling into consultations due to competing priorities or may not utilize standardized protocols for blood pressure measurement. To overcome these barriers, continuous professional development and training opportunities must be provided to healthcare workers. Furthermore, integrating hypertension management into electronic health records (EHRs) can help standardize care and prompt providers to follow established guidelines, ensuring that patients receive consistent and evidence-based treatment.

v. Patient Adherence and Behaviour Change:

Encouraging patient adherence to hypertension management plans is a significant implementation issue. Many individuals may struggle with lifestyle modifications, such as dietary changes and increasing physical activity, due to various barriers including lack of motivation, social support, or resources. Additionally, the complexity of medication regimens can lead to nonadherence, especially if patients do not fully understand the importance of their medications or experience side effects. Effective implementation strategies should include tailored education and support for patients, such as motivational interviewing, patient-centred counselling, and the use of technology for reminders and tracking progress. Providing resources that facilitate behaviour change, such as access to nutritionists, fitness programs, and community support groups, can further enhance adherence and improve health outcomes.

In conclusion, the implementation of hypertension prevention and management strategies faces multiple challenges that require comprehensive approaches to address. By focusing on improving healthcare system coordination, ensuring adequate resource allocation, engaging communities, integrating evidence-based practices, and supporting patient adherence, stakeholders can create an environment conducive to effective hypertension management. Overcoming these implementation issues is essential for reducing the burden of hypertension and improving health outcomes on a population level.

9.7.2 Cultural and Behavioural Barriers:

Cultural and behavioural barriers significantly impact the prevention, diagnosis, and management of hypertension, often leading to disparities in health outcomes. Understanding these barriers is crucial for developing effective public health interventions tailored to diverse populations. Cultural beliefs, social norms, and individual behaviours can all influence how individuals perceive hypertension, their willingness to seek care, and their adherence to treatment plans.

i. Cultural Beliefs and Perceptions:

Cultural beliefs about health and illness play a pivotal role in how individuals understand hypertension. In many cultures, chronic conditions like hypertension may be perceived as inevitable aspects of aging rather than preventable or manageable health issues. This perception can lead to a fatalistic attitude, where individuals may not prioritize monitoring their blood pressure or making lifestyle changes. Additionally, cultural interpretations of symptoms and health can affect whether individuals seek medical attention. In some communities, there may be a preference for traditional remedies or alternative medicine over conventional treatments, which can delay appropriate medical care. Furthermore, stigma surrounding chronic illnesses can discourage individuals from discussing their hypertension or seeking help, particularly if they fear judgment or social repercussions. Public health interventions must consider these cultural beliefs and work towards creating culturally sensitive educational materials and outreach strategies that resonate with the target population.

ii. Social Norms and Support Systems:

Social norms significantly influence health behaviours related to hypertension. In communities where unhealthy eating habits, such as high salt consumption or low fruit and vegetable intake, are the norm, individuals may find it challenging to adopt healthier dietary practices. Social gatherings and cultural traditions often revolve around food, making it difficult for individuals to make dietary changes without feeling isolated or disconnected from their community. Moreover, individuals with hypertension may lack social support for making lifestyle changes. If family and friends are not engaged in healthy practices themselves, individuals may struggle to maintain motivation or adherence to treatment plans. Addressing these social norms through community-based programs that promote collective lifestyle changes can help foster an environment that supports healthier behaviours. Engaging community leaders and influencers can also amplify the message of healthy living, encouraging collective participation in hypertension management.

iii. Behavioural Factors and Lifestyle Choices:

Behavioural factors, including physical inactivity, poor dietary habits, and substance use, are significant contributors to hypertension. Many individuals may struggle to engage in regular physical activity due to various barriers, such as a lack of access to safe spaces for exercise, time constraints from work and family obligations, or a lack of knowledge about effective exercise routines. Similarly, dietary choices are often influenced by convenience and accessibility;

individuals may opt for processed, high-sodium foods due to limited access to fresh produce or the demands of a busy lifestyle. Additionally, stress and mental health issues can contribute to unhealthy coping mechanisms, such as overeating or substance abuse, which further exacerbate hypertension risk. Public health initiatives must address these behavioural factors by promoting accessible resources, such as community exercise programs, nutrition education, and mental health support, to empower individuals to make healthier choices.

iv. **Health Literacy and Education:**

Low health literacy is a significant barrier that can hinder effective hypertension management. Individuals with limited understanding of health concepts may struggle to comprehend their blood pressure readings, the importance of medication adherence, or the implications of their lifestyle choices on their health. This lack of knowledge can lead to poor self-management and increased health risks. Effective health education tailored to the literacy levels and cultural contexts of individuals is crucial for empowering patients to take control of their hypertension. Educational programs that use simple language, visual aids, and culturally relevant examples can enhance understanding and engagement.

v. **Misinformation and Myths:**

Misinformation about hypertension and its management can also present a barrier. Myths surrounding hypertension—such as the belief that it only affects older adults or that medication is unnecessary if one feels fine—can deter individuals from seeking care or adhering to treatment plans. This misinformation may spread through social networks, traditional media, or cultural narratives, leading to widespread misconceptions. Public health campaigns that address these myths directly and provide accurate, evidence-based information are essential for overcoming these barriers. Utilizing trusted community figures or healthcare professionals to disseminate information can enhance credibility and encourage behaviour change.

In conclusion, the public health implications of our findings highlight critical areas that require immediate attention and action. The data indicates that specific health disparities persist across different demographics, revealing an urgent need for targeted interventions that address these inequities. By focusing on prevention strategies—such as vaccination campaigns, health education, and early detection programs—we can significantly reduce the burden of disease within vulnerable populations. Moreover, increasing access to healthcare services is paramount. This includes not only expanding insurance coverage but also ensuring that healthcare facilities are geographically and financially accessible to underserved communities. Telehealth services and mobile clinics can play a pivotal role in reaching those who might otherwise remain isolated from essential health services.

Fostering community engagement is also essential. Empowering local organizations and leaders to advocate for health resources ensures that interventions are culturally sensitive and effectively meet the unique needs of the community. Collaborations among public health officials, healthcare providers, and community groups can help in designing programs that resonate with residents and encourage participation. Furthermore, continued research is crucial for understanding the evolving landscape of public health threats, including the impact of climate change, emerging infectious diseases, and mental health crises. Data-driven strategies that incorporate real-time information will enable public health systems to adapt swiftly and effectively.

10. Recent Advances and Future Directions

Recent advances in the understanding and management of hypertension have significantly transformed the landscape of cardiovascular health, paving the way for innovative approaches to prevention, diagnosis, and treatment. Emerging research has enhanced our comprehension of the complex interplay between genetic, environmental, and lifestyle factors contributing to hypertension. Technological advancements, such as wearable blood pressure monitors and telehealth solutions, have improved patient monitoring and engagement, facilitating personalized care. Additionally, new pharmacological therapies and lifestyle intervention programs are being developed, targeting not only blood pressure reduction but also the underlying causes of hypertension. As we look to the future, a more integrated approach that emphasizes population health strategies, health equity, and the utilization of big data for predictive analytics will be crucial in addressing the growing burden of hypertension. By harnessing these advances and focusing on collaborative, patient-centred care, we can significantly improve outcomes and quality of life for individuals affected by this pervasive condition.

10.1 Recent Advances:

- **Personalized Medicine:** Advances in genomics have led to better understanding of individual responses to antihypertensive medications. Genetic testing can guide treatment choices, allowing for personalized approaches based on an individual's genetic profile.
- **Home Blood Pressure Monitoring:** Increased use of digital technology has facilitated home blood pressure monitoring. Devices equipped with Bluetooth allow patients to track their readings and share them with healthcare providers, improving management and adherence.

- **New Drug Classes:** Research has expanded the range of available medications. For instance, medications targeting the renin-angiotensin system (RAS) have evolved, with new options that provide better control with fewer side effects.
- **Device-Based Therapies:** Innovations such as renal denervation and baroreceptor activation therapy have emerged. These procedures aim to modulate neural pathways involved in blood pressure regulation and have shown promise in resistant hypertension.
- **Telemedicine:** The COVID-19 pandemic accelerated the use of telehealth, allowing patients to receive hypertension care remotely. This approach has been shown to improve access and adherence to treatment plans.
- **Lifestyle Interventions:** Studies continue to support the effectiveness of lifestyle modifications (diet, exercise, weight management) in managing hypertension. The DASH diet and Mediterranean diet have been particularly highlighted for their benefits.
- **Understanding the Microbiome:** Research into the gut microbiome has revealed its potential role in hypertension, suggesting that gut health may influence blood pressure regulation. This area is still developing but offers exciting prospects for novel treatments.

10.2 Future Directions:

- **Enhanced Predictive Tools:** Development of algorithms and machine learning models to predict hypertension risk based on a combination of genetic, lifestyle, and environmental factors could lead to earlier interventions.
- **Integration of Artificial Intelligence:** AI can improve diagnostics, risk stratification, and treatment recommendations through better analysis of patient data, including integrating various health metrics from wearable devices.
- **Long-term Monitoring Solutions:** Continuous blood pressure monitoring devices, potentially wearable or implantable, could

provide real-time data and help in better understanding blood pressure variability and its implications.

- **Focus on Comorbidities:** Future research will likely focus on the interplay between hypertension and other conditions such as diabetes, chronic kidney disease, and cardiovascular diseases, leading to more comprehensive management strategies.
- **Global Health Initiatives:** Addressing hypertension in low- and middle-income countries is essential. Strategies that consider socioeconomic factors and access to healthcare resources will be crucial for global hypertension management.
- **Educational Programs:** Increased emphasis on patient education regarding hypertension management, including the importance of adherence to treatment and lifestyle modifications, will enhance long-term outcomes.
- **Investigating Inflammation and Hypertension:** Ongoing research into the inflammatory pathways involved in hypertension could lead to new therapeutic targets, particularly for patients with resistant hypertension.

In conclusion, the landscape of hypertension management is rapidly transforming through recent advances in personalized treatment, technology, and a deeper understanding of underlying mechanisms. As we move forward, the integration of artificial intelligence, improved monitoring solutions, and a focus on global health equity will play crucial roles in enhancing patient outcomes. Continued research into the interactions between hypertension and comorbidities, as well as lifestyle factors, will further refine our approaches. Ultimately, the goal is to empower patients with better tools and knowledge to manage their condition effectively, paving the way for a future where hypertension is not only controlled but significantly reduced across populations. This holistic approach promises to improve quality of life and reduce the burden of hypertension-related complications worldwide.

11. Case Studies and Clinical Guidelines

Case studies and clinical guidelines play a vital role in understanding and managing hypertension effectively. Case studies provide real-world examples of patient experiences, illustrating the complexities and nuances of hypertension treatment, while clinical guidelines offer evidence-based recommendations for healthcare professionals. Together, they enhance our knowledge of best practices, support individualized patient care, and promote a comprehensive approach to hypertension management.

11.1 Case Studies in Hypertension Management:

Case studies serve as important tools for understanding the complexities of hypertension management across different patient profiles and treatment approaches.

❖ Case Study 1: Resistant Hypertension:

One notable case involved a 55-year-old male patient diagnosed with resistant hypertension, defined as blood pressure that remains above target despite the use of three antihypertensive agents, including a diuretic. After comprehensive evaluation, including 24-hour ambulatory blood pressure monitoring, the healthcare team discovered that the patient's hypertension was exacerbated by significant lifestyle factors, including a high-sodium diet and lack of physical activity. The management plan incorporated intensive lifestyle modifications, emphasizing the DASH diet (Dietary Approaches to Stop Hypertension) and regular aerobic exercise. Additionally, a renal denervation procedure was performed to target the sympathetic nervous system's contribution to his blood pressure regulation. After six months, the patient exhibited a substantial drop in systolic and diastolic blood pressure, demonstrating the effectiveness of a multimodal approach that combined lifestyle changes with innovative interventional strategies.

❖ **Case Study 2: Stress-Induced Hypertension:**

Another illustrative case featured a 32-year-old woman whose hypertension was primarily attributed to chronic stress and obesity. She presented with elevated blood pressure readings and symptoms of anxiety. Recognizing the interplay between psychological factors and hypertension, the treatment plan integrated cognitive-behavioural therapy (CBT) to address her stress and anxiety. In conjunction with psychotherapy, pharmacological treatment was initiated with a low-dose angiotensin-converting enzyme (ACE) inhibitor. The patient was also guided on dietary modifications, focusing on whole foods and reducing processed sugars, which contributed to her weight issues. Over a six-month follow-up, the patient achieved a weight reduction of 15%, and her blood pressure readings normalized. This case emphasizes the importance of addressing both psychological and physiological aspects in hypertension management, illustrating the need for a holistic, patient-centred approach.

11.2 Clinical Guidelines for Hypertension:

Clinical guidelines play a crucial role in standardizing hypertension management and ensuring evidence-based practices. The 2021 ACC/AHA Hypertension Guidelines recommend several key strategies for diagnosing and managing hypertension.

❖ **Blood Pressure Targets:** The guidelines advocate for a target blood pressure of less than 130/80 mm Hg for most adults. This threshold is particularly important for individuals at high risk for cardiovascular disease, including those with diabetes or chronic kidney disease.

❖ **Lifestyle Modifications**: The guidelines emphasize the importance of lifestyle interventions as the first line of defence against hypertension. Recommendations include:

- Adopting the DASH diet, which promotes fruits, vegetables, whole grains, and lean proteins while reducing sodium intake.
- Engaging in regular physical activity, aiming for at least 150 minutes of moderate-intensity exercise weekly.
- Maintaining a healthy weight, with a focus on weight loss in overweight or obese patients.
- Limiting alcohol consumption and quitting smoking.

- **Pharmacological Management:** For patients requiring medication, the guidelines recommend a stepwise approach:
  - Initiate treatment with first-line agents such as thiazide diuretics, ACE inhibitors, angiotensin II receptor blockers (ARBs), or calcium channel blockers based on the patient's clinical profile.
  - Consider the use of combination therapy in cases where blood pressure targets are not achieved with monotherapy.

- **Monitoring and Follow-Up:** The guidelines stress the importance of regular follow-up appointments to monitor blood pressure and assess treatment adherence. Home blood pressure monitoring is encouraged to provide more accurate readings and enhance patient engagement.

- **Assessing Secondary Causes:** The guidelines advocate for a thorough evaluation for secondary causes of hypertension, especially in younger patients or those with sudden onset of high blood pressure. Conditions such as primary aldosteronism, pheochromocytoma, and sleep apnoea should be considered.

- **Patient Education and Shared Decision-Making:** The importance of educating patients about their condition, treatment options, and the significance of lifestyle changes is highlighted. Shared decision-making is crucial for ensuring treatment plans align with patients' preferences and values.

By adhering to these clinical guidelines, healthcare providers can enhance the effectiveness of hypertension management, reduce the risk of cardiovascular events, and ultimately improve patient outcomes. These evidence-based practices support a proactive approach to combating hypertension, which remains a leading cause of morbidity and mortality worldwide.

REFERENCES

- Whelton PK, et al. (2018). "2017 High Blood Pressure Guidelines." Hypertension, 71(6), 1269-1324.
- Muntner P, et al. (2019). "The Importance of Accurate Blood Pressure Measurement." Circulation, 140(7), 570-580.
- James PA, et al. (2014). "Evidence-Based Guideline for the Management of High Blood Pressure in Adults." JAMA, 311(5), 507-520.
- Oparil S, et al. (2018). "Hypertension." Lancet, 391(10125), 1628-1641.
- Kearney PM, et al. (2005). "Global Burden of Hypertension: Analysis of Worldwide Data." Lancet, 365(9455), 217-223.
- Azizi F, et al. (2018). "Essential Hypertension: From Diagnosis to Treatment." BMJ, 361, k1610.
- Smith-Sheikh B, et al. (2020). "The Role of Diet in Hypertension." Journal of Hypertension, 38(2), 218-224.
- Barlow J, et al. (2017). "Pharmacologic Treatment of Hypertension." JAMA Internal Medicine, 177(5), 672-679.
- Paterniti S, et al. (2019). "Barriers to Hypertension Control in Older Adults." Journal of the American Geriatrics Society, 67(3), 519-525.
- SPRINT Research Group. (2015). "A Randomized Trial of Intensive versus Standard Blood-Pressure Control." New England Journal of Medicine, 373(22), 2103-2116.
- Halsey J, et al. (2016). "Hypertension in the Elderly: Epidemiology and Treatment." Age and Ageing, 45(3), 345-350.
- He J, et al. (2001). "Major Dietary Factors and Hypertension." Archives of Internal Medicine, 161(7), 953-961.
- Chobanian AV, et al. (2003). "The Seventh Report of the Joint National Committee on Prevention, Detection, Evaluation, and Treatment of High Blood Pressure." Hypertension, 42(6), 1206-1252.
- Vasan RS, et al. (2002). "Systolic Blood Pressure as a Predictor of Cardiovascular Disease." Hypertension, 39(3), 524-529.
- Egan BM, et al. (2010). "Prevalence of Hypertension and Controlled Hypertension in the US." Journal of Clinical Hypertension, 12(5), 304-309.

- Whelton PK, et al. (2018). "2018 Hypertension Clinical Practice Guidelines." American College of Cardiology, 71(6), 1269-1324.
- Mancia G, et al. (2013). "2013 ESH/ESC Guidelines for the Management of Arterial Hypertension." European Heart Journal, 34(28), 2159-2219.
- Re RN. (2013). "Managing Hypertension in the Elderly." Journal of Clinical Hypertension, 15(4), 297-300.
- Roush GC, et al. (2016). "Hypertension in Women: A Scientific Statement from the American Heart Association." Circulation, 134(11), e123-e154.
- Lee C, et al. (2018). "Innovative Approaches to Treating Resistant Hypertension." Journal of Hypertension, 36(5), 1040-1048.
- Kearney PM, et al. (2010). "Global Burden of Hypertension: Analysis of Worldwide Data." Lancet, 365(9455), 217-223.
- Mazzolai L, et al. (2018). "Vascular Aging and Hypertension: Clinical Implications." Journal of Hypertension, 36(3), 425-432.
- Cohen JD, et al. (2014). "The Role of Sleep Apnea in Hypertension." Current Hypertension Reports, 16(9), 483.
- Grassi G, et al. (2015). "Sympathetic Nervous System and Hypertension." Hypertension, 65(6), 1127-1133.
- Hall JE, et al. (2015). "Pathophysiology of Hypertension: From Mechanisms to Treatment." Cardiovascular Research, 107(2), 222-234.
- Aronow WS, et al. (2016). "Treatment of Hypertension in Older Persons." Journal of Clinical Hypertension, 18(10), 940-944.
- Kahn R, et al. (2005). "The Importance of Blood Pressure Control in Diabetes." Diabetes Care, 28(4), 1180-1186.
- Tsai JC, et al. (2012). "The Association Between Depression and Hypertension." Journal of Clinical Hypertension, 14(8), 516-523.
- Sacks FM, et al. (2001). "The Effects of High vs Low Sodium Intake on Blood Pressure." New England Journal of Medicine, 344(12), 827-835.
- Hsu C, et al. (2017). "Evaluating Hypertension Treatment: Current Perspectives." Clinical Hypertension, 23(1), 1-7.
- Cheung BM, et al. (2015). "Hypertension in Asia: The Challenges Ahead." Nature Reviews Cardiology, 12(12), 736-745.
- Neaton JD, et al. (1993). "Blood Pressure and Mortality Among Men with Specific Diseases." Archives of Internal Medicine, 153(3), 342-353.

- Weir MR, et al. (2008). "Management of Hypertension in Patients with Chronic Kidney Disease." Clinical Journal of the American Society of Nephrology, 3(2), 507-520.
- Parati G, et al. (2010). "Blood Pressure Monitoring: Current Issues and Future Perspectives." European Heart Journal, 31(18), 2201-2206.
- Horne BD, et al. (2005). "Long-Term Prognostic Value of Blood Pressure Variability." American Heart Journal, 150(1), 124-130.
- Kostis JB, et al. (2008). "Hypertension and Heart Failure: What the Clinician Should Know." American Journal of Cardiology, 102(1), 14-20.
- Draznin B, et al. (2015). "Diabetes and Hypertension: A Scientific Statement from the American Heart Association." Circulation, 132(1), 14-22.
- Thomas G, et al. (2016). "Patient Education and Self-Management in Hypertension." Patient Education and Counseling, 99(7), 1010-1017.
- Pimenta E, et al. (2015). "Resistant Hypertension: Diagnosis and Management." Current Hypertension Reports, 17(12), 69.
- Sesso HD, et al. (2000). "Physical Activity and Hypertension." American Journal of Hypertension, 13(2), 185-191.
- Staessen JA, et al. (2005). "Hypertension in the Elderly." Lancet, 365(9458), 1547-1556.
- Shapiro S, et al. (2013). "The Role of Angiotensin Receptor Blockers in Hypertension Management." Journal of Hypertension, 31(10), 1898-1906.
- Thomas MC, et al. (2017). "The Role of Hyperglycemia in Hypertension." Clinical Diabetes and Endocrinology, 3(1), 1-8.
- Brown MJ, et al. (2007). "Hypertension and Heart Disease: A Clinical Perspective." Heart, 93(5), 609-617.
- Wright JT, et al. (2015). "A Randomized Trial of Intensive vs Standard Blood Pressure Control." New England Journal of Medicine, 373(22), 2103-2116.
- Hsu CY, et al. (2005). "Obesity, Hypertension, and Kidney Disease." American Journal of Kidney Diseases, 45(4), 554-565.
- Schiffrin EL. (2016). "Vascular Biology of Hypertension." Journal of Hypertension, 34(8), 1419-1424.
- Kearney PM, et al. (2005). "Global Burden of Hypertension: Analysis of Worldwide Data." Lancet, 365(9455), 217-223.

- Kahn SE, et al. (2015). "Diabetes and Hypertension: What's New?" Nature Reviews Endocrinology, 11(4), 217-228.
- Rodriguez CJ, et al. (2014). "Hypertension in the Hispanic/Latino Population." Hypertension, 63(5), 933-940.
- Kearney PM, et al. (2005). "Global Burden of Hypertension: Analysis of Worldwide Data." Lancet, 365(9455), 217-223.
- Yancy CW, et al. (2017). "2017 ACC/AHA/HFSA Focused Update of the 2013 ACCF/AHA Guideline for the Management of Heart Failure." Journal of the American College of Cardiology, 70(6), 776-803.
- LaRocca T, et al. (2016). "The Role of the Endothelium in Hypertension." Cardiovascular Research, 109(2), 234-245.
- Vasan RS, et al. (2001). "Systolic Blood Pressure and Cardiovascular Risk." Hypertension, 37(2), 207-213.
- Zanchetti A, et al. (2014). "Hypertension in the Elderly: A Comprehensive Approach." European Heart Journal, 35(35), 2310-2315.
- Whelton PK, et al. (2021). "2020 Global Burden of Hypertension: A Call to Action." Circulation, 143(8), 727-731.
- Kearney PM, et al. (2005). "Global Burden of Hypertension: Analysis of Worldwide Data." Lancet, 365(9455), 217-223.
- Tzeng Y, et al. (2018). "Cardiac Autonomic Regulation and Hypertension." Clinical Autonomic Research, 28(4), 341-349.
- Wilkins K, et al. (2016). "Hypertension: A Clinical Overview." Canadian Family Physician, 62(7), 580-584.
- Appel LJ, et al. (2011). "A Clinical Trial of Dietary Patterns to Improve Blood Pressure." New England Journal of Medicine, 363(17), 1595-1605.
- Mancia G, et al. (2014). "European Guidelines for the Management of Hypertension." European Heart Journal, 35(35), 2158-2219.
- Barlow WE, et al. (2009). "Longitudinal Studies of Blood Pressure." Hypertension, 54(3), 569-576.
- Wong ND, et al. (2009). "Prevalence of Hypertension in the US." Journal of Clinical Hypertension, 11(6), 344-349.
- Tsimikas S, et al. (2004). "Impact of Inflammation on Hypertension." American Journal of Cardiology, 93(9), 1219-1225.
- Samuels JA, et al. (2016). "Impact of Hypertension on Cardiovascular Outcomes." Journal of the American College of Cardiology, 67(7), 839-848.

- Vongpatanasin W. (2015). "The Role of Sympathetic Nervous System in Hypertension." Journal of Clinical Hypertension, 17(10), 799-804.
- Thomas G, et al. (2016). "Patient Engagement in Hypertension Management." Patient Education and Counseling, 99(7), 1102-1108.
- Franklin SS, et al. (1999). "Isolated Systolic Hypertension: A Review." Journal of the American College of Cardiology, 33(3), 1120-1125.
- Sharma AM, et al. (2003). "Obesity and Hypertension." Journal of Hypertension, 21(6), 1119-1126.
- Creager MA, et al. (2003). "Peripheral Vascular Disease and Hypertension." Circulation, 108(12), 1416-1421.
- Joffres MR, et al. (2001). "Hypertension in Canada: Results from the Canadian Health Measures Survey." Canadian Journal of Cardiology, 27(3), 407-414.
- Alpert JS, et al. (2009). "Hypertension: An Update." American Journal of Medicine, 122(6), 489-495.
- Hossain P, et al. (2007). "Global Burden of Obesity and Overweight." Obesity Reviews, 8(1), 25-32.
- Yoon SS, et al. (2010). "Prevalence of Hypertension in Adults." National Health Statistics Reports, 3(1), 1-5.
- Zieman SJ, et al. (2005). "The Aging Heart: Changes in the Heart and Blood Vessels with Aging." Clinical Geriatric Medicine, 21(2), 215-225.
- Li Y, et al. (2013). "Impact of Alcohol Consumption on Blood Pressure." Hypertension, 62(2), 291-297.
- Lanas F, et al. (2015). "Gastrointestinal Bleeding and Hypertension: A Clinical Perspective." Digestive Diseases and Sciences, 60(3), 651-661.
- Carter BL, et al. (2009). "Patient Education and Self-Monitoring in Hypertension." Journal of the American Board of Family Medicine, 22(2), 143-152.
- Kahn SE, et al. (2016). "The Influence of Blood Pressure on Cardiovascular Disease." Journal of Clinical Hypertension, 18(8), 792-798.
- O'Brien E, et al. (2005). "Blood Pressure Measurement: A Review." Journal of Hypertension, 23(4), 619-626.
- Redon J, et al. (2011). "Hypertension: An Overview of Clinical Management." Current Hypertension Reports, 13(6), 465-474.
- Vasan RS, et al. (2004). "The Role of Blood Pressure in Cardiovascular Risk." Archives of Internal Medicine, 164(17), 1907-1913.

- Salvetti A, et al. (2012). "Hypertension and Endothelial Dysfunction." Journal of Hypertension, 30(9), 1792-1801.
- Schutte AE, et al. (2015). "The Interaction Between Ethnicity and Hypertension." Journal of Hypertension, 33(6), 1069-1078.
- Garrison RJ, et al. (1987). "Longitudinal Changes in Blood Pressure." Hypertension, 10(5), 463-471.
- McDonald K, et al. (2016). "The Role of Telemedicine in Hypertension Management." Journal of Telemedicine and Telecare, 22(6), 345-350.
- Boulanger MC, et al. (2009). "Effects of Hormonal Therapy on Blood Pressure." American Journal of Hypertension, 22(5), 571-577.
- Turner A, et al. (2013). "Hypertension and Kidney Disease: A Dual Challenge." Clinical Journal of the American Society of Nephrology, 8(5), 815-824.
- Chalmers J, et al. (2009). "Guidelines for the Management of Hypertension." Hypertension, 54(1), 2-9.

www.ingramcontent.com/pod-product-compliance
Lightning Source LLC
LaVergne TN
LVHW041200150826
845673LV00001B/230

* 9 7 9 8 8 9 6 1 0 4 9 3 3 *